A SUPREME *QUESTION*

LEE RICHEY

Copyright © Lee Richey, 2020. All rights reserved.

ISBN: 9781090443137

Cover photo from NASA:

"Hubble Goes to the eXtreme to Assemble Farthest Ever View of the Universe"

https://www.nasa.gov/mission_pages/hubble/science/xdf.html

Cover design (and center star brightened) in Photoshop by Maegen Worley.

To

my parents:

David Frank Richey

and

Elaine Lee Richey

Thank you for giving me life, love, music, and a passionate curiosity

CONTENTS

Prologue   vi
Introduction   viii

PART I
SOME FOUNDATIONAL ISSUES

Dream, Discover, Define, Delight!   2
"In the Beginning, God..."   22
Absolutely *Right*?   41
Fundamentalism   53
Creation and Evolution   77
Scientific Thought and Method   88
Faith   103
Miracles   122
Proof and Free Will   129

PART II
A SAMPLING OF NOTED AUTHORS

C.S. Lewis   158
Sheldon Vaunauken   171
Tenzin Gyatso   181
Stephen Hawking   186
Gerald L. Schroeder   193
Patrick Glynn   197
John Polkinghorne   208
Stephen Jay Gould   214
J. P. Moreland and Kai Nielsen   218
Ken Ham and Bill Nye   226
Keith Ward   230
Neil deGrasse Tyson   238

PART III
PERSONAL PERSPECTIVES

The Hard Line   247
A Lenient Tack   270
In Tentative Conclusion   286

Epilogue   300
Acknowledgments   305
Notes   307
Index   319

Prologue

I want to first express gratitude to you, the reader, for your interest and curiosity in this book. I have always known that this project might appear presumptuous on my part, particularly since I have no scholarly training in either religion or science. It has been a fascinating journey for me but it has also felt risky. I know that some of you will be intrigued and perhaps very much in agreement. But I also know that, regardless of how fair and balanced I have attempted to be in giving equal consideration to all viewpoints, there will be many whom I will unintentionally but undoubtedly offend. I only hope that in addition to hearing a few things you might not have considered, you might have the same appreciation for my courage in writing the book that I have for you and your willingness to give it a try.

This book is the culmination of many years of thought, reading, research, conversation, exploration, and a tremendous dose of humility. Though most reputable authors have deep backgrounds and credentials in the field of study about which they write and don't need to offer disclaimers, I feel ethically and emotionally obligated to explain my motivation for delving the depths of the religious and scientific waters. Although I am neither a scientist nor a theologian, I am a curious person and feel the desire to share and encourage thoughts and ideas regardless of my lack of scholarly training in either of these distinguished disciplines.

Needless-to-say, there have been a great many books written about this subject and many contentious debates. As with this entire book, my voice and perspective are only one of many, and many far more specifically educated in these subjects than I. But it is a deep interest of mine and I cannot think of a more fascinating and intriguing (albeit sensitive) issue to discuss and debate than the question of the meaning of God.

I need to make an additional clarification. Though I am primarily interested in what the concept of God means—the focus of this book—there are many people (myself included) who also question the *existence* of God. Because I think that questioning the meaning of a concept is very nearly the same as questioning its validity or existence, I ask the religious reader to be patient when I use the words meaning and existence, interchangeably, in questions about the concept of God. I intend both words inquisitively but respectfully.

I have heard mixed feelings about discussing the subject of God from family, friends, and colleagues. Most say that they find it intellectually stimulating and are happy to share their point-of-view or faith. But some say that they avoid it, or loathe even contemplating the attempt. Since for many people the subject is so steeped in emotion, it is understandable that discussions and/or debates about God can become uncomfortable and emotionally charged. Significantly, the topic, and questions about it, can reveal how much of a person's own self-esteem and view of the world is centered and invested. One can feel challenged, judged, that their belief is not respected, that someone might find an error in their thinking, and that an argument is likely to (or does) ensue. However, it is also one opportunity and litmus test for what I feel is one of the most admirable human qualities: the ability to admit one's own error, about anything. It's easy to be convinced of error in others. It's much harder to see error in ourselves.

The most consistent reason that I have heard expressed as to why the discussion would be avoided is that the conversation often becomes more personal than about the ideas. My own philosophy is that discussions about ideas should never become personal, at least not negatively personal. (Personal compliments almost always feel *flattering*. Personal criticism almost always feels *painful*.) However, as understandable as is the fear of feeling personal criticism, the necessity of exercising our thinking and emotional responses, both in general and about this specific subject, is why I propose that the issue and its discussion *not* be avoided. I hope that by adding my voice to this healthy and ongoing conversation, I might help encourage others to do the same.

— Lee Richey

Introduction

When I looked up at the sky on an early summer night in May, 1997, I was delighted to behold the slightly fuzzy, but unmistakable head and tail of Comet Hale-Bopp. I've had only scattered luck seeing rare celestial phenomena, but Comet Hale-Bopp gave a particularly spectacular performance in its passage through the inner solar system—a full 18 months—so it would have been difficult not to have seen it at least once.

After spending some moments just staring at this cosmic visitor, I walked inside my Madison, Wisconsin apartment, picked up my cordless phone, and called my mother.

"Richey's residence," she answered.

"Hi, mom!"

"*He-llo*, honey!"

"Hey, where are you right now?!"

"At home, talking to you. Where do you think?!," she retorted playfully.

"No, no!," I said, laughing. "I mean are you inside or outside?"

"Oh!," she said, also laughing. "I'm in the living room playing with Jo-Mouse!" Jo-Mouse was her very thin, but sprightly cat. My mother was a deep lover of cats, and enjoyed imagining *herself* as a cat in a possible past life!

"Well," I said, "stay on the phone (she had also graduated to a cordless phone) and go outside. If it's a clear night, look up at the stars and tell me at you see."

After a moment or two, she said, "Okay, I'm outside and looking up. What am I looking for?"

"Do you see anything significantly different, any object even slightly brighter? Do you know what's visible?"

"Hmm...I'm not sure. But I'm still looking..." Then, a bit quizzically, "Well, there's the Big Dipper...and I see Orion...honey, what else am I supposed to be—" Suddenly, she slowly, quietly, almost in a whisper exclaimed, "Oh...my goodness...I *see* it! Is that the *comet*?!"

Like me, my mother had expressed frustration and disappointment in the past that she never got to witness cosmic sightings. This time, she was neither disappointed nor frustrated.

After another moment, and a little bit louder than a whisper, she said giddily, "Just think...I'm having fun imagining where it's *been*!"

Her sense of wonder and awe at the comet's travels and the universe is, I think, at the heart of all religious and scientific thought and feeling. It only takes looking up on even a reasonably clear night to see a sky strewn with stars. And those stars in our view are but an infinitesimal fraction of the stars in our own Milky Way galaxy, and of course then, the universe. Like my mother, the exhilaration that I have felt and still feel when I gaze up on a clear enough night makes me imagine not only the incomparable expanse of time and distance though which all the matter and energy in the universe has traversed and journeyed, but I feel a respectful and empathetic understanding of why those who are deeply religious are intrinsically moved to feel a benevolent Creator lovingly at the helm. The universe, as presently known, is the grandest of phenomena, and its origin one of the deepest mysteries.

But regardless of our individual lives and backgrounds, most of us have had the experience of the stirring sensation of looking up at the night sky and feeling connected. That feeling is completely normal and real. The reason is because we, and all of life on Earth, owe our lives to the stars. We are the result of universal molecular showers. We sprang from cosmic confetti. As one of my science heroes, Carl Sagan, said, "We are *starstuff*."

Comet Hale-Bopp

April 2, 1997

<u>www.rocketroberts.com</u>

PART I

SOME

FOUNDATIONAL ISSUES

Chapter 1

DREAM, DISCOVER, DEFINE, DELIGHT!

*The Gospel of Thomas relates that when the disciples asked Jesus where
they should go, he said only,
"There is a light within a man of light, and it lights up the whole world.
If he does not shine, he is in darkness."
Far from legitimizing any institution, both sayings direct one instead to
oneself — to one's inner capacity to find one's own direction,
to the "light within."*

Elaine Pagels
The Gnostic Gospels

*Another way in which he [Carl Sagan] was Old Testament:
he couldn't live a compartmentalized life,
operating on one set of assumptions in the laboratory
and keeping another, conflicting set for the Sabbath.
He took the idea of God so seriously
that it had to pass the most rigorous standards of scrutiny.*

Ann Druyan,
in the Editor's Introduction

*The Varieties of Scientific Experience:
A Personal View of the Search for God*

Carl Sagan
(published posthumously)

Besides "Refrains From Unnecessary Talking," another comment on my report card by my 3rd grade teacher was, "Very inquisitive." With only those two words, I wasn't sure if she was giving me a compliment or a criticism. At first, I thought she meant I was annoying and irritatingly persistent with my questions, or even unaccepting of her authority as our teacher. But maybe it was a surprise compliment intentionally hidden in vocabulary education. Perhaps she purposely and playfully chose the second word knowing that I would inquisitively look it up!

My initial confusion by what she actually meant reminds me of a drawback with today's "texting," where the desire for convenience, speed, and brevity often sacrifices specificity and clarity. Texting—often in acronyms for even short and simple phrases to write—nearly resembles the monosyllabic "grunts" we humorously imagine of our ancient ancestors before words and more complex language were invented. Though seemingly harmless, rather amusing, and obviously understood by its billions of daily micro-journalists, texting still seems to me like a regression in communication rather than an improvement.* But since my 3rd grade teacher's two-word comment, I have come to know that being inquisitive is an asset, one of the prerequisites to learning. And asking and receiving questions is fun. It indicates interest.

Along with my love and passion for music, another one of my joys has always been reading and writing. Words.

Invented by the Sumerians in 3,000 B.C., words are the human technology of imparting and receiving knowledge. My mother shared with me once that, as a young child, I made an observation of the spelling of a word on the plastic bag of a loaf of bread. The word, *wheat*. It evidently puzzled me that it was spelled beginning with *wh* but, when pronounced,

---

* A funny but serious article by Niall Ferguson titled, "Texting Makes U Stupid" in *Newsweek/Daily Beast* on October 20, 2011, addresses this point exactly. http://www.niallferguson.com/journalism/finance-economics/texting-makes-u-stupid. I came up with a silly phrase when I caught several spelling errors in my own hasty texting: "Txting eets brane sells."

sounded like it began *hw* : h-weat, not w-heat. Any language is, of course, full of exceptions, but I realized in hearing my mother relate that to me (I have only a dim memory of asking her the question), that I had an affinity for words and enjoyed noticing, imagining, and discovering unique things about them.

One of the first more sophisticated words I learned in my early youth was the word *visceral*. I enjoyed learning that it meant the gamut of feelings that exist, move, and vibrate within us with anything we experience. I experience visceral feelings about everything I enjoy, the same feeling as that tingly sensation of staring at the stars. For me, the visceral verges on the infinite. Thinking about our connection to the universe—whether by natural law through science or the concept of God through religion, or both—is clearly concerning and contemplating the infinite.

In addition to the beauty and variety of global languages, I think that there are two tools of communication that, although not thought of as languages, are essential parts of being human, and have deep visceral roots. They are the intellect[*] and the emotions. They are usually thought of as the two areas of our brain—the left-brain and the right-brain—but I think that they can also be treated as foundation languages: the dual neural tools to be developed and utilized in assisting all other languages. (We all have intellect and emotions, but none of us speak every language. If our intellects and emotions worked more healthily in tandem, perhaps we could all become more foreign language fluent!) They are also frequently treated as separate qualities, designed for entirely different functions. For me, however, they are inseparable. I enjoy experiencing the gamut of my senses together, my intellect and my emotions. The specific and the visceral. The infinite.

It is for this reason that, in addition to my passion and profession in music and the performing arts, I have spent a lot of my wondering and inquisitive life considering how and why humans think and behave as they do and how we generate our philosophies, sciences, arts, and religions. Though I only have formal training in the arts, I am fascinated by thought in general. And since the visceral includes the specific for me, I have always yearned to help the visceral become more specific. The concept of and

---

[*] The intellect is not defined as visceral. Visceral is defined only as the emotions and instinct. For me, however, my intellectual inquiries and discoveries feel very visceral.

connection to God is certainly in the category of the visceral. Such is my motivation for seeking a more specific meaning and understanding of God.

Another favorite word of mine is one I learned much later (actually from Garrison Keillor while listening to A Prairie Home Companion). It is the word, *perspicacious*, or deeply discerning. In addition to my late parents, this book is dedicated to the perspicacity in all of us—whether awake or in need of awakening—to strive to better understand the universe, the concept of God, and to love one another unconditionally.

~~~

All of us arrive at our respective points of view about the origin of the universe and life based on a variety of factors: our family backgrounds, our education, our life experience and study, and perhaps most deeply, our wonder and imagination. The varieties of thought are nearly as numerous as there are individual people. This is apparent because of the diversity of points of view and the fact that if any of our views were indisputable, we would all perceive the world around us and the universe essentially the same way.

Most of us have similar perceptions and knowledge about some basic things of course. We know that we are human beings and need to breathe oxygen to live, water to drink, and food to eat. Because of our own heartbeats, and our daily life routines, responsibilities, and recreations, we understand something about the difference between involuntary and voluntary impulses. We know our own birthdays—and why we had an *original* birthday—so we know at least something about sexual reproduction. We understand something about weather; why our star, the Sun, generates light and heat; gravity; centrifugal force; the existence of the boiling point of water; some national and global history; basic and adequate math skills; what feels good physically and emotionally; how to maintain basic cleanliness and hygiene; and so forth.

Philosophically or religiously, and regardless of the issue of divinity, we know that Jesus, Muhammad, and Buddha, for example, all existed, lived, and died in history. What this book is attempting to do is not only pose specific questions about how and why we think the way we do about ourselves, life, and the universe, but to encourage and challenge our thinking about one of the largest questions that any human faces regarding our own origin and that of the universe: the question of the meaning and existence of God. The two main disciplines that have spawned from human thought, and continue to tackle this question the most often, are religion and science.

I also want to share, honestly and respectfully, that though I am deeply curious and motivated to think, write, speculate, discuss, and creatively debate about religion, science, and God, I am by nature and intellect a scientist. I am not motivated by religious faith, and I am seldom moved or inspired by church sermons. That does not mean that I don't admire some religious authors, respect the ministry, and hold some ministers in particularly high regard, particularly some of those with whom I am close personal friends. And although I am more intrigued and stirred by science, for me the topics of religion and science are *both* extremely interesting, profoundly thought-provoking, and not mutually exclusive. Ideally, they should be mutually inclusive, instructive, and inspirational. I am inspired by and care deeply for love, life, humanity, and origins, so I'm interested in the origin of both religion and science.

I also want to admit and offer that because I am a native and citizen of the United States, and primarily a resident of the southern states, I have the most awareness of Christianity. That said, though many of my religious examples reference the Christian religion, this book is in no way or fashion an indictment against Christianity, any other religion, or science. It is an open and respectful discussion comparing science with *all* religions, cross-culturally. Specifically, the meaning of the Deity, God.

Since religion and science seem at times to be deeply divergent and I am advocating their symbiosis, I want to look briefly at the original definitions of both the words.

The word *religion* originally came from two words, the root word *re* meaning "again," and the Latin, *ligāre* or *ligio* meaning, "to bind," "to tie," or "to fasten." I also like thinking of another meaning, "to link." Since link means nearly the same thing as bind and tie, and link and ligio sound similar, the inference, then, is a rebinding, retying, or relinking of all matter and life in the universe: universal (the definition of the adjective, *catholic*, from which the proper noun, Catholic, derives).

The word *science* originally came from the Latin *scientia* which means, simply, "knowledge." The word, knowledge, has two root words, *know* and *ledge*. The word, know, means "to perceive, understand, and apprehend clearly and with certainty." The word, ledge, in this instance, does not mean a narrow exterior shelf or precipice. It more likely comes from the Middle English suffix, *leche* or *lāc,* meaning "action, or practice." So the word, knowledge, can mean, "the act or practice of understanding."

Together, religion and science could mean rebinding, retying, or relinking all knowledge. In other words, universally comprehensive and inclusive. I can think of no greater global goal.

∼∼

For me, religion—or spirituality—has a different shade of meaning from some standard definitions and practices. My religion and spirituality are what I like to think of as my own creative "trinity." * They are:

1. My own inner peace
2. Loving all human beings and all of life
3. Feeling a deep and respectful connection to the cosmos

In following the "Golden Rule," I have deep respect for all perspectives and points of view, and I hope to receive that respect. Not included in my personal trinity is any sense of an external entity or being that is responsible for creating the cosmos. I think it's our tendency and need to ascribe human-like causes or human allegory and characteristics to the universe and its origin so that everything makes sense from our familial and experiential point of view.

In the Christian religion, for example, God as the "Father," Jesus Christ as the "Son," the Virgin Mary, as the "Mother." In various secular metaphor, "Mother Earth," "Mother Nature," "Mother Ship," "Mother Lode," "Father Time," "Father Christmas," "Absentee Father," "Old Man Winter," "Old Man River," "Franco Zeffirelli's, *Brother Sun, Sister Moon*, George

---

* Though I begin with myself, I do not intend the order to be selfish or ego-centric. I feel it more as personal peace and health. If one is not happy and healthy within themselves, it is more difficult to love life and the universe. Of note: In the Kathleen Price Bryan Y.M.C.A. in Greensboro, N.C., a wall motto reverently reads the opposite order: "God is first, Others are second, I am third." It is also lovely, but I think that the principles are more important than the order.

Orwell's, "Big Brother," "The Man in the Moon," the "Seven Sisters" (the Pleiades) a computer's "Motherboard," personifying a motor vehicle or a water vessel as "She," etc. Clearly, the human parental, familial, noun and pronoun projection in religion, spirituality, and life-in-general is ubiquitous.[*]

Christianity goes farther and asserts that God and Jesus Christ are both divine, but differ only in name. They are simultaneously separate and synonymous deities, one-and-the-same. This simultaneity also results in a third and equally synonymous entity, the Holy Spirit. These three separate but unified entities—God, Jesus Christ, and the Holy Spirit—comprise the Triune, "three-in-one," "trinity-in-unity," or simply, the *Trinity*: The Father, Son, and Holy Ghost (the first two, once again, referenced by human male nouns; the third by a supernatural term).

By contrast, in Judaism and Islam, the concept of the Trinity is not only non-existent, it is blasphemous and hints at polytheism. In both these faiths, there is one and *only one* God (in Judaism, God; in Islam, Allah), not one God simultaneously divided by three.

In the four largest global monotheistic religions—Christianity: Catholicism and Protestantism; Judaism; Islam—the divine distinction of the Deity (whether united *and* separate, or undivided) also makes the Entity perfect, omnipotent, and immortal. The words, divine and divinity, are mostly associated with God and the supernatural. I imagine another, non-supernatural definition. It is only natural when offering love and kindness that one anticipates acknowledgment and appreciation (and hopefully not indifference or rejection). I think divinity might also be the ability for one to offer unlimited love and kindness with *no need* of receiving acknowledgment or appreciation. That would certainly fit with the reputations of many, if not all, of the world's great religious/spiritual leaders.

---

[*] In an opinion column for Fox News on April 14, 2017, entitled, *The 'Mother of All Bombs' is actually the mother of all warmongering*, former U.S. Representative from Ohio, Dennis Kucinich, made the following insightful but disheartening observation about human mother and father analogies: "Russia, in response to the U.S. development of the 'mother,' [Mother Of All Bombs (MOAB)] has developed the 'father of all bombs' which supposedly has five times the devastating power of mother. Not to be outdone, the U.S. has taken steps to have a new "mother" brought forward, this one weighing 30,000 pounds. How unbelievable it is to live in a time where the life-creating symbols of mother and father became the agencies of the destruction of life. Our metaphors are signposts to the end of the world."

The Catholic religion teaches, if not quite the divinity, at least the sanctity of the womb of the Virgin Mary. Her conception of Jesus Christ is given an additional adjective accolade which is unique to her: immaculate (the Immaculate Conception).* Though most often descriptive of Mary's virginity in conceiving Jesus, this adjective actually has additional religious interpretations. First, it is a gesture that is interpreted by many of those religious as rare respect to women in an otherwise patriarchal religion. Second, it can be attributable not just to the Virgin Mary, but to the heredity of Jesus, implying an immaculate lineage. However, and third, to many feminists it has been felt by some women as patronizing and demeaning of Mary, implying that she had no choice in the divine decision to be a vessel for the Messiah.

Tellingly, *perfection*, *omnipotence*, and *immortality* are three qualities that humans, and all of life, do not possess. We do have the ability to be *immaculate* with our personal health and environment, but women, not commonly, with conception! It is curious that many religions tend to ascribe those four unattainable qualities to their deities, and the vessels of deities. Is that an envious and vicarious motivation? A yearning that, unlike Adam's and Eve's fall from grace and expulsion from Eden, at least our ultimate origin was free from error?

In my experience, I am not aware of a perfect, immortal, omnipotent, or immaculate *anything*, unless the laws of nature can be considered omnipotent and immaculate associated with cleanliness. For example, even celestial bodies, like the Earth or any other planet, that appear to our eye as perfectly round spheres are not perfectly smooth on the surface. They only look perfectly round from a great distance. They are, in fact, only approximate spheres, with very rough surfaces. This is because, though all mass and matter contain gravity, their central gravitational pull is not strong enough to make their surfaces pristinely and omnidirectionally smooth. This

---

* There is also a funny twist of an analogy on the "Immaculate Conception" in sports. It occurred on December 23, 1972, in the final thirty seconds of the AFC division playoff game between the Pittsburg Steelers and the Oakland Raiders. With the score tied 7-7, Steelers wide receiver, Franco Harris, caught a deflected forward pass from quarterback, Terry Bradshaw, on the Raiders's 35-yard-line—in his outstretched fingertips!—and ran for the winning touchdown. His phenomenal reaching catch was dubbed, "The Immaculate *Reception*!"

difference in perspective is true of everything of course when compared from the macroscopic and the microscopic perspectives. Perfection is an illusion and pretense. A myth. Might our Deity be the same?

Like the misconception and misattribution of the above four words, I also think that the word *spiritual* is misunderstood. The word, spiritual, is frequently used by those non-religious as a substitute for the word, religious (personal profile choices in online dating websites occasionally include the category, "Spiritual, But Not Religious"), a kind of reverence for one's *inner* being rather than an *external* Being. But, like the external deities of religion or mythology, the word, spiritual, often seems to be interpreted as a part of us that is separate from our bodies. (Spiritual is not interpreted synonymously with corporeal.) There is no strong evidence, however, that our sentience—our intuition, feelings, and other senses associated with spirituality—are in our bodies but not a part of our biological structure, our physics, like all our other atoms and molecules. It is certainly possible that our bodies and our "selves," "spirits," or "souls" are just different combinations of atoms within the same DNA. There is physical evidence to support this. We are certainly made of atoms and our DNA is the building-block of our genes. Unless there were evidence of some other molecular mechanism separate from our DNA and the atoms that contain that DNA, there is no reason to think that all of our senses—including that part of our deep awareness which may *feel* separate—are anything other than additional components of our DNA, our physical and biological chemistry.

Journalist and author, Cate Montana, argues against that point, that the soul or spirit might be defined by physics. In an article in The Huffington Post on May 24, 2016, entitled, *Proof of the Soul*, she starts by describing the neurological hypothesis of the soul as, "...the much maligned intangible essence that far too many scientists, materialists and behavioral psychologists like to marginalize as 'brain epiphenomenon.'" To offer her proof, she continues, "...my face had been providing 'proof positive' that the soul or spirit—whatever you want to call it—exists all along...'I' haven't changed at all. Never mind it's not the same face looking back at me from the mirror. Never mind it's definitely not the same body...Yes, my body is definitely older. But 'I' am not. The essence that I call my 'self' has not aged a day." [1] I will be examining the concept of proof in a later chapter, but simply sensing that oneself—the "I" as she states—is unchanged though their body is clearly changing does not negate the possibility that the "self," "spirit," or "soul" may also be defined by physics. Sensing alone is not "proof positive."

The word, spiritual, comes from the word *spirit* which derives from the Latin words *spiritus* and *spirare* which mean *to breathe*, or just *breath*; in Greek, *pneuma* (whence comes the medical word for disease in breathing, pneumonia). My translation and experience of spiritual is that definition, and visceral. It is my deep breathing as a result of my intellectual and emotional equilibrium. When I feel emotionally and intellectually healthy I breathe more deeply and peacefully. Therefore, I think that whatever helps one breathe more easily and deeply *is* spiritual. That actually may be the strongest litmus test to being spiritually healthy. Again, I suspect that our spirit (breathing) is not a separate or intangible part of ourselves unrelated to our biological physics. I like to think of our spirit, alliteratively, as our breathing biology.

In the songbook, *Singing the Journey: A Supplement to Singing the Living Tradition*, used by the Unitarian Universalist Church, Hymn 1009, "Song of Centering," contains this simple and beautiful phrase:

Breathe-in peace, breathe-out love

The text in this phrase of the song is borrowed from a "guided mettā[*] meditation" in the book, *Who is My Self: A Guide to Buddhist Meditation*, by German Buddhist and teacher, Ayya Khema. Breathing-in peace[**] and breathing-out love is very simple and soothing imagery. It reminds me immediately of the symbiotic relationship between oxygen-breathing life and carbon-dioxide-breathing life. Mammals (including humans), reptiles, and birds all breathe-in (inhale) oxygen and breathe-out (exhale) carbon dioxide. Trees and all other plants do the opposite. They absorb (breathe-in, figuratively) carbon dioxide and emit (breathe-out, figuratively) oxygen. Figuratively or not, if most of the energy exhaled by humanity was love, imagine what more abundant peaceful energy we would all inhale! I like to think of that potential cycle with another alliterative phrase:

The Summit of Spirituality

---

[*] The word, *mettā*, means *benevolence*.
[**] See: http://www.breatheforpeace.org

The primary and most successful outlet for spiritual connection and healing are Twelve-Step recovery meetings. Bill Wilson, one of the founders of the original Twelve-Step meeting, Alcoholics Anonymous (AA), struggled not only with alcoholism but with the meaning of God. Significantly, it was suggested to him that he think of his own understanding of God. That is, in fact, the genesis of the ending phrase of Step 3: ...*as we understood God.* Though early Twelve-Step meetings did include readings from the Bible, Twelve-Step groups were not intended as religious sanctuaries or services. They were initiated as spiritual gatherings. In keeping with that, Twelve-Step meetings have adopted the term, Higher Power, as a substitute or synonym for the word, God (similar to the substitute of *spiritual* for *religious*). Higher Power is perhaps a reference to the energy that feels like an undefinable force, greater in power than any individual person, and connecting all of life.

I have attended many Al-Anon and other Twelve-Step meetings, and my impression is that Twelve-Step groups use the term Higher Power not only as a secular and alternative option to the word, God, but also to refer to the focus on spirituality rather than religion in their meetings and personal work. Since spirituality originally meant breathing, I wonder whether one form of that higher power is the peace we feel when we breathe well, deeply, and easily, and feel that peaceful breathing with others. That sounds, to me, like a simple, but profoundly higher power. Again, peaceful breathing might encapsulate the ideal of spiritual health.

Consistent with my desire to be specific and clear about the meaning of the word God, what might be the specific meaning of the words *higher* and *power* in the term Higher Power? Just as with the word, God, it can be confusing when any word is used with deep and profound intention without clarifying whether it is meant literally or metaphorically. As with any good writing, metaphors are a wonderfully creative and literary tool, but their use in conjunction with words used literally should be very distinct and clear. Like the word, God, the term, Higher Power, is an example of a phrase that is caught between literal and metaphor. Unlike the word God, I think its meaning is probably general on purpose. It is designed to accommodate a wide range of spiritual and religious viewpoints, to avoid confusion with a literal or religious interpretation of God, and to demonstrate respect for the various perceptions of God. It is a very benevolent and sensitive practice; the focus of Twelve-Step groups is on spiritual healing, not on religion.

It is also consistent with the final phrase of AA's 12th Tradition which emphasizes to, "...place principles above personalities." (This phrase is spoken in unison in many 12-Step meetings when the 12 Traditions are read.) In other words, the principles of healing are emphasized more strongly than the people to whom they are credited. Since God is interpreted by many people as a personality, offering the alternative phrase Higher Power is consistent with that emphasis.

As I mentioned above, I think the phrase Higher Power might mean our own deep emotional awareness (spirit/breathing) and that awareness shared with others. But this all-inclusive phrase, Higher Power, can be as confusing as the word, God, and in a very specific way. Like the word, God, in Twelve-Step literature the two words in the phrase, Higher Power, are always printed with their first letters capitalized. In standard and correct English, a word with its first letter capitalized indicates a proper noun, a word that describes a *specific* person, place, or thing. Just as with the word, God, it is unclear (which is exactly my point) whether the capital letters in the phrase, Higher Power, are intended to indicate a proper noun.* So as well-intentioned and compromising as the latter phrase is, that small disparity is also unclear and confusing. I suggest that the confusion would be eliminated altogether by dropping the capital letters. Simply, higher power.

Granted, the focus of Twelve-Step groups is less on what words mean or to what they're actually referring, and more on how the individual person *feels* about the words, how they best help to reconnect the person to their own inner peace and to the universe/God. They are there for spiritual healing and recovery, to breathe more easily and deeply. I would suggest, though, that clear intellectual thinking and understanding is *also* part of spiritual healing. It certainly is for me.

As I've mentioned, I have attended many Twelve-Step meetings, and *I* find the term, Higher Power, unclear and confusing (just as I find the word,

---

* I have heard the point made that capitalizing God and Higher Power could refer to proper nouns, but to *things* instead of *people*. That seems somewhat clearer to me, but still unnecessary. And I think it might also incite rebuke from those who would consider referring to God as a living "thing" blasphemous.

God, unclear and confusing). Though I think I understand the *reason* for substituting the proper noun, God, with the proper noun term, Higher Power—perhaps a compromise between honoring those who believe in a personal God and those who do not—since the words in Higher Power are capitalized, I have found this substitute phrase equally vague, distracting, and annoying. Though not a hindrance to my own spiritual healing and recovery, to me the capitalizations seem silly and superficial. Other than metaphorically personalizing the sense of human unity, why is there any need to personify the sense of cosmic connection?

Since spiritual originally meant breathing, and deep, comfortable breathing is inexorably connected to our feelings and sense of well-being, let me relate a simple phrase that a good friend of mine once said: "Your feelings are your most important thing." I completely agree. However, in my opinion, the key word (used twice in the statement) is *your*. Feelings are subjective. My larger point is that although feelings are without a doubt an immensely vital part of personal security, life experience, and understanding, they are not the only part. As my friend offered, I think being healthy with one's feelings is probably *most* important. But intellectual understanding is *also* important (very nearly equally for me). It completes the dual functions of the brain—left-brain/right-brain—that I mentioned earlier. Therefore, understanding what words mean and how to use them well is as deeply important to me as the feelings stimulated and aroused by words, particularly in the context of as profound a question as the meaning of a deity or a higher power.

And even though I think our feelings are our most important and vulnerable trait, I'm not certain that the answers to the deepest of life's riddles and puzzles are primarily about feelings or with what one is most comfortable. Comfort is certainly *part* of the answer to problems. But a more complete answer to any problem should be a combination of what feels good *and* what works. Actually, "what feels good" and "what works" could be brief encapsulations of religion and science, respectively. In fact, what works well usually *is* comfortable and feels good. Therefore, shouldn't a more complete and healthy approach to solving life's problems and challenges be an applied combination of the two? The intellect and the emotions, the visceral?

When it comes to one's own well-being and privacy, I think one's feelings definitely come first. But when it comes to communicating large thoughts, ideas, and concepts to many people (no longer private), I think understanding the *specific meaning* of words is more important and feelings less important. Feelings fluctuate. The meaning of words lasts much longer. This is because words are a result of clear, long-term thinking and use. And clear, deep thinking is the profound evolutionary advantage humans have over most other life forms. The word I want to better understand—and am proposing that the reader more fully understand—specifically and clearly, and in any religious concept or translation, is the word, *God*.

~~~

I have been asking "why" about everything at various stages of my life for as long as I can remember. It has always been important for me to understand, and hopefully experience, how and why things work. Though I often err by making premature conclusions, I try to be mindful of the hazard of assumptions (the old phrase, "to assume makes an ass of you and me"). Assumptions, although sometimes accurate, are often wrong and tend to be weak in specifics and detail. The detailed questions of why, who, how, where, when, and what are always relevant to any subject. Detailed questions are particularly relevant with regard to subjects or concepts of large magnitude. The larger the concept the more need for detailed questions. Shouldn't these questions be applied to a subject as large as the concept and meaning of a deity? Christopher Hitchens and Carl Sagan said the same thing in slightly different ways about the need for profoundly detailed evidence to bolster large propositions. Hitchens stated, "Exceptional claims demand exceptional evidence." And Sagan averred, "Extraordinary claims require extraordinary evidence." The proposition or assertion of a deity is certainly an exceptional and extraordinary claim.

The concept and claim of God (by any name, in any religion) is probably the largest proposition put forth by humans (and, in religious texts, purportedly put forth by the deities themselves) so it follows that the topic would generate many questions. If it were safe to conclude the meaning and existence of God—if there was *indisputable evidence* of God's existence—then there would be far fewer people, if any, who did not believe in God. Conversely, since there is no indisputable evidence refuting God's existence, it is also not safe to conclude that God does not exist. Still, while it is true that there are millions of wonderful people who *do* believe in God, it is certainly not the case that *everyone* (or even the majority of people) believes in God. Therefore, the evidence for God must not be entirely conclusive for everyone.

Some detailed questions might be: What exactly is meant by God? Does God have a physical appearance? If so, what does he/she/it look like? If not, then why not? Is a pronoun appropriate for God? If so, which one and why? If not, why not? And since God is known to most believers by faith, why is there such a thing as a scientific viewpoint or the scientific method? Why would the Deity create the potential for asking questions about its existence if its existence and meaning was obvious? Is that another intention by the Deity of free will? Not only creating our ability to choose right from wrong, but to believe or not believe? There is an incongruity in a perfect Creator creating imperfect creatures. If the answer to that is that the Creator's motivation is mysteriously didactic, a masked moral lesson, is that the only answer? How could the perfect Deity create our deep capacity to think and ask questions, *and* be unaware of the conflict that its very existence would be elusive to our questions? That seems to me an egregious error; by God, religious writers, or both. Or, if divinely intentional, a pointless paradox. Why would the Deity create confusion in its creations? Faith aside, it is plainly illogical. And it not only makes no logical sense, it makes no *loving* sense. Shouldn't the concept and experience of God be the opposite of confusion: the deepest and clearest connection and love?

For many religious people, however, logic applied to faith is itself illogical. They use the trust of faith to support their belief in God, particularly when answers to questions about religion are not readily, if ever, forthcoming. But could unquestioning religious faith be interpreted as an unconscious excuse and/or a proxy apology for the Deity? And if faith is the foundation for the largest question in religion, what role does faith play for religion in the smaller questions? Is faith the predominant or only tool in religion, or is there another religious tool to tackle smaller questions? Is that the function of prayer? And how are prayer and meditation different? How are they similar? Many non-religious (spiritual) people derive deep peace from meditation. Are prayer and meditation really the same thing with different terms (prayer to God or other deity; meditation for self-reflection and inner peace)? Meditation certainly seems to work to quiet the mind, but does prayer to God really work to connect with the Deity?

In the following extract from John Steinbeck's, *The Grapes of Wrath*, the former preacher, Jim Casy, expresses doubts about prayer while talking to Tom Joad as he ponders what he thinks all the poverty-stricken people really want. "Ever' place we stopped I seen it. Folks hungry for side-meat, an' when they get it, they ain't fed. An' when they'd get so hungry they couldn' stan' it no more, why, they'd ast me to pray for 'em, an' sometimes I done it...I use ta think that'd cut 'er...Use ta rip off a prayer an all the troubles'd stick to that prayer like flies on flypaper, an' the prayer'd go a-sailin' off, a-takin' them troubles along. But it don' work no more...An' Almighty God never raised no wages." [2] It is hard to have faith in the power of prayer when you are staving off starvation.

Meditation and prayer are very personal experiences, so are difficult to substantiate scientifically. Are either of them compatible with science? Is prayer only applicable to or dependent on faith? Is meditation solely a spiritual (breathing) exercise? Are prayer, meditation, and the scientific method equally effective, or are they each only effective for their respective disciplines: religion, spirituality, and science? Perhaps the answer depends on the participant(s).

On the other hand, how many, if any, of the greatest accomplishments by humans have been achieved almost exclusively through prayer or meditation? Is inner reflection ever effective without prior and subsequent thought, preparation, and action? (That is the origin of the contemporary colloquial term *proactive*: *action* taken *before*.) And when preparatory and subsequent action are taken, is credit due to the individual or a deity? Or both? Where does science end and divine intervention begin? Or the inverse, where does divine intervention end and science begin? Are they indistinguishable?

Organized religion and religious practice have been responsible for some of the greatest and most compassionate good in human history. Millions of charitable religious organizations have housed the homeless and fed the poor: Catholic Charities USA, Catholic Relief Services, The Salvation Army, Habitat for Humanity, St. Jude Children's Research Hospital, the New York City Metro Baptist Church's rooftop vegetable garden, Compassion, Christian Children's Fund (In 2009 it was renamed ChildFund International to broaden its reach. This is a commendable example of a religious organization recognizing the importance and effectiveness of global rather than denominational outreach.), Lutheran

Services of Georgia, Tzu Chi (Buddhist) Foundation, Islamic Relief USA, Heifer International, International Fellowship of Christians and Jews, to name only a significant few. There are clearly many religious organizations which actively help and assist their fellow human being.

Much of the success of science is also evident and obvious. Medical science, for example, can certainly credit the use of the scientific method for many, if not all, of its progress and achievements: its painstaking testing of new methods and chemical combinations (drugs, herbal, and homeopathic remedies) that have prolonged and bettered human (and other) life. Humans used science to invent the now commonplace transportation technologies of the wheel, the bicycle, the automobile, the railroad, and airplane flight. In outer space technology, a handful of humans have successfully left and returned to the Earth by orbiting and lunar space vehicle. A phenomenal telescopic camera (the Hubble Space Telescope) which maintains permanent Earth-orbit, has photographed a cornucopia of exhilarating images of the Solar System and the universe. And unoccupied space vehicles have not only landed on Mars, a moon of Saturn, and a comet, but five are still en route permanently: Pioneers 10 and 11; New Horizons; and Voyagers 1 and 2. The two Voyagers—both have already entered the heliosphere, and Voyager 1 has crossed the heliopause—are equipped to continue traveling through interstellar space for a staggering one billion years! These are no meager feats of human thought, innovation, and ingenuity. Should credit for these scientific successes be given to humans or to God? Or both? Depending on one's perspective, God could either be the obvious cause or obviously unnecessary?

And yet, though the scientific method clearly works consistently and brilliantly, many millions of people find faith, prayer, and meditation preferable alternatives and seem to find greater personal and spiritual fulfillment in religion? What are the functions of religion and science, and why do we treat them differently? Is one a more effective tool than the other and why? How can religion and science find common ground to understand the universe and God more fully together? Why bother to ask or understand any of these questions at all?

The common ground, I think, is ourselves and our collective curiosity and compassion. We are all human and striving to make sense of the vastness of the universe. We are still a long way from understanding much of the universe, but we have also come to understand a remarkable amount, which is a testament to the evolution of our intelligence. But our evolution has also generated two distinct and, at times, seemingly opposite and conflicting methods for understanding and surviving in the universe. They both consist of feelings, senses, instincts, techniques, practices, and conclusions concerning the origin of the universe and life and manifest themselves in religion and science. It would probably behoove us all to better understand both.

～～～

The religious perspective understands the universe as having been generated or created by an entity or a being of incomprehensible power and love that is responsible for everything we observe in the universe. This entity also created human beings as the predominantly intelligent species to live on one planet in that universe, the Earth. The entity is a benevolent (and sometimes malevolent) being that is both proud and occasionally ashamed of its creation. But this entity is alive and intelligent, is the being which created the universe, and to which we owe the existence of our lives.

The scientific perspective understands the universe as having potentially always existed through its own inertial natural law. This perspective does not require a creator, entity, or being to be responsible for the existence of the universe. In this perspective there may or may not have been an actual *beginning* to the universe. But if there was a beginning (an initial spark that began the inertia of the universe, as opposed to the idea of an infinitely old universe), then, except for the plausible (and largely substantiated) theory of the Big Bang, humans have simply not found enough evidence to corroborate a definite beginning of the universe. Science is getting a better and better picture of how the universe works and how it came to be, but it has not come close to a final conclusion. In contrast to the religious perspective, however, this perspective avoids forming a decisive conclusion about any assertion until strong, detailed physical evidence is found. The only thing assumed is that no assumption should be made. This is because the universe is always changing, and assumptions are vulnerable to change. Compared with the suggested benevolence or malevolence of a religious deity, the beauty and chaos (respectively) in the universe are simply the natural, random constructions and destructions of matter and energy rather than a "Being" approving or disapproving of aspects of its creation (i.e. The Great Flood and Noah's Ark).

Probably the biggest difference between the two perspectives is the following: Religious scripture, principles, and dogma tend to be taught and accepted as accurate *before* evidence for them are examined and substantiated. Scientific findings, discoveries, hypotheses, principles, theories, and facts tend to be taught and accepted as accurate *after* evidence for them are examined and substantiated.

This book is not about which perspective is right and which is wrong. It is about why we formulate our viewpoints about these two topics, a look at comparing them, and what we do with them in our continuing quest for knowledge and survival.

Chapter 2

"IN THE BEGINNING, GOD…"

*The fundamental proposition of Paul Tillich's theological system is that
'God is being-itself.'*

He has being, he is being, but he is not a being.

The Systematic Theology of Paul Tillich: A Review and Analysis
Alexander "Sandy" J. McKelway

...the subject [the idea of God] *is further confused by the fact that prominent theologians such as Paul Tillich, for example, who gave the Gifford Lectures many years ago, explicitly denied God's existence, at least as a supernatural power. Well, if an esteemed theologian (and he is by no means the only one) denies that God is a supernatural being, the subject seems to me to be somewhat confused.*

The Varieties of Scientific Experience: A Personal View of the Search for God
(From Sagan's appearance and discussions at the Gifford Lectures in Scotland in 1985. Published posthumously in 2006 by his widow, Ann Druyan)

Though I never met Paul Tillich, Presbyterian Minister, Sandy McKelway is a friend of mine and a close friend of my late parents. I find it very interesting that the renowned theologian, Tillich—whom McKelway wrote about and Sagan verbally referenced—asserted that God was "not a being." In other words, neither a living entity external to life and the universe, nor the creator of either. Clearly, the assumption of the existence of God continues to be confusing enough to generate questions and challenges not only from some scientists, atheists, agnostics, and a curious person like myself, but from others like the above distinguished theologian and scientist.

I also find it curious that, in addition to the assumption of the existence of God, the opening phrase of Genesis makes the clear assertion that there was a *beginning* to the universe. In my awareness and experience, modern science has come to no such conclusion.[*] In fact, more and more evidence is being offered and demonstrated which seems to indicate that there may have been *no* beginning of the universe, at least not in the sense that humans associate the beginning of life; the former theory of an expanding/contracting, or cyclically oscillating universe of infinitely multiple "big bangs," would have all but eliminated a definite beginning. And a new discovery of differing quantum speeds of expansion of the universe stirs even quantum physics, much less a single beginning. We are extremely influenced by the beginning of our *own* lives, which creates an immediately subjective bias. Furthermore, scientists are discovering evidence for multiple universes in quantum physics, which implies an infinite existence of universes, which, in turn, also nearly negates the idea of a single beginning. Genesis also does not offer any more explanation than simply "In the beginning..." *How* that beginning happened is immediately assumed by the fourth word of the phrase, "...God...."

As I've already mentioned, like the contemporary term Higher Power, God is introduced as a proper noun. And God is not defined in any detail in

---

[*] Exception can confidently be made for the *known* or *observable* universe. That beginning is called the "Big Bang." But the known universe may be only one of infinite multiverses.

the opening sentence. But the implication (by the subsequent verses of Genesis and the teaching by most religions) is not that God is the name of a specific place or a specific thing, but a specific *person*. And not only a specific person, but a specific *gender*: male, with the pronoun, *He* (Genesis 1:4). That pronoun is inconsistently capitalized or not capitalized, apparently at random within the biblical text, or depending on the edition of the Bible. However, it is made unequivocally clear in the opening verses of Genesis that God is assumed, is introduced as a male deity, and is presumed responsible for having created the cosmos.

With respect to all religious faith, this is an enormous assertion (or the extraordinary or exceptional claim proffered by authors Sagan and Hitchens, respectively). So it is all the more curious that detailed explanation of God is scant or nonexistent. It is as if at some point the Bible had a preceding or subsequent chapter in which God was introduced, described, and explained in much greater detail, but is now missing. Granted, the Bible and the other monotheistic texts were written long ago, by scribes who were writing in the language and style of their time, so some lack of modern clarity can be excused.

But there are many verses/assertions later within the Bible and other religious texts which state that they were not written by men but by God *Himself*. John 1:1, for example, says: "In the beginning was the Word, and the Word was with God, and the Word was God." I have heard it offered that the capitalized term, "Word," is referencing Jesus Christ rather than text, or "words" in the Bible which implies Trinity authorship rather than solely by the Deity. And like the Deity, in Christianity the Trinity is an assumption, even if the three names are referenced separately. That kind of assumed assertion, though, raises the question of why so powerful an entity as the creator of the universe would leave such crucial information to assumption and be so relatively non-meticulous and vague in its (I'm purposely avoiding a personal pronoun) dictation, and in the opening of the first chapter. Within most secular printed text, the noun (and small case) *word* does not obviously indicate a person. It is a *thing*. And even though the Deity and the Trinity are presumed synonymous in Christian teaching, since the Trinity includes God, Jesus Christ, and the Holy Spirit, it is *not* immediately clear or conclusive to the non-Christian reader that the Word is only Jesus. God, or the Holy Spirit, could be debated as the sole and independent author of the Bible. This confusion between the scribes who wrote out the text, and the purported authorship of the Deity makes me think of a humorous reference. In the words of the British comedian, Eddie Izzard, perhaps any confusing religious text can be called a "scribo!"

Creative and clever humor aside, I think it apparent that, in addition to many beautiful words of wisdom, biblical scripture and other religious texts abound in ambiguity. Granted, too, in many well-written books, characters are not necessarily defined or even introduced immediately at the beginning of the book. Books often begin "in progress" keeping the reader waiting in anticipation for more detailed information and action. However, to my knowledge and reading, this is not the case with Genesis, nor anywhere in the Bible or any other religious text. The existence, form, description, history, explanation, or any other physical detail about the Deity—God, Allah, Yahweh, the main character* —is simply missing, omitted, or at least not present. This specific character's existence, definition, and existential properties are simply and completely *assumed*. In all other literature, this omission would be considered sloppy, unclear, and poor writing. In the Bible and other religious texts, this basic assumption is taken unquestioningly for granted. It is for this reason that I feel the desire to raise what I think is the most important question about the Deity: What is *meant* by God?

Carl Sagan spoke to this directly in his book, *Broca's Brain*. "Some people think of God as an outsized, light-skinned male with a long beard, sitting up on a throne somewhere up there in the sky, busily tallying the fall of every sparrow. Others—for example, Baruch Spinoza and Albert Einstein—considered God to be essentially the sum total of the physical laws which describe the universe. I do not know of any compelling evidence for anthropomorphic patriarchs controlling human destiny from some hidden vantage point, but it would be madness to deny the existence of physical laws. Whether we believe in God depends very much on what we mean by God." [3]

---

* Speaking of characters, if there is a God, I could imagine God like Gandalf, Glenda the Good Witch of the North, or Aslan, the Lion. Kind, benevolent, wise, and with supernatural powers. I know that this contradicts my point about not assigning form or gender to the concept of God. But there is a difference to me between my fanciful imagination of God, and if I were to seriously assign form or gender to God. I think it is abundantly clear that most monotheistic religions don't consider their Deity as fanciful imagination.

Marcus J. Borg makes the same point in his book, *The God We Never Knew: Beyond Dogmatic Religion to a More Authentic Contemporary Faith.* "How are we to think of God?...What is our concept of God (or the Sacred, or Spirit, terms that I use interchangeably)? ...My central claim is very direct: our concept of God matters...Is it about believing in God as a supernatural being separate from the universe or about a relationship to the Spirit who is right here and all around us?...Both are found in the Bible and the Christian tradition. They are fundamentally different. The first...I will call...'supernatural theism.'...The second concept of God in the Christian tradition...I will call...'pantheism'...in our time, thinking of God as a supernatural being 'out there' has become an obstacle for many. It can make the reality of God seem doubtful...[but] many people are not aware that there is a second root concept of God within the Christian tradition—namely, pantheism." [4]

Reza Aslan made a similar point about pantheism in his book, *God: A Human History.* He writes, "One need not arrive at pantheism through religion at all, but rather through philosophy...the rationalist, Benedict Spinoza argu[ed] that since there could be but one 'substance' in the universe...whether that substance is called God or Nature, it must exist as a single, undifferentiated reality...Or ignore God altogether and simply look to science and its unifying conception of nature...Either way, the fundamental truth remains: All is One, and One is All. It is simply up to the individual to decide what 'the One' is: how it should be defined and how it should be experienced." [5]

Like Aslan, though I suspect that pantheism might be synonymous with the perception of Spinoza and Einstein, I think Sagan and Borg are representative of those scientists and theologians, respectively, who recognize the need for greater clarity with respect to the exact meaning of God. And while I'm sure that there are many religious people who feel very clear about their own meaning of God—including God as a transcendent, yet living being—and consider physical evidence for proof pointless, I think it would be fair to presume that there are also many people who imagine God metaphorically instead of literally. The notion to them of God as anything approaching supernatural, much less an "anthropomorphic patriarch," would seem silly and even preposterous. But those with a deep belief in God as a conscious and living entity would undoubtedly agree with Marcus Borg and disagree with Paul Tillich. They not only sense God (supernaturally or pantheologically) as *a being*, but refer to God as a "*Supreme* Being" (in capital first letters, again implying a proper noun). That term is, of course, the origin of the title of this book.

～

Because I am interested in origins and definitions, and this chapter pertains to *the* beginning, in a moment I would like to carefully examine the word associated with that beginning: God. However, before specifically defining the word, here is a short synopsis of what I have observed that God means to the deeply religious and then to the scientist.

A religious person uses the term, *God*, to define the creator of the universe and life and uses a proper noun—with the convention of the capitalized first letter—which attaches a "persona" or "being" to the Creator, Entity, or Deity.

A scientist stops short of professing a persona, entity, or separate "being" to explain the vastness of the universe, nor do they necessarily use a capital first letter to create a proper noun. They use the term *cosmos* or *universe* (they are different words which refer to the same thing, and I will use them interchangeably throughout this book).

All these terms, *God/cosmos/universe*, it seems to me, could be interpreted as the totality of the observable universe. The only remaining problem is more accurately defining the terms. Here is where a potential problem arises and where both the religious person and the scientist need to be flexible. Although terms are of secondary importance, it is nonetheless very important to know what is specifically meant by terms—and certainly by *these* specific words—if it is not simply the suggestion that I just made of *the totality of the observable universe*. These may be among the largest terms that humans use, so it is much more important to define them well.

The word *cosmos*, derived from the 13th century Greek word *kosmos*, means, "an orderly harmonious systematic universe—compare [as opposed to] CHAOS; and "a complex orderly self-inclusive system."

The word, *universe*, means (at dictionary.com), "the totality of known or supposed objects and phenomena throughout space; the cosmos; macrocosm" or (in the Miriam-Webster Dictionary), "the whole body of things and phenomena observed or postulated: cosmos." Clearly, dictionaries define the words cosmos and universe similarly.

The etymology of the word, *God*, is (surprisingly, or unsurprisingly) elusive and ambiguous. There seems to be no scholarly certainty of an original source or meaning. The closest concrete candidate derives from the Gothic word, *gheu* meaning, "to invoke," or "to sacrifice." In Francis J. Hall's ten-volume tome, *Dogmatic Theology*, after offering those two definitions for gheu he writes, "Thus God is the One to whom sacrifice is offered." [6] And the word, invoking, can be interpreted as referencing, requesting, or even beseeching, all of which are consistent with the religious ritual of prayer. Though invoking or sacrificing are only two of many characteristic demonstrations to the Deity, they are certainly plausible suggestions as etymologies* for God.

In the Webster's New World College Dictionary, the word *god*, in its common noun form, means, "any of various beings conceived of as supernatural, immortal, and having special powers over the lives and affairs of the people and the course of nature; deity, esp. a male deity: typically considered objects of worship." In the same dictionary, but as a proper noun, *God* means, "in monotheistic religions, the Supreme or ultimate reality, as the Being perfect in power, wisdom, and goodness whom men worship as creator and ruler of the universe."

Besides it being interesting that a male reference is given in both of the definitions of the word *god*—the first with "a *male* deity" and the second with, "whom *men* worship" (to describe people in general) —there is a similarity to the definitions of *cosmos/universe* and *god*. All the definitions describe a subject of the most monumental scale and perception. A "complex orderly system," "orderly harmonious universe," and "the totality of known or supposed objects and phenomena throughout space" are similar to "ultimate reality." A god as an "object of worship" is similar to how all of us feel when gazing up on a brilliantly clear and starry night: beholding the

---

* Contrary to another opinion, though they only differ by one letter and are conceptually identical, the word *God* is not thought to be derived from the word *good*. I actually thought it might be a convenient coincidence. I imagined that since both are one-syllable words, the choice between the two might have been that two consonants and *one* vowel are easier to spell and pronounce than two consonants and *two* vowels! There is also the obvious and comical question in the palindrome, God/dog. Is our relationship to God similar to a dog's with us?

universe with wonder and veneration. The scientist and the religious person both feel *awe*.

~~~

In the vein of defining words, another word that is utilized in much religious teaching, also not as a proper noun but given very weighty emphasis, is the word *believe*. This word is used in religion as both an infinitive verb, *to believe*, and as a common noun, *belief*. In both those word forms, it is often used as the strongest evidence for the existence of God; at least the strongest personal evidence. In John 3:16-18: "For God so loved the world, that he gave his only begotten Son, that whosoever believeth in him should not perish, but have everlasting life." Obviously, the Greek derivative of believe, *believeth* (translated from the Greek verb *pisteuo*), in this passage of scripture is not confusing, but it is completely clear that the focus is on belief: first on God, then on his Son (capital "S" like capital "G"), and then on the importance of believing in the two, God and His Son. (In math, it very closely resembles the Transitive Property of Equality: If $a = b$ and $b = c$, then $a = c$. In Christianity, God would be "a," Christ his Son would be "b," and believing in God (through Christ) would be "c.") This example in the Book of John, of the focus on belief, is one of many throughout the Bible.

Richard Dawkins questions this stress on belief in his book, *The God Delusion*. He asks, "But why, in any case, do we so readily accept the idea that the one thing you must do if you want to please God is *believe* in him? What's so special about believing? Isn't it just as likely that God would reward kindness, or generosity, or humility? Or sincerity? What if God is a scientist who rewards honest seeking after truth as the supreme virtue? Indeed, wouldn't the designer of the universe *have* to be a scientist?" [7]

I share Dawkins's feeling, but I have an additional perspective on one of his words: *humility*. Though believing too often connotes blind following to me, I also understand that, for many religious people, belief evokes the sense of humility that Dawkins suggests. It is a humble sense of trust, respect, and reverence, which, for the believer, honors the universe and its "Designer" and brings them inner peace and security. Belief in God becomes a psychological but universal belief. Scientific assertions and knowledge can be perceived as pompous and arrogant; ironically, pomposity and arrogance can often be exactly what the extremely religious exhibit under the veil of humility.

While I deeply admire humility, I do not think that humility should outweigh or negate detailed questions or knowledge. Too often, religious humility evokes supplication and submission rather than intelligent wonder. The humility to which Dawkins is referring is both similar and dissimilar to the religious sense. It is humility with our minute size and remote location in the universe, coupled with a passion for inquiry and knowledge, just absent a deity.

Now let's look at the word, believe, in a non-religious context and compare it to a couple of other, similar words that could be (and often are) substituted for the word, believe, in religion. The substitute words are *think* and *know*. These latter two words are not primarily religious words, but they are often used in place of the word believe to express religious conviction. I would like to define each of these words in turn—first by the dictionary definitions and then in my own imaginary examples—to try to shed some light on what I suspect might be near the root of understanding at least a few of the word choices in religious teaching.

In the Merriam-Webster Dictionary, as might be expected the first definition of the word *believe* means, "to have a firm religious faith." The remaining definitions do not reference religion specifically. For example, the second definition is, "to accept something as true, genuine, or real." Since the word *something* is not specific, there is plainly no specific religious inference in that definition. It is curious to me that the first definition pertains to religion even though the word has other, non-religious meanings. Granted, the choice of the Miriam Webster Dictionary is mine, but the question that occurs to me is that, regardless of who chose the order of the definitions, why did they decide to put the religious definition first? There is always some subjective bias with any choice. It would appear that subjective religious bias played some role in the order of those definitions. On the other hand, if the word, believe, originally meant to have a firm religious faith, then how did the word come to have other, more general definitions expressing at least some reservation? It is curious to me that in this particular dictionary the religious definition is listed first *and* that there is only one religious definition of several definitions. Mostly, given the fact that there are several variations of meaning for this word, most of which are non-religious, it intrigues me as to why religion gives the word such strong importance.

To me, the word believe is more like the non-religious definitions. It indicates an expression of a strong thought, sense, or feeling, but with some reservation. Before I offer examples of my own, here is an interesting example of the word, believe, used in a television script. It is during a moment in the episode, "Criminal Stories," from the Emmy Award-winning and longest-running prime-time television detective series, *Law and Order: Special Victims Unit (S.V.U.)*. This scene also illuminates perspectives on the words, fact, and faith (which I discuss in detail in Chapters 5 and 7, respectively). The prosecutor, John Buchanan (Delaney Williams), is cross-examining detective, Odafin "Fin" Tutuola (Ice T):

> Buchanan: Detective, when an interview subject lies to you initially, is it harder to trust them going forward?
> Tutuola: Yes
> Buchanan: Didn't the victim in this case lie *repeatedly* at the outset and make up and stage an entirely false scenario?
> Tutuola: That's right, but given that her brother was...
> Buchanan: ...so she lied to you and fabricated evidence in the past. Can you be sure she's telling the truth now?
> Tutuola: I believe she is.
> Buchanan: You *believe*? So it's more about faith than fact. Can you see how others might have some doubt?

Like the prosecutor's point, I think it is quite understandable that the word, believe, can leave too much room for doubt or reservation.

Here is an example of the word believe from my own imagination (the italics imply hypothetical conversations, not quotes):

Would the building be open Saturday morning if it's open Saturday afternoon?

Well, I believe so, but I'm not sure. You'd have to check the building schedule to make sure.

Granted, the choice of words above are my own, but I suggest that the word, believe, may not the best word to choose to indicate the deepest devotion or conviction. Again, it is curious that a word that usually refers to thoughts with some reservation and doubt would be used by many religions to express the strongest conviction.

The two other words that are used by both science and religion, but are sometimes used by religion as substitutes for the word believe, are *think* and *know*.

All of the dictionary definitions of the word *think* are non-religious. To me, the word *think* indicates slightly stronger conviction than the word *believe*. An example of my sense and use of the word *think* is as follows (again this example is from my imagination, and the italics are a hypothetical conversation; this example also reveals a point of my socio-political thinking):

What do you think should be done with the problem of immigration in the United States today?

Well, I think that since we were all once immigrants—or descendants of immigrants, and thus a nation of immigrants—that the problem should be dealt with as if it were we ourselves who were trying to immigrate and allow the immigration as long as some basic legal security measures are administered, thus making immigration simple, but legal. In other words, I think that any and all immigrants who pass a reasonable, but non-invasive legal security process should be welcome.

So, in my view, the word *think* is used to express a strong opinion, with a little less reservation than the word *believe*.

All of the dictionary definitions of the word *know* are also non-religious. I concur with the dictionary definitions. To me, the word *know* indicates the most surety of a thought or idea beyond a reasonable doubt. Here, again, is my hypothetical example (which will also reveal some of my strongest feelings about life):

Tell me some of the things that you feel you know or are reasonably sure about, or as sure as you can be based upon what you've learned.

Well, I know that I feel love for people and all of life. I know that I also need love. I know that life as we know it, or are aware of it, is highly complex but inordinately beautiful. I know that I have a desire to be as sure and convinced about something as I possibly can be before I can say that I know it; although that knowledge needs to be flexible so that, if it is shown to be incorrect or misguided, I can comfortably adjust my point of view, even excitedly so, and enjoy knowing the new information. I know that the Sun is a medium-sized star. I know that the planets revolve around the Sun and constitute our Solar System. I know that it's nearly impossible to foresee that any knowledge will be consistent without the passage of time. I know that the universe contains most if not all of the chemical/physical properties that constitute our own physical chemistry and that are found on Earth, so that it is easier now to deduce that what we are made of, and what the universe is made of, appear to be one and the same. I also know that there are many different points of view in humanity, both scientific and religious (and everywhere in-between!) and that this is part of what makes life and learning extremely interesting.

My point in all my hypothetical examples with the three words above—believe, think, and know—is not to further my own opinions (though I obviously expressed a few in them), but to demonstrate that I think we should be clear, careful, and conscious about the words we invent and use. I hope I was clear in my examples. Words should be used less loosely, especially in writing. We invented words for the express reason of trying to be understood more clearly. Using words too loosely completely defeats that purpose. That is particularly so in writing because writing is much more permanent; hence the need for any verification or confirmation, "in writing." Of course, there are words that are classified as, "usage," meaning that they are intended to be, and are, understood well enough when used more loosely. But usage words are the exception not the rule. In general, words need to be used properly and specifically so that as little confusion results as possible. Of the words I discussed above, I think that the most vague and misused is the word, believe, particularly in a religious context. Like the prematurity of conclusion that its use fosters, I suggest that the word, believe, is too frequently and mistakenly used as a *substitute* for the word, know.

Carl Sagan's widow, Ann Druyan, made the succinct and separate distinction between these two words when she was asked by an interviewer about her late husband's religious feelings. The interviewer asked, "Didn't he [Sagan] want to believe?" Ann Druyan replied simply and earnestly, "He didn't want to believe. He wanted to know." [8]

This would address my first confusion with religion, and specifically with the definition (or lack of a definition) of God—the assumed *know*ledge of the meaning and existence of God. I certainly don't know whether God does or does not exist. I think either is possible. I have senses about what I think is closer to the truth about the meaning, existence, or non-existence of

God, but I certainly can't be sure. Either way, I don't have enough evidence, nor have I read or heard of indisputable evidence.

That's only my opinion of course. I would hope and guess (and it is a humble, hopefully non-arrogant guess) that many religious people, if honest, might say the same: that they might *think* they *know* what they mean by *believing* in God, but that they might not fully understand what their belief means—what is actually *meant* by God, or even what *they mean* by God—or have an accurate and clear understanding of these italicized words, both separately and within the context of their belief. In other words, I suspect that the reason for my confusion with the first sentence of Genesis is because the words used in the text have never been clearly enough defined within the specific religious context, and have been allowed to remain loosely defined. My encouragement for the clear use of words in this context is a paraphrase of the quotes of Sagan and Hitchens: the larger the concept, the greater the need for clarity (in the language/words used) in describing the concept.

~~~

To many skeptics, the idea of a Supreme Being is a fairy tale, as are many religious stories: divinity in general, the Immaculate Conception, the Resurrection, the Burning Bush, Jesus walking on water or feeding 5,000 people with only five loaves of bread and two fish, Moses parting the Red Sea, etc. These are fairly tales to skeptics in the same way that Santa Claus, the Easter Bunny, a Pooka (Harvey, the rabbit), the Tooth Fairy, the Sandman, Groundhog Day, etc. are obvious fables and fairy tales to the great majority of us as we get older. They are fun and fanciful fiction for children and all of our playful imagination, but not to be taken seriously as adults. Sagan put this comparison well in his book, *The Demon Haunted World*, "We tell children about Santa Claus, the Easter Bunny, and the Tooth Fairy for reasons we think emotionally sound, but then disabuse them of these myths before they're grown. Why retract? Because their well-being as adults depends on them knowing the world as it really is. We worry, and for good reason, about adults who still believe in Santa Claus." [9] Stephen Hawking stated it similarly to Ian Sample, science correspondent of *The Guardian* on May 11, 2011, "I regard the brain as a computer which will stop working when its components fail. There is no heaven or afterlife for broken down computers; that is a fairy story for people afraid of the dark." [10]

Following Sagan's and Hawking's points above, as children mature into older children, teenagers, and then young adults, maybe strongly reinforcing the concept of God as lovely, historical metaphor and mythology rather than literal divinity would be a much healthier practice. Yes, there is documentation and its purported history in the form of religious texts, but, as I touched on before, the actual source/authors of religious texts and the clarity of those texts are debatable to the extent of rendering the validity of that documentation as dubious as many fantasy and fairy tales. So why should the idea of the existence of God be taken so seriously by adults when there is no better evidence for the existence of God than there is for the existence of fabled characters?

A sobering reason may be that the most dramatic religious stories could have been (and perhaps still are) adopted and utilized as a mass organizational tool; groups of people are more unwieldy than individuals. And because the concept of divinity in the imagery of a male *personal* God is rooted in terms that humans already know, a father-figure ("God, the Father"), that organizational approach can be easily and consistently effective. We all have a father and want to emulate him. If he is still living, we want to be like him, reside safely with him, be protected by him, and be loved and nurtured by him, unceasingly and unconditionally. Don't we all want and need unencumbered and unconditional love from our fathers? Though we want the same from our biological mothers, and they are the sex/gender that carried us in-utero and gave birth to us, it can be argued that our biological fathers are the dominant sex/gender by the strength of pure physics. Charles Darwin's "Survival of the Fittest," for better or worse, seems to suggest that the *physically strongest* beings tend to dominate and influence many of our deepest needs, including those psychological and metaphoric.

This is, I think, one origin of misogyny, or *assumed* male superiority. Muscle and mind are both physics, but muscular strength is arguably inferior to mental strength, and I think that women have often proven themselves stronger in the mental category. Frankly, I suspect that misogyny originates from an obviously simple reason: A man's fear of an unsuccessful erection. Every man fears this loss of his most vital physical function. For more insecure men, it's easier to blame the female for impotence. This might have been the subconscious reason in the Bible's *Genesis* story for casting Eve as the original sinner, and the choice of God as a male deity. Both are establishing assumed and arrogant male dominance, and false female gullibility and inferiority. However, wiser men honor a woman's keen intellect and curiosity. They innately respect, revere, and love women. Like the saying, "Respect your elders," men who love women know to, "Respect their *betters*."

Thus, regardless of one's personal, family, and life background and circumstances, how comforting it must feel for some people to imagine (believe in) a powerful *fatherly* God rather than a tender and vulnerable *motherly* God: an infinite, strong, and powerful male entity, immune to the foibles, inconsistencies, and vulnerabilities of human nature, offering an ultimate and eternal residence of happiness ("Heaven"), and always able and available to love. A perfect patriarch.

We also like the idea of that protective patriarch being an assumed truth and immediately available, both as a balm and cure for our emotional pain, and as a defense against the cataclysmic and annihilating forces of nature. In other words, if all one needs to do is *believe* that such an entity is going to help us survive, and even forever, that's much easier and more appealing than the idea of our being alone in life and vulnerable to nature. Perhaps *most* discouraging is the hard reality that life seems to be a finite amount of time. We long to be spared from both pain *and* death. If, however, we are alone in the universe, there is no such divine patriarch (no God), and/or our lives are indeed finite, then we have no recourse but to figure things out entirely for ourselves, including averting death when faced with the extreme forces of nature. If there is no deity, then we are left with the primary tool we have to survive against the natural forces: our brains (I suggest that this is an advantage we have, not a disadvantage). That's harder work, and harder work is more daunting and frightening, less immediately secure, and therefore less immediately appealing. In short, it is possible that for many people, and for all these reasons, it is simply more emotionally reassuring to believe in God.

My general sense is that humans have cast God (by any name, in any religion), the story of *Genesis*, and many other religious stories into human terms because that is how we understand our own birth, lives, survival, and death, and particularly our fear of the latter. As in the father-figure, we crave to superimpose human-like characteristics on the cosmos. The likely reason—as many authors, far more learned and scholarly than I, have also offered—is cosmic loneliness. A universe created by its own natural law, possibly with no other life but on our planet, would feel inconceivably isolated, abandoned, and marooned. The possible fact that all of life on Earth may be the only life in the universe would be dismal and harder to bear than if the universe were teaming with life or at least evident elsewhere. Even if life does exist elsewhere in the universe, it is probably disappointingly distant.

Another inherent and intriguing fact of life is that it doesn't seem to exist well *completely alone*. In addition to simply reproducing for survival, we (and really most all life) need love and companionship (hence the story in Genesis of Eve being "created" for (and from) Adam). So even if we aren't alone in the universe, the fact that other beings are probably very far away is like a cosmic long-distance relationship. And since there is as yet no evidence of possible life anywhere else in the universe (except the evidence of water, or the remnants of water, on Mars and Saturn's moons, Titan and Enceladus), it is as yet an *imaginary* cosmic long-distance relationship. And even if there is other life in the universe, it will likely be a very long time before we ever make contact, either through our efforts or theirs.

I think the subconscious possibility of cosmic loneliness is one reason why our ancestors like astronomer Claudius Ptolemy thought in terms of a geocentric Solar System, or evangelists like Billy Graham reinforced the idea of a God who created the universe and then human beings as the dominant life form. If we *are* alone in the universe, both of those perspectives allow us to think and feel that the Earth, and we, are of central importance. That comforting focus of the Earth and humans as the intended and inevitable goal of the universe is the basis of the curious and often misconstrued *anthropic principle* (which I will discuss in more detail in Part II): the universe produced the requisite physics for the primary purpose of forming the Earth and us.

So, we might feel the need to exaggerate our own, human importance on the Earth (and in the whole universe) in order to not only feel less alone and more secure, but that we feel *most important*. It's a kind of cosmic egoism (really ego*tism*), which I also think has its roots in insecurity, survival, and fear of death. We feel bolstered thinking that the Earth and humans are the focal point of the universe. And if a Creator, God, made the Earth as that focal point, it would follow that the first human made by that God would be the focus of *life*. Everything about humans from this perspective would be special and less lonely because the cosmos had been created specifically for us. However, it also smacks of Dr. Seuss's, *The Sneetches*, or cosmic superiority and segregation. Frankly, regardless of the reasons, I don't think superiority or segregation is ever a healthy or mature way to feel secure or special.

This self-centered and egotistical thinking is, to me, a possible underlying reason for many if not all of the antagonistic political conflicts and violence of any kind in human history. If the Earth and humans beings are special and important in the universe to God, by extension, and like *The Sneetches*, one person or group could feel the need to be more important (self-centered) than another person or group, generated by the same innate fear of cosmic loneliness and our individual death. If we feel like we are individually, or as a group, the most important, we feel more secure and more like our own survival is guaranteed. This seems to me quite plausible since the size of our planet and the laws of nature, not to mention the immensity of the universe, offer us very little or no control. It's much more difficult to feel secure and/or survive with minimal control.

My strongest feeling and encouragement is to abandon all pretension and presumption of cosmic human importance. Besides the well-established fact that modern humans have only been in existence a scant 200,000 to 500,000 years[*] of the estimated 13.799 billion-year-old universe[†], in the human tenure on Earth this has translated all too often into human arrogance and conceit, which are never valuable, productive, or admirable qualities. Importance is best gauged by loving kindness, compassion, assistance, and accomplishment, not dominance. Better to simply enjoy the sweetness, love, and phenomenon of life—no matter where and how it all began and no matter when and how each of us will inevitably die—and make the most of the opportunities in life, through love and hard work rather than trying to be better, more right, or more important than anyone or anything else. In my

---

[*] http://en.m.wikipedia.org/wiki/Timeline_of_human_evolution

[†] A very recent discovery by scientists strongly suggests that the universe may be one billion years younger, at approximately 12.5 billion years old. Like the discovery of quantum physics, this new discovery is confounding scientists. The new evidence is both unmistakable *and* elusive to clear detail. https://www.nbcnews.com/mach/science/universe-may-be-billion-years-younger-we-thought-scientists-are-ncna1005541

opinion, one becomes better and has a more fulfilling life by sharing love and pleasure with others, not by being *more important* than others.

My late paternal grandmother, Jaime Grace Yeager Richey, had a small plaque that hung on her kitchen wall and had a lovely message. It read: "It's nice to be important, but it's more important to be nice." I always thought that was a sweet and unique kernel of truth. There probably is no *more important* anywhere in the universe, just as there is no *right to life* anywhere on Earth, and maybe in the universe. (That latter statement—partly a paraphrase from the Sagans's chapter on abortion in *Billions and Billions*—is in complete disagreement with the opinion of the Christian belief in the "Right to Life" for human beings, which I will address more in the next chapter. But then my argument here takes complete issue with that belief/opinion.). Nature doesn't seem to work with "right." But that's where intelligence comes in and probably how life evolved. Once in a while, life springs up because the chemistry of nature generates organisms that figure out how to create a little bit on their own. And a "little bit" evolves into "more" and "better" which generates better and better intelligence. Humans are one phenomenal example. We are creatures who have developed intelligence to be able to figure out, understand, and live with some of the sporadic beauty and chaos of the universe. That in itself might be the "purpose" of life, if there is one: Regardless of how the universe began, the more we love and understand the more we are able to perceive the beauty of the universe, and create a little of *our own beauty* despite the chaos.

Chapter 3

ABSOLUTELY *RIGHT* ?

The method we have followed [his earlier stated "analytic description of the presence of absolutes within the universe of relativities"] *liberates us from thinking in terms of questions and arguments about the existence of an absolute being, whether it is called God, the One, or Brahman-Atman, Fate, Nature, or Life. That to which our analysis led us, the Absolute itself, is not an absolute being, which is a contradiction in terms.*
It is Being-Itself.

Paul Tillich
My Search For Absolutes

There is probably no such thing as anything being permanently or eternally true. The phrase, "There are exceptions to everything," is a reflection of that probability. Even the laws of physics might prove vulnerable or inapplicable on as yet unknown worlds. Taking into consideration exceptions and other workable scenarios requires more flexibility, effort, and risk. It's harder work. Fear of the slippery-slope can occur—the concern that leaving the door open for other solutions might mean that even preposterous propositions will be adopted. That is why, in my view, it is very *easy* to think in absolutes. It takes less thought. It is a position of extremity which avoids the interest, necessity, and pleasure of complexity and nuance.

It is also a stance that indicates discomfort with an issue. Instead of finding a solution or set of solutions that would solve a problem more comprehensively, a general, broad-based, or *absolute* solution is often adopted which covers too much in fear of covering too little. I think part of the discomfort comes from realizing that, in some situations, it is apparent that the absolute does not apply. If the discomfort is ignored, objection to the absolute almost always increases. That is to be expected. If an absolute worked in all situations there would be no objection. This speaks well of human intelligence. When something works poorly, there tends to be great outcry. When something obviously works well, there tends to be less serious objection.

For example, not since the Boston Tea Party have American citizens rebelled in such demonstration against the levying of a tax. Granted, the destruction of the British tea by the early colonists was in response to a tax imposed by the British Parliament—there was, as yet, no United States of America, so no United States federal government—but the severity of that objection to paying a tax is unique in pre-American and American history. The objection was not handled with diplomacy. The rejection of the tax was demonstrated drastically and absolutely. Though it resulted in the American Revolution—independence from Britain and the eventual formation of the

United States of America—American citizens now acknowledge with much less severe protest that some taxation is necessary.*

Sure, we grumble that taxes are too high, that there are too many taxes; that there be no more new taxes, or that the tax revenue is being spent inequitably or poorly. But most of us acknowledge that some taxes are necessary in order to insure a common benefit. Taxes are like a public insurance policy. When everyone contributes to it fairly, everyone benefits from how the government then puts the revenue to use (if governments use the revenue wisely, which is always questionable and should be questioned). We may object to the *way* our tax money is utilized or, more recently, to how *much* of our money is apportioned for taxes, but we have not protested in a long time to the degree of *refusing to pay* a tax (tax "loopholes" are a surreptitious exception). So, by-and-large, we agree that taxes work to help pay for public benefits.

Another example of something that raises very little serious objection, both here and in much of the rest of the world, is our form of government in the United States. We have essentially retained our form of government since its inception in 1776—a democracy. Even though there are extremists in the United States (just as there are extremists in every country) who have little confidence or trust in democracy, it is obvious that extremism is still not tolerated by the majority of us; which is why democracy continues to work here and why there is less extremist activity from the citizens of the United States compared with some other countries.

---

* Though the Boston Tea Party was understandably motivated by anger that the early colonies were not yet represented by their own government, the newly-formed Tea Party in the United States—named for the December 16th, 1773 Boston incident—is an ironically contradictory form of protest cloaked in a political party. The Tea Party's resentment is not directed toward a foreign government. It is directed at its *own* federal government, the very entity from which the early colonies desired representation. The Tea Party seeks to significantly shrink the influence and legislative capacity of the federal government, which is, in effect, less representation, exactly the opposite of the desire of the early colonists. It is consistent, however, with the desire of the early American colonists for less restrictive and regulated government. Less regulation and restriction allows the unimpeded, unrestricted, and unlimited acquisition of land and wealth. It is also, in my view, an example of an extreme or absolute position.

In the 2000 presidential election, however, between then-Governor George W. Bush and Senator Al Gore, it appeared to many American (and likely many foreign) citizens that the Supreme Court of the United States violated our democracy by ordering a halt to the recounting of the confusing voting ballots (the "hanging chads") in Florida. The Supreme Court's decision gave the impression of curtailing the democratic process of ensuring that every vote was important and counted. Though the Supreme Court was successful in that particular and isolated interruption of the democratic process, the Supreme Court certainly felt the negative ramifications of its action and the displeasure of many of the American citizens. That displeasure took the form of protest, an action or ritual that is still permitted under the Constitution. That is evidence itself that democracy in the United States is still functioning and is arguably one of the better, if not the best, forms of government.

But even as we profess by our Constitution to support diversity, liberty, and freedom for all, when it comes to a question of morals, we are still too inflexible and tend to adhere too strongly to absolutes that work less well or are dysfunctional. Religion errs with this more often than science since, between religion and science, it is religion that professes more often to be the domain of morality; religions frequently argue that science cannot answer moral questions. The very adoption of the word *right* by many religions, conservatives, and Tea Party politics, while labeling the liberal media and politics and the sciences as *left*, shows the presumption of religious conservatives that their viewpoint is "right," or correct.[*] It is an extremely arrogant posture.

I do not mean that as a solution to such inflexibility that we should be loosely moral or amoral. And I don't think that either science or religion alone should be our sole moral barometer. But I would argue that our criteria for deciding what we think is a moral position can tend to be absolute and inflexible, and does not match the levels of intelligence and compromise, or non-absolutist positions, manifested in the two examples above of tax

---

[*] I have seen the alliterative phrase about Rush Limbaugh, "Rush is Right." That translates both that he is politically right (conservative of center) and that he is correct. It is an attempt at a clever double-meaning. In my view, it is much more pompous than clever.

compliance and practice of democracy. It is with the category of *morality* that we consistently continue to adopt an absolutist position.

An example of how absolutist positions on morality affect public life is the "Right to Life," or "Pro Life" campaign of Christians and Fundamentalists (politically, the "Right Wing"), and the "Right to Choose" of progressives and feminist supporters (politically, the "Left Wing"). These extreme positions constitute the renewed and ongoing debate on abortion; this contrasted with the 1973 Supreme Court decision of Roe vs. Wade. Both campaigns take an absolute position. In essence, they are all-or-nothing stances. They seem unwilling to compromise.

In an effort to offer a compromise, Carl Sagan and Ann Druyan wrote an article for Parade magazine in the April 22, 1990 issue of Parade magazine entitled, "The Question of Abortion: A Search for Answers." They expanded that article into a complete chapter in Sagan's last book, *Billions and Billions*, called, "Abortion: Is It Possible To Be Both Pro-Life And Pro-Choice?" Both the article and the chapter pose a unique, and scientifically testable middle-ground as a solution between these two absolutist positions.

The authors suggest that the subconscious motive fueling the "Right-to-Life" campaign of conservatives is the deep awareness of human intelligence: our ability to *think*. They pose this because the "Right-to-Life" campaign is all-but-silent on the indiscriminate killing of other, less intelligent forms of life by humans which are not defined as murder. Killing a chimpanzee, for example—the primate that shares 99.6 percent of our genes—is not, they point out, classified as murder (it probably should be). And since laws such as murder are enacted, they remind, to protect the weak from the strong, a fetus needs and deserves protection from the state against *indiscriminate* abortions. The Sagans suggest the earliest detection of fetal brain development as their main criteria for limiting legal abortions. Fetal brain waves, akin to normal adult brain wave patterns[*], they say, are initially detectable only after the beginning of the *third trimester* of gestation. At that point, they aver, the fetus should be assumed to be an aware person because it can think, hence more likely conscious of the horror of being aborted. From that point on, indiscriminate abortions should be defined as "murder."

---

[*] A notable comparison is the medical definition of death. "Brain death *is* death." https://www.kidney.org/atoz/content/braindeath Thus, it could be argued, (fetal) brain activity *is* life.

The pregnant woman no longer has sole choice. Conversely, from conception to the commencement of the third trimester of gestation, abortions performed by a physician should be legal, available, and primarily the pregnant woman's choice.

The documented evidence of the earliest recorded fetal brain waves is available but sparse. Two sources[*] assert 40 days as the earliest; these early detections might be other fetal nervous signals misinterpreted as brain waves. The Sagans's report, however, is consistent with an undated but highly thorough op-ed article by Margaret Sykes.[†] Sykes argues that, because the brain is not fully formed in utero until approximately 150 days (21 weeks), distinctive fetal brain waves prior to that are not biologically possible. One potential indication of a time-frame for the Sykes article is in another article written both in support and rebuttal of her article, in TheMediaReport.com,[‡] October 30, 2006. That article wisely takes care not to conclusively substantiate the 40-day fetal brain wave detection hypothesis. I offer that even if brain waves *are* barely perceptible at 40 days in gestation, it still allows the woman to easily notice if she misses her next menstruation (which would likely be sooner than 30 days from her last sexual activity). That would more greatly ensure that she got an early, safe, and less traumatic abortion—well within the first trimester—if that is her choice. The Roe vs. Wade decision continues to protect that right, *and* the more developed fetus later in gestation against murder, thus preventing irresponsible and indiscriminate abortions.

The Sagans suggest, as I am, that the Roe vs. Wade law simultaneously allows for early, safe, and ethical abortions *plus* protects the "thinking" human fetus later from murder. The Sagans's reasoning and proposition in support of the current law on abortion is both a pragmatic compromise and a sensitive solution to a deeply divided and complex issue.

Another perspective on absolutist political positions in general, and then on morality specifically, was offered by my maternal and late uncle, Frank Ayre Lee. In one of many in-person and phone interviews I conducted with

---

[*] http://www.pregnancy.org/article/overview-fetal-development
http://prolifeaction.org/faq/unborn.php#brainwaves

[†] about.com(http://www.svss-uspda.ch/pdf/brain_waves.pdf

[‡] http://www.themediareport.com/2006/10/30/a-response-to-margaret-sykes-and-the-brain-waves-issue/)

him (and recorded, with his permission), I asked him first to clarify what to me is the inconsistency of the Republican position against "big government." I asked why Republicans consider most any federal domestic initiative—the Roe vs. Wade abortion law, health care, housing, transportation, education, raising the minimum wage, gun-control, tax increases for the wealthiest Americans, etc.—"big government," but other government-invasive initiatives—the effort to criminalize abortion, funding the Vietnam, Gulf War, Iraq, and Afghanistan wars, unlimited and indiscriminate individual and corporate campaign contributions, tax breaks for the wealthy, etc.—*not* "big government." All of the latter were also proposed or instigated at the federal level or by the Supreme Court, which could be equally interpreted as intrusion by the federal government.

I asked from where the idea of the federal government being too intrusive in public life came. I asked if it descended from the Church of England's domination of the lives of the British citizens which motivated the pilgrims' departure and subsequent settling in the "New World." My uncle responded. "No, no, no, no...I think this is 'home grown.' I think this came out, essentially, of the south, which, even at the time of the signing of the Declaration [of Independence], didn't want any interference by a *central* governmental authority in what they considered to be the states' rights. And I think the Republicans—and of course they weren't called Republicans in those days...I think they were called Whigs—they were opposed to government regulation of almost anything they wanted the states to handle...I think that that same philosophy then shifted to the south in post-Civil War-era, after the abolition of slavery, when the south became solidly Democratic...but *only* because Abraham Lincoln was a Republican. But Abraham Lincoln bore very little resemblance to today's Republicans. So, no, I think that whole attitude is "home grown," and I think it evolved out of the concept that an active federal government might *interfere* with the amassing of great fortune and might be contrary to the spirit of the "Frontier." There was an American "mystique" having to do with the wide-open western frontier...cowboys...all this jazz...and I think that became...it's kind of a myth...but it became imbued in the American psyche. Anything that tramples on what they regard as the right to shoot your neighbor, deny 'em water rights, foreclose on his ranch the first time he misses a payment, all that stuff...I think that became the mantra of the Republican party...and "big government" [the Federal government] tends to try to limit those things.

State governments have been *notoriously* unable to limit that stuff, and so the Republicans have adopted...what was [in Lincoln's day] solidly the Democratic south. And as a consequence, [since the turn of the 20th century] the south has voted solidly Republican for *how many campaigns now*? You know...*today's* southern Republican is *yesterday's* southern Democrat. The name [Whig/Democrat then, Republican now] is a little misleading...[but] the *idea* that nobody should interfere with 'em—even when they're bein' crooked (chuckles) —is the *same*! And...so...no...I think this is a 'home grown' thing."

I followed up by asking why the Republicans today don't seem to realize that when they push their own agenda—like attempting to criminalize abortion—they are perceived by Democrats as hypocritical, as *also* being "big government." He continued. "Well, my feeling is that that's when their *ideology* gets 'in the road' of their theory of government. The big trouble—and the Republicans have always had this problem—is that they are an ideological group, generally speaking...Christian right, anti-abortion, anti-gun-control, and so forth...and I think that the difficulty is that when that conflicts with their aversion to "big government," the ideology takes over. So it's alright for the government to invade your bedroom—gay marriage, for instance—but that's not "big government," that's *morality*...in the Republican 'eye.' So they ["big government" and "ideology"] get very confused."

On the issue of morality, the religious or ideological mindset tends to reach too quickly for an absolute position—and invoke a deity—without seeing the inconsistencies in its own thinking.

Granted, it is difficult and practically unrealistic to find a solution to a problem that would satisfy *everyone's* objections (which is another reason that the absolutist position tends to be adopted in the first place). But choosing an absolute solution that leaves many peripheral issues unsolved doesn't seem practical either. Curiously, what is often interpreted as "waffling" (such as George McGovern or John Kerry in their respective presidential campaigns, or any person in public service who is perceived as frequently changing their mind) might be the best solution in many cases: that of adopting some form of middle-ground—as the Sagans attempted to do—and being willing to have the flexibility to change or adjust the decision with time. That is, in fact, the premise of science.

50   A Supreme *Question*

~~~

The following is a very extreme example (and I ask the reader to be patient with *my* momentary exploration with extremes), but perhaps even murder can't be said to be absolutely or purely evil in *all* cases. For example, maybe Lizzie Borden had one of the few legitimate reasons or motives for murder (I think not, but bear with me). Perhaps she would never have dreamed of murdering her parents were it not for experiencing the utterly helpless situation of being victim to their horrific child abuse. I still think that she probably could have, and should have, thought of and utilized other options (though her parents had been hideous examples). But I think we are not assessing each situation fully when we habitually reach for absolutes as solutions and are not willing to solve problems through their own circumstances. I do think that murder is one of the human atrocities that should still be absolutely wrong. But we also need to be willing to reexamine what we consider absolutely wrong. As in the example of Lizzie Borden, there were certainly reasons for her action which challenged the assumed absolute (of murder always being wrong) and the apparent obviousness of her due punishment. As if in consideration of this, and as many who followed her story and her trial know, she was acquitted of both murders.

In a much more obviously sympathetic example, Jean Louise "Scout" Finch recognized this at the end of Harper Lee's beloved novel (and later, brilliant motion picture), *To Kill A Mockingbird*. At the end of the story and the film, she told her father, Atticus, that she agreed with Sheriff Tate: that Boo Radley should not be tried for murder even though he killed Bob Ewell (Radley killed Ewell to save her older brother, Jeremy Atticus "Jem's" life). Atticus had told Scout, Jem, and Walter Cunningham earlier in the story that when his own father gave him his first rifle, his father had said that though he preferred that he only shoot at tin cans, he knew Atticus would become tempted to shoot at birds. Atticus was allowed to shoot all the blue jays he wanted but not a mockingbird. Killing a mockingbird, his father said, would be a sin. When Jem asked why, Atticus replied, "Well, I reckon they don't do anything but make music for us to enjoy...they don't do one thing but just sing their hearts out for us." Sheriff Tate said it would be a sin to connect Boo Radley in any way with the death of Bob Ewell. Tate warned that, if tried (much less convicted), Radley, a very shy but lovingly sweet-natured man, would become the "side-show" of the town, a humiliating and tragic scenario that he would not tolerate as long as he was sheriff. Because he understood Radley's reason for murdering Ewell—that he was saving the children's lives—Tate ignored a seeming absolute: the condemnation of murder. He also recognized that Boo needed sensitivity, compassion, and love more than Ewell needed justice for his murderer. In Tate's words, "Let the dead bury the dead, Mr. Finch." (Allegorically, deceased Tom Robinson burying deceased Bob Ewell.) Most importantly, Boo loved Atticus's children. It was he who left all the mysterious gifts for them in the tree, and who folded and hung Jem's pants for him across the fence. It would have been a sin to try him for murder even though he did indeed murder Ewell. Boo Radley was the "mockingbird."

Another example—and much less severe than considering whether or not murder is absolutely wrong—might be considering and acknowledging the medicinal and relatively benign recreational effects of marijuana. I agree with the argument that marijuana is treated with excessive, or absolute strictness in the laws against its use. Though now fully legal in some states, the fact that marijuana is still illegal for use in any form and for any situation in many states corroborates that excessive severity and is an absolutist position.

Therefore, I want to support a somewhat innocuous two-word principle: *Everything depends*. Everything depends on the circumstances involved. Abortion is probably not abhorrent or murder in all cases. Socialism is not a global evil in all cases. Capitalism; communism; drugs; premarital sex; pornography; obscene language; guns; etc. To suggest and consider that these or other examples might not all be absolutely wrong or right means being willing to take the position of burrowing further to find workable solutions as each situation arises. The only thing that could be helped by burrowing further is coming up with better and better solutions, thus expanding human knowledge and our ability to solve problems. If we adhere to absolutes, especially in the most difficult situations, we prevent ourselves from the discipline of discovering better solutions. In the short-term, it may seem easier and seemingly obvious to use an absolute solution. But in the long term, choosing an absolute is likely to be less gratifying and effective than a well-crafted, strongly specific solution. (The United States Constitution is one such well-crafted and specific solution.).

It could also be evolutionarily damaging. In the long-term, choosing an absolute position prevents us from experiencing the collective brain exercise which eventually contributes to the progress of our intelligence. The mental effort may seem uncomfortable and tedious, but doesn't any work feel tedious until you finish it satisfactorily? Of course, the more we take the time to problem-solve the more it becomes something that we actually look forward to, because we get better at it and we feel good and proud of ourselves as a result. Any serious or recreational puzzle-solver can attest to that.

I propose, very respectfully and non-confrontationally, that when we succumb entirely to an absolute it indicates that we are unaccustomed to the satisfaction of careful and creative thinking. Thinking almost always feels good when ideas come quickly, but thinking can feel laborious (which it is to some degree) when the ideas and solutions take longer. I feel strongly, though, that it is the ideas that take longer to develop that are the most valuable, hence thinking for the *long*-term. We need to be able to recognize and admit when we find ourselves impatient with thinking. Surely it is less embarrassing to be noticed for our momentary inexperience with thinking than it is to be observed at having arrived at a faulty conclusion because we dispensed with the required thinking in the first place. It's like never balancing your checkbook because of being embarrassed to admit that you *feel anxious* about balancing your checkbook. More often than not, being uncomfortable with thinking is the problem and the time thinking takes. But we need to be able to admit that we're uncomfortable with careful thinking and be willing to try to improve.

Careful and creative thinking is an extremely important skill to develop and as fundamental, in my view, as reading, writing, and arithmetic. So, though it is an easy, weighty, and assertive two-word phrase, it may be a detriment to deeper thinking—particularly on the subject of morality—to insist on being "absolutely right."

Chapter 4

FUNDAMENTALISM

*Fundamentalism as it is called is not confined to the Muslim world.
It is something that we have seen in different parts of the world.
Let us hope that a dialogue between the followers of the
three great monotheistic religions
could help in putting an end to this.*

King Hussein I

*We must fight back against those radical minorities who are trying to
remove God from our textbooks, Christ from our nation.
We must take back what is rightfully ours.*

The Reverend Jerry Falwell
Moral Majority Sermon
March, 1993

Traditional fictional fantasy stories, such as Santa Claus and the Easter Bunny, are treated as such by adults when relating to young children, but similar religious stories that sound much like fantasy or fiction—the serpent verbally convincing Eve to eat the apple of the Tree of the Knowledge of Good and Evil, Moses parting the Red Sea, or Jonah swallowed by and living in a great fish for three days and three nights—are accepted by many adult religious people literally. It's a very curious paradox. Clearly, if a large premise (such as the existence of God) is believed strongly enough, one can overlook some of the seeming improbabilities associated with that belief.

I've always wondered why many adults take the latter religious stories so seriously, but consider the former tales and characters of childhood fairytales? Just like the childhood fictional stories, the above biblical tales never occur in everyday life experience. I suggested possible reasons for this as emotional and psychological comfort, and cosmic loneliness in the Introduction and Chapter 1, as well as adhering to absolutes in Chapter 2. But an additional and related reason is a posture that some of the strictest of the religious community have adopted and is a form of absolute thinking. It is called *fundamentalism*, or a focus on the fundamental, non-interpretive meaning of religious scripture. It has also become an extreme or absolute position. This point-of-view teaches the necessity that religious texts be understood, accepted, and taken *literally*, word-for-word.

The noun, fundamentalism, is of course a derivative of the noun, fundamental. The noun, fundamental, means (at dictionary.com): a basic principle, rule, law, or the like that serves as the groundwork of a system; essential part. The noun, fundamentalism (often spelled with a capital "F"), is defined (at the Merriam Webster Online) as: "a movement in 20th Century Protestantism emphasizing the literal interpreted Bible as fundamental to Christian life and teaching." It follows then that a *fundamentalist* is a person who practices fundamentalism.

Applying the first category of the first definition above, "a basic principle, rule, law...," a fundamental principle, element, or idea is very practical and useful because it can be applied to almost anything and does not interfere with any personal or public goal. However, a fundamental system, while potentially useful (El Sistema is an obvious and glorious example!), can also risk being imposing and intrusive because it tends to project the personal, or subjective goal of one or several people onto society as a whole, the public. This is rarely a wise goal because personal perspectives proposed to the public frequently feel imposing and invasive; at its root, personal perspectives are self-centered, even if the "self" is a group rather than an individual. This is, in fact, how religious fundamentalism often manifests itself in society.

In, *Under the Banner of Heaven*, Jon Krakauer relates the following anecdote of a woman named Debbie Oler Blackmore Ralston Palmer. She is the former wife ("wife" really meant "property") of the three Mormon Fundamentalist men whose above names—Blackmore, Ralston, and Palmer—she carried by polygamist (plural) marriage. "…Debbie…even as young girl, was proving to be intelligent and willful and disinclined to defer blindly to authority. Debbie tended to ask questions and think for herself—qualities not regarded as attributes in the Fundamentalist Church." [11] A striking but typical example of one serious problem created by polygamy—not to mention the horrific child abuse—is exemplified in the last sentence of the above excerpt. It illuminates the conflict of Debbie's personality with her strict polygamist family: the incompatibility of thinking for oneself within the mores of fundamentalism.

Personally, I wish that there was no such thing as being a fundamental*ist* at anything. I feel the same about atheism, or the extreme conviction of the non-existence of God. I think it's equally erroneous and folly to be unwaveringly convinced that God does not exist. Just as there is no proof for God, neither is there substantial evidence to disprove God.

As I have shown, there is a difference between the word *fundamental* and the word *fundamentalist*. Once again, a fundamental is a single principle, a part of an idea or ideas, and is flexible to change. A fundamentalist is one whose lifestyle is based on the literal interpretation of religious text, and is much less, if ever, open to change. As a result, fundamentalism is an example of a viewpoint that is considered unerring, or absolutely right (and politically "Right"), as I explored in Chapter 2. And absolutes are usually based on a personal or collectively subjective idea or interpretation of something and are rarely open to question, discussion, debate, much less change. In my opinion and observation, anything that is not open to question, discussion, debate, or change is unwise because it is an impediment to progress. Progress is change by improvement, with discipline but flexibility. Fundamentalism does not recognize the need for improvement (other than becoming more and more strictly fundamentalist) and is inherently inflexible. Inflexibility to change is also unwise because one thing that I think most everyone could agree on is that the universe is *always changing*. The universe doesn't appear to operate by any *one* fundamental principle or absolute, so adhering to any single fundamental principal is really going against-the-grain of nature and the universe. It is true that scientists/physicists are searching for a *unified* theory (I will explore that more in Part II with Stephen Hawking and John Polkinghorne) and a strong candidate for the unifying principle or force in nature is *gravity*. But even a unified theory in physics may reveal varying attributes, attenuations, and amplitudes of gravity rather than cosmic rigidity.

Though not necessarily a rigid absolute in itself, I have observed, to myself, what seems to be a disappointing fact of nature and the universe. Though I express it here somewhat poetically, it is still discouraging: *The hand of destruction is swifter than the hand of construction*. It takes time to create. It takes almost no time to destroy. Seeming absolutes in the universe are destroyed all the time. Stars explode. Asteroids, meteors, and comets collide with and disfigure planets, moons, and other celestial objects. Even allowing for human proliferation and overpopulation of the planet, nature on Earth destroys more life than it creates. Life is the exception. Extinction is the rule. Change is the norm.

The details, circumstances, and perceptions in our lives also change. Everything we sense, feel, and have discovered are valid only to the extent to which those properties in the universe continue to operate in the same way. Therefore, any life that operates or functions in the world based on one fundamental idea that is not open to change is probably more *vulnerable* to change. It could also be said that any form of fundamentalism is a denial of nature.

Evidence of problems with religious fundamentalism are abundant. All the Inquisitions; terrorism; extreme positions of intolerance on issues such as abortion and gay rights; ethnic genocide; the debate between creation and evolution (about the origin of the universe and life); prayer in public schools; religion given equal weight in the public science classroom; and extreme religious influence in elections for public office are just some examples of issues that are adversely affected. Atheism does not have the same tendency.

Though a fundamental—a principle, not a system—is an ingredient of a fact that has been proven to work in practice, it should be subject to the same scrutiny, and is in the same category, as hypotheses, theories, and eventually, facts. A fundamental is only firmly established by experiment and the test of time.

Similar to Don Miguel Ruiz's, *The Four Agreements*, four fundamentals that I perceive as basic and vital to humanity (though they are certainly not the only important ones, and may be different from what others might choose) are a combination of the three that most of us were taught as children (at the end of the preceding chapter) plus one that gets much less attention, at least by American society.

My Four Fundamentals:

1. **Reading** (The phrase, "Reading is fundamental.")
2. **Writing**
3. **Arithmetic**
4. **The performing arts**

These four I group under the umbrella of another, larger fundamental, one that I have already discussed:

Creative and critical thinking.

These creative/critical thinking fundamentals of reading, writing, arithmetic, and the performing arts are inventions by the first two categories within my personal trinity, the self and other life. I also feel that these four fundamentals are the most valuable ones of the human creative output. They have allowed us to persevere, accomplish, and present beauty and knowledge. The umbrella fundamental of creative and critical thinking is a genetic, and subsequently developed characteristic and skill that has enabled us to discover and create the other four. Driving all of these, I feel deeply, is the energy and power of love.

The most productive way to perceive and think deeply about life and the universe is with as few preconceptions as possible. This is, of course, almost impossible. We are all products of our genetics, environment, and education which, collectively, give us some preconceptions before we are able to consciously think, choose, or filter preconceptions for ourselves. So the closest we can come is to be encouraged during our earliest years to acknowledge our preconceptions and view them seriously but skeptically.

However, not all preconceptions are unhealthy. Everyone would undoubtedly agree that the need to love and be loved seems to be inherent in us genetically (as well as inherent in other living things) and needs regular nurturing. It would follow that any behavior that causes anyone not to feel love would be damaging to life, and that the eradication of that behavior would be a healthy preconception to cultivate.

Another preconception that is, in my view, also vital to functioning within a loving environment would perhaps be agreed to less by everyone. That is my umbrella fundamental above: the principle of applied creative and critical thinking. As Carl Sagan and Ann Druyan proposed, the ability to think and think deeply is what seems to separate humans from every other life form. I also suggest that anytime one engages in any kind of healthy, careful, and creative thinking (about any subject, including religion and science), one is automatically utilizing the scientific method and not fundamentalism. The scientific method (which I will reference in this chapter but discuss at more length in Chapter 6) is simply proceeding step-by-step to a solution. That means that one does not conclude a concept, idea, or proposition as truth or fact until steps have been taken to clearly demonstrate that the proposition or idea is a result of its steps, the sum of its parts. This is the exact opposite of fundamentalist thinking. Fundamentalist thinking begins with an inflexible, inerrant, and infallible doctrine prior to (or devoid of) deductive deciphering. In the scientific method, the specific number of steps required to reach a given solution is not necessarily known in advance (except, for example, if the solution is something like a pilot's checklist or an established mathematical proof). When a solution is reached it is simply reached by the number of steps each individual problem takes. And, once a solution is reached, the result must be *repeatable*. The practice or use of the scientific method should also not be associated solely with a laboratory and chemistry beakers. It only means being taught to think in small steps to reach solutions. I have found that this principle works across nearly all disciplines; conversely, I have found almost no discipline in which it would not work. The only syndrome that seems to completely shun the scientific method is fundamentalism, because it is not open to questions, careful steps toward solutions, or the avoidance of assumptions. In addition to the assumption of the meaning and existence of God, fundamentalism, by definition, makes rigid, literal presumptions. And I would propose strongly that assumptions and presumptions are care*less* not care*ful*.

The discipline of religion then, particularly fundamentalist religion, seems to work in the reverse of the scientific method: starting with an assumption of the result—that God (the Deity) exists and created the universe—with steps taken to understand the result *after* assuming/accepting the idea. In other words, religion teaches acceptance (intuitively; emotionally; by faith) first and understanding (intellectually) second. To me this is backward, not only because of my own upbringing and experience, but because no other discipline that I can think of operates that way. Why should religious questions be approached differently than any other questions?

Regarding the order of any thinking process, and using another analogy to math, the Order of Operations seems apt to mention here. In mathematics, there are several specific methods of computation. From simple to more complex, addition, subtraction, multiplication, division, exponents, parentheses, and square roots are some of the most familiar examples. But computation equations with multiple methods cannot be performed randomly and get the same result. Though numbers may look random and arbitrary, they are not and cannot be calculated arbitrarily. Each number and/or symbol represents a specific item or groups of items in physics. Calculations combine those physical items. In algebra, for example, in an equation with two or more different methods of calculation, to maintain consistent results this is the established order: Parentheses, Exponents, Multiplication/Division, Addition/Subtraction. Again, this computation order is strictly performed to prevent discrepancies in the results caused when calculating any equation randomly. It is failsafe advanced arithmetic.

Similar to religious teaching of belief in God before questions are asked about God—apparently contrary to the scientific method of simple to complex—the Order of Operations in math is clearly from complex to simple. Though the Order of Operations is a principle of mathematics, and mathematics is a branch of science, a computation or calculation in math is not exactly the same as a scientific question. However, even with that similarity to religious teaching, the Order of Operations is actually more similar to science than resembling of religion.

Rather than beginning with smaller calculations first, in math it is probably more expedient to tackle larger, more difficult calculations first, leaving smaller, easier calculations for last—like the principle while driving a motor vehicle of reducing speed before and during a curve (more difficult), then gradually resuming the speed limit when the road straightens (easier).* That is less true for questions. Scientific inquiry works from small questions to larger solutions—baby-steps. Using, for example, the natural development of self-transportation in every human being as an analogy, natural progress proceeds from crawling, to baby-steps, to walking, and finally to running and jumping (unfortunately, we cannot fly). Learning safe and effective mobility is instinctive scientific experiment, from simple to complex. Priority of mathematic calculation is the reverse, from complex to simple; that would appear to be analogous to religious instruction.

What strikes me, though, about the Order of Operations in expediently beginning with the most complex computation, is a different and larger point than its apparent similarity to the religious teaching of an unerring large concept (God) before smaller questions are asked (about God): It is the difference in *logic* when comparing religion with science. Even though the process of the scientific method and one of its techniques, the Order of Operations, work in reverse order, *both* employ logic. In religion, *faith precedes logic*. Religion would probably assert that logic *must* take a back seat to faith, because of the (assumed) transcendence of God from physics. God is taught and believed as outside of and the Creator of physics. To the believer, God also dictates logic. Religion, then, works in the reverse from science, from one large solution to smaller steps, and is different from the Order of Operations in its unscientific lack of logic: The existence of God is initially assumed to be the creator of physics and the solution to all questions

---

* An exception to this is in Euclidean Geometry where the process of *deductive reasoning* is not only the same as the scientific method, it is the definition—from simple to complex. Those steps are the following: axioms (These resemble "assumed truths," which science supposedly shuns, but axioms are rudimentary and accessibly apparent.), postulates, theorems, and proofs.

about physics, whether or not the solution works with the questions, or whether any questions are asked. That is certainly scientifically illogical.

The problem for many non-religious people is that the assumed solution of in most modern monotheistic religions—the Deity or God—is ambiguous and abstract, and the definition of the Deity is almost entirely subjective. Solutions in science and mathematics are neither ambiguous, abstract, nor subjective. Therefore, those non-religious (and I) would ask why one would begin with an assumed, ambiguous, abstract, and subjective solution and try to make all non-abstract, objective, and rational questions fit the abstract solution? It seems like trying to fit a square peg into a similarly-sized round hole—God is the square peg, with questions trying make sense of God the round hole; or if you are religious, maybe God is the perfectly circular round hole, and skeptical thinking the square hole futilely trying to make God conform to the human limit of logic. But even allowing doubt for the legitimacy of logic, it certainly doesn't make enough sense. So why, logically, would one have such deep faith and belief in something that doesn't make enough logical and rational sense? Why *begin* with ambiguity?

However, sometimes even the question of something making sense is a matter of perception. One person's ambiguity might be another person's clarity. And perhaps religious thinking only seems illogical to adherents of logic. Religion likely considers logic a human limitation, and maybe it is indeed. Or, it might be that religion could use a larger dose of logic. Regardless, just as the logic and wisdom in the mathematical Order of Operations and the scientific method seem not to matter in religion, so does a clear, consistent, objective, and unambiguous solution—explanation of God—seem to be unimportant. However irrational and illogical it might seem to a skeptic, religion seems to revere not the distinctly clear, but the ambiguous and abstract, the mysterious (i.e. "God moves in mysterious ways."). Because those attributes are bestowed on the divine, to many religious people logic is a smaller part, not a part, or even an obstacle in the theological equation.

If there *is* logic in any religion, I have observed four steps in this order:

1. **Acceptance of the truth of the Deity**
2. **Belief**
3. **Reading of religious scripture**
4. **Prayer**

An umbrella fundamental for all the above steps might be the following (the topic of Chapter 7):

Faith

The first step of the four above is the initial acceptance of the result, and the following three (2 through 4 above) are the steps taken to attempt to better understand that result. Again, it is interesting that for a concept as magnificent and extraordinary as a claim of an omnipotent deity, that the result is established and accepted first. It would, of course, be naturally logical for it to be the other way around (perhaps order 3,4,2,1 above). There are also relatively few steps involved. (Granted, the steps I outlined are my own opinion and formulation, but they are consistent with most religions I've observed and studied). In other words, in religion there is relatively little experiment and the result is accepted *prior* to any experiment. In science, there is no prior accepted truth, and the number of steps cease when the questions cease. Or when the questions minimize to the point of greater certainty. Or when a simple, workable solution is found that can be repeated with the same solution.

I don't intend to say that religion doesn't utilize science at all nor that the emotional instinct and passion for religious feeling shouldn't be taken seriously. Religious instincts and passions should be taken very seriously, and with great respect. However, since the scientific method seems to be applicable across disciplines and begins with only the *proposition* of an idea (with steps then taken to determine the idea's validity), a discipline which begins with the acceptance or assumption of an idea—and then takes relatively few steps to understand the idea—is, it seems to me once again, non-meticulous and going at it backwards.

So why can't religion be allowed to operate somewhat differently than science, to enjoy its own nuances? It can. This is one of the primary reasons for the separation of church and state in the First Amendment of the Constitution. Just as religious organizations are immune to the tax laws by which secular institutions are bound, so does religion seem to desire to be immune to intellectual logic and scrutiny and to emphasize more of a focus on emotional peace and trust than intellectual understanding. I maintain that the most satisfying application of science and religion is a stirring blend of the two!

In practice, though, many religions, particularly fundamentalist religions, tend to voluntarily cross the emotional, psychological, and private lines and enter into the public arena, such as politics. When you cross the line from an area that was previously private (religious feeling, faith, churches) into an area which is considered public (neighborhood, community, media, metropolitan, political, national, global), you enter into a larger area that requires the same rules and regulations for everyone—objective rather than subjective. Those objective regulations, I propose, more often utilize the principle of science than religion. Public regulation should never be the platform for or dictated by fundamentalist religion. The Framers of the Constitution knew this, which is the reason for the First Amendment.

If religion can be said to operate with deep personal, subjective, and emotional conviction, science can be said to operate with specifics about physics. It is about how things in the universe work physically (physically is the adverb of physics). And science has done well as an applied principle in acquiring knowledge of physics consistently. With that in mind, isn't it "reinventing the wheel" to approach a curiosity or problem, even if deeply emotional, exactly opposite to science? What sense does it make to firmly assume a solution in advance and then force the steps to work within the assumed solution? Isn't it always possible that the assumed solution is incorrect, was reached prematurely?

I once had a grade-school art teacher instruct our class to paint the objects first and the background last. This seemed backwards to me even then. If you painted a tree with many small branches (which I did), it was much more difficult to then paint the background between the already-painted branches; the "objects" in the painting are, of course, analogous to God (the solution, or the point-of-focus), and the "background" the questions asked and investigation undertaken to understand the solution. Would it not have been wiser to have painted my background first and then my objects or subject overtop the background? Or better yet, we could have learned how to paint only the *suggestion* of a background, while we then easily painted the objects on and around the emerging background so that both took shape together. In avoiding fundamentalism, perhaps we could learn to do the same: make only a *suggestion* or *proposal* of an idea or solution (of God), then test the proposal with questions, allowing the solution to gradually emerge. An exact science scenario.

Another point: If you begin with an assumed solution or never question the assumed solution, and you run into a problem, how will you ever know which is the problem, the assumed solution or the steps? And when science has helped us conclude that the universe now appears to operate by the same physical laws that govern our Solar System (and obviously the Earth), why doesn't the religious discipline adjust, or better, abandon fundamentalism and attempt to relate its emotional connection to the cosmos more from physical logic—including seeking physical evidence for a "Creator?" Clearly, science has not revealed one. Wouldn't it make more sense that, if the rest of the universe seems to operate physically, that any religious concept would probably also have physical explanations? Why the severe resistance from, or reinventing of the wheel for, this one discipline?

The immunity from and near-complete resistance by fundamentalist religion from the rigor of the scientific method is a curious and confusing one. I have never understood the need for the separation of religious feeling and scientific finding (distinguished from the separation of church and state) or why physical explanations—ones that require proof—are often considered a nuisance and less inspiring in religion. For me, discovering how a natural phenomenon—that was once thought of as beyond physical explanation—is eventually explained by physics, it becomes *more interesting and beautiful* not less. It illuminates or reveals that the more we continue to observe about ourselves, our planet, and the universe, the more everything seems to be deeply and elegantly connected by physics. That is not the result of *scientific fundamentalism*. It is the result of slow and careful *avoidance* of fundamentalism.

For example, I think that it is exhilarating to learn that a comet is a huge asteroid covered with ice, and that the stream of a "tail" we see flowing behind it is the ice melting as it is pulled around the sun by the latter's gravitational force. It seems far less compelling (and really very silly) to imagine that traveling just behind the comet is an alien spaceship that has come to take a few spiritually chosen people to eternal life. As the reader will recall, this was, in fact, the contention of the cult of "Heaven's Gate." Its followers committed suicide in 1997 following the dictates of their director, Marshall Herff Applewhite, a man who called himself, Do, after the first note of the C Major scale. His wife, Bonnie Lou Nettles, was called, Ti, the final note and "leading-tone" of the C Major scale. (Though seemingly a patriarchally Fundamentalist cult, I wonder if it occurred to

Applewhite that Nettles's alias implied that she was the more prominent "leader" of the two!) At least these leaders were attaching the concept of musical beauty to their fundamentalist belief.

These fundamentalists firmly believed that, upon their suicidal death, they would be "astrally projected" onto that spaceship where their alien "God" was waiting for them on board. There is certainly no evidence that alien spaceships regularly follow behind comets (much less having enacted a surreptitious rendezvous for a few specially chosen humans), but there is well-documented evidence for the physical construction and properties of comets.

Actually, claims like astral projection to a comet post-mortem are, to me, not so different than the claim of a resurrected Jesus Christ (Applewhite and his followers clearly believed that, upon their mass suicide, *they* would be resurrected.). Nor are either of them much different from the familiar myth of the Phoenix Bird. The multi-colored bird, after burning to death by the Sun, rises to life again from its ashes. It is a fictional tale of resurrection.

The belief that Christ defied death, with God's intervention by the Resurrection, and was brought back to life in his physical human form and as God, simultaneously, is an *enormous* claim. If indeed true (as many Christians firmly believe, and not just Christian Fundamentalists), it would be an extraordinary phenomenon of the highest magnitude. Perhaps it *is* true. Or, perhaps there is (or will be in the future) a very clear scientific explanation of what a resurrection is and the phenomena might change from supernatural to natural. On the other hand, if a resurrection is indeed supernatural, the evidence would need to be *very* substantial, particularly if it involves returning from death both to one's former physical body *and* as a divine being.

I am limited by my own personal experience, of course, but I have never heard of a resurrection apart from Christ's Resurrection and the word resurrection used as a metaphor. Undoubtedly, a Christian would argue that it is precisely because I have never heard of a resurrection other than Jesus Christ that is itself the clear evidence. In other words, proof that Jesus was the Son of God is because he was the *only* human to ever have been resurrected. Perhaps Christians are correct. But they could also be mistaken. Practically speaking, Christ's resurrection is likely an example of a tenet of belief wholly elusive to either proof or disproof.

In Carl Sagan's, *The Demon-Haunted World*, the Fourteenth Dalai Lama made a similar, but very circumspect point about the related tenet of Buddhism: reincarnation. Sagan wrote: "In theological discussions with religious leaders, I often ask what their response would be if a central tenet of their faith were disproved by science. When I put this question to the current, Fourteenth, Dalai Lama, he unhesitatingly replied as no conservative or fundamentalist religious leaders do: In such a case, he said, Tibetan Buddhism would have to change. Even, I asked, if it's a *really* central tenet, like (I searched for an example) reincarnation? Even then, he answered. However—he added with a twinkle—it's going to be hard to disprove reincarnation. Plainly the Dalai Lama is right. Religious doctrine that is insulated from disproof has little reason to worry about the advance of science. The grand idea, common to many faiths, of a Creator of the Universe is one such doctrine—difficult alike to demonstrate or to dismiss."[12] The same is clearly true for resurrection.

Though intriguing and enchanting to contemplate, resurrections and reincarnations are not the beauty of the universe based on physical explanations that inspire my interest. For example, the pictures taken by the Hubble Telescope magnificently show both the beauty and destruction of the universe. For me, they are spine-tinglingly gorgeous!! And they are unmistakable physical evidence.*

Other than the biblical account, what physical evidence is there for a resurrection? And in at least a minimally scientifically advanced world such

---

* Physical evidence insofar as our normal senses perceive the universe. It has been proffered that all of what we perceive in the universe as reality, including all physical and metaphysical evidence, may in fact be one gigantic computer simulation. In an article entitled, "Do We Live in the Matrix," in the December, 2013 issue of *Discover* magazine, Zeeya Merali poses just that. Because computer programming and simulation has reached extraordinarily complex proportions, it is as yet impossible to determine whether we and the universe we observe are "real" or only illusions within a far more vast computer program (e.g., Paramount Pictures *The Truman Show*)! In other words, that we might be artificial intelligences in someone else's computer simulation. Perhaps that *someone else* is the entity that some of us perceive as *God*. But how does one test for *that*?! Is there even any point in worrying or focusing on that eerie and disturbing scenario? The folly of that paradox and seeming paralysis for human investigation is exactly Merali's point.

as ours, where physical evidence is required of most other proposals, why are Christ's resurrection and other religious supernatural stories—such as the premise of the existence and meaning of God—accepted by fundamentalism without question and scrutiny? Why is physical evidence not sought for all these elusive questions by even the more moderate and progressive religious community? The latter could set a stronger example of interest and inclusion for their less flexible, fundamentalist fellow-believers.

My only guess is not a flattering one: fear of the possibility that any search for physical evidence for religious stories (particularly if found to be erroneous), could cause deep embarrassment for the religious community in general if the evidence suggested, and even proved, that religious stories were fallible, or even fiction. Perhaps that risk feels too great to embolden most believers (not just fundamentalists) to search for better physical evidence and probe the principles of their faith more critically. A friend of mine once said, "Familiar demons are better than unknown saints." Better not to know and believe in the fantasy than to risk having the fantasy exposed and suffer disorientation and embarrassment, even if the truth would turn out to be spectacularly beautiful. That's a lot to keep hidden—with many potential gold mines—to prevent risk of embarrassment. But then the courage and honesty that risk takes often feels too daunting, thus easier to deny. As Ricky Fitts (Wes Bentley) said to Lester Burnham (Kevin Spacey) in the film, *American Beauty*, "Never underestimate the power of denial." Evidence of denial seems readily available.

~~~

I was raised in a non-religious family and encouraged to think for myself about any subject, including philosophical, religious, and spiritual matters. However, though I'm stressing the importance of guarding against any excessive or extreme perceptions, my upbringing was not without preconceptions, preconditions, or values. My preconceptions, preconditions, and values were not taught by my parents as distinct subjects, nor were they taught from a rigid or fundamentalist viewpoint, but their principles were practiced and very much a part of our lives. Without stressing any belief in the supernatural, they were the same as those of any genuinely loving and inclusive religious practice: love and respect for myself and others; love and respect from and for my family; dignity and health and love for all living beings and things; the health and beauty of the arts; respect for and appreciation of the point of view of others; and basic human kindness, ethics, and love. I suppose I could be considered a *humanist*, and I have sometimes thought of myself with that term. But by focusing on the word "human," the term humanist also, unintentionally, excludes all other life, which I *include* in the second part of my personal trinity.

I've been challenged by some of my religious friends as possibly being preconditioned by freethinking or the scientific method, just as I suggest to them that they might be preconditioned by religion or religious fundamentalism. This is a legitimate suggestion/criticism both ways and one that I think is probably impossible to test. We are all preconditioned by our upbringing, regardless of what it happens to have been.

So, what does it mean to be preconditioned? The Webster's Collegiate Dictionary definition is, "to put in a proper or desired condition or state of mind." Like the preconditions of my youth, three of those preconditions, the values of love, the arts, and kindness/ethics were certainly instilled in me by my parents as a desired set of experiences and state of mind. I was not, however, told that I had to "believe in" the arts, love, or ethics. I was also not taken to church by my parents, but I was allowed to attend church if I chose to go (even though my parents themselves did not).

The difference to me is that none of the preconditions from my parents were professed to be unalterable truths, or fundamentalist. Everything was open to debate (save, for example, arguing with them before we were mature enough to have knowledgeable arguments!). I was simply encouraged to freely consider and think about *everything*...hence a "free-thinker." The difference in the method of instilling preconceptions and instilling a fundamentalist mindset, in my view, lies in the ability to retain the capacity to *acknowledge the possibility of other perceptions.*

I acknowledge that God may exist, but I think it's equally important to acknowledge the opposite, that God may not exist. Some of my religious friends simply cannot acknowledge that God might not exist. They say that since they believe in God they can't imagine it any other way. I have not asked them to say that God does not exist, only that it is *possible* that the Entity doesn't exist. I suggest this partly because of my own perception, but primarily because of what I think are legitimate arguments for the non-existence of God: insufficient physical evidence of God, and the lack of clarity of what is meant by God. All of the explanations of God can, it seems to me, be *interpreted* in a non-religious way as well. That should not be so easy. A strong, concrete idea or proposal is less vulnerable to interpretation. Plus, interpretation is only an attempt, an approximation, a step toward a conclusion, not a definitive conclusion. There are many interpretations of an original, but only one original, and the original is sometimes (and often) not available.

Musically, for example, a conductor or performer "interprets" the composer's original score through rehearsal and performance, but only the composer knows (or *knew*, if the composer is no longer living) what they were originally hearing. There has, therefore, never been one definitive performance of anything, only attempts, approximations, or variations of interpretations with varying levels of success, which is the best one can do. (So far, that has been brilliantly and wonderfully satisfying!) Just as with taking an absolute position, advertising a *definitive* or *authentic* performance has been and will always be futile. It doesn't exist because no one but the composer (the "creator," if you will) really knows. So it should be with extreme fundamentalism or atheism: the professing of a definitive knowledge of the existence or the non-existence of God. Definitive knowledge of the Deity, either way, really doesn't exist.

I will offer an admission of my own, which the reader has undoubtedly already sensed. Though this book is about encouraging us all to be willing to ask questions about everything, both scientifically and religiously, and promoting a non-prejudiced view of both science and religion, I have at times noticed myself being prejudiced toward and against religion, especially fundamentalist religion. I suppose I *could* be accused of being a science fundamentalist. I don't feel that way and don't necessarily think that I am, but I'm sure that I have struck many people that way. Again, however, one difference I think between my point of view and a fundamentalist's (extremely religious or atheist, or an extreme and strict opinion of any kind) is that I am open to religious or atheistic explanations as possibilities for ultimate answers (if there is such a thing as an *ultimate* answer). I am also willing to change my point of view if I hear a very convincing religious or atheistic argument. But along with my feeling of the need to be open-minded comes a definite need for strong physical evidence to verify claims, regardless of the discipline. Since physical evidence is the kind of evidence provided for every theory other than religion (including atheism), I am among the skeptics who hold out for physical evidence for religious claims.

If physical evidence is not immediately or even ultimately available for the largest religious claims, I feel that each lack of clarity needs to be addressed by some other form of strong evidence which has, as yet (that I am aware of), not been presented. I certainly reach for science much more than I do religion because science is, for me, more interactive both intellectually and emotionally. But I am also interested in the intellectual history, discoveries, and knowledge in religion, and in the history and biographies of religious leaders. Frustratingly, I have often been disappointed with the sparsity of detail and clarity in the latter.

In fact, a Catholic chaplain in Madison, Wisconsin, once told me, "Religion is not an intellectual pursuit." I thought then, and still think, that the chaplain was right. But it is also very revealing about religion. What the chaplain didn't say, but implied, is that religion does not use or encourage the intellect. I don't think the chaplain meant it quite that strictly or severely, but I do agree that religion uses and encourages less of the intellect than other disciplines or fields of study. I think that extreme religious faith/fundamentalism is perhaps one byproduct of insufficient intellectual attention. As a result of less use of the intellect, religion—particularly fundamentalist religion—relies more on faith to compensate.

In my humble opinion, humans invented science because we *had to*, both intellectually *and* emotionally. We either figured out how to survive in all ways, and do it repeatedly, or we died. We invented religion and our deity or deities for a slightly different reason: in order to feel at more emotional peace with the same cosmos that science helps us to better understand both intellectually and emotionally.

I stress that we need the healthy combination of the two, the intellect and the emotions, in every endeavor of human pursuit. My observation and opinion is that with the tool of religion we tend to think less rigorously and intellectually about *detail* (physical evidence) and rely more exclusively on the *general emotions* (faith, belief) than we do with the tool of science, and that perhaps religion could benefit with more detailed intellectual attention.

But my opinion is only that and not the focus of this book. I do, however, want to offer, admit, and clarify that while presenting the material here that I am, and must always continue to be, acutely aware of my own prejudicial and fundamentalist tendencies.

~~~

The Inquisitions are, without question, among the darkest and ugliest atrocities in the history of organized religion and in human history. They are all historical examples of fundamentalist religion. The modern equivalent, however, is not sanctioned or condoned by any one denomination or center of theological belief, but is perpetrated by radical individuals and groups acting in violent and murderous distortion of a specific faith. It is called *terrorism*.

Ever since I was a young boy, I have loved aviation and flight. I am thrilled at every opportunity to travel by air, whether on a commercial airliner or in a private plane. But I remember well when I first felt fear of flying. It was when I saw a television news report of a hijacking. Until then, everything about being on an airplane felt safe. My family was with me, the plane looked sleek and strong, the stewardesses and stewards (now, of course, all called "flight attendants") and pilots (captains) were all warm and friendly, the complimentary meals were usually fun and delicious, and I always requested a window seat. I loved looking out the window. I could pretend that *I* was flying!!

But the sudden thought of the possibility that among one of the *passengers* was a criminal who would, with a gun, force the plane to divert to another destination, and likely life-threatening danger, terrified me. It is obviously because of the feeling of terror that the act of creating mass fear and committing mass murder is called *terror*ism.

Obviously, terrorism is by no means always instigated by fundamentalism or religion. Terrorism is radical. Though extreme, fundamentalism is not necessarily radical. But any terrorist attack, extermination, and/or genocide is unspeakably heinous. It takes no debate to know that the Holocaust was terrorism. So were the atomic bombs that were dropped on Nagasaki and Hiroshima. But terrorism and radical fundamentalism are often dealt in the same hand. The most obvious and largest example is the attack and destruction of the World Trade Center in New York City on September 11, 2001. The terrorists that flew all three jet airliners that morning were members of Al Qaida, the Islamic fundamentalist terrorist organization. Another hideous example is the multiple bombing attacks in Paris on November 13, 2015. The terrorist organization responsible in those horrific incidents was the fundamentalist organization called the Islamic State of Iraq and Levant (ISIL), also called the Islamic State of Iraq and Syria (ISIS). Whether combined or separate, clearly fundamentalism and terrorism can breed hate and murder, the opposites of love and life.

Fundamentalism is frequently advertised and fueled in the news media, even among those networks most impressively educational and neutral. It is my strong personal feeling that no one should ever receive credit, momentarily or historically, for harming or killing another human being or other form of life. So I always feel incredulous when any of the news media announce an individual or organization suspected or confirmed of perpetrating a terrorist attack with the phrase, "claimed responsibility." It almost sounds as if they have been awarded and are claiming a prize. It seems like fuel for terrorism by the news media: the news media gives terrorists the credit and notoriety, so terrorists keep terrorizing. Even if the cycle is unconscious and unintended by the news media, in the process of informing the public (often dramatically for higher ratings) they are certainly doing nothing to *discourage* terrorism or fundamentalism.

Of great importance, too, is the separation of beautiful and loving religious belief and practice from religious fundamentalism. In response to the Paris bombings, columnist David Gushee emphasizes this in an article for the Religion News Service entitled, "After Paris: Christians, don't forget that we too have killed in God's name." Gushee points out commendably and necessarily that it is fanatical fundamentalism, not the genuine and loving core in religious faith, that is the cancer perpetuating terrorism. Like my suggestion of avoiding absolutes, he reminds and emphasizes that no religion is intrinsically evil. Gushee writes, "As a Christian scholar and minister, I have made it a practice not to point fingers at supposed problems in other religious communities but instead have focused on helping my fellow Christians practice our own faith better. It has always seemed to me the responsibility of religious leaders to put their own house in order, which gives us plenty to do. So the problem is not an abstraction called 'Islam.' And it's not 'Christianity.' It's human nature. But leaders in these and all religious communities do have a sacred responsibility. They must teach versions of their religion that produce believers who will love rather than murder their neighbors." *

---

* **http://davidgushee.religionnews.com/2015/11/17/paris-attacks-religion-violence/**

I enthusiastically applaud the article. Like Gushee, and the entirety of loving humanity, I deeply mourn the death of all the beautiful people in Paris who were murdered by these radical religious extremists. And I agree wholeheartedly that the culprit is not in any way religions that teach and practice love. I disagree, though, that the fault lies with human nature. I feel strongly that radical fundamentalism is born not from human nature, but from human insanity. I think that this particular insanity is an extreme byproduct of the focus, and decisions based, on the dogmatic authority of a supernatural entity rather than on the simplicity of loving independently and unconditionally. So many religions have justified murder—including the perpetrators of the November 13, 2015 annihilation in Paris—because of a twisted interpretation of a dictate from a deity (killing by following orders from an invisible god). If, however, religions in general taught less emphasis on a deity and more on independent unconditional love, extremism and fundamentalism in any form might diminish significantly.

My late Uncle Frank, who I have previously quoted, was a paratrooper in World War II. Even though he felt a strong sense of loyalty and duty in his military service, in his later life he freely acknowledged the scourge of war. He described war as, "...the ultimate triumph of terrorism." Then he added, "War is *terroristic*." He did not verbally equate terrorism with radical fundamentalism, but I'm certain that he associated the two. He strongly discouraged fundamentalism.

All I have ever tried to stress with my religious friends is that the possibility of God's existence or non-existence is as yet inconclusive. Adherence to strict belief in any form seems premature and folly. Perhaps it's the uncertainty or insecurity of not believing that feels anxious. But sometimes uncertainty is exactly the position that should be taken until better evidence can be found in order to be certain. One of my friends, who was raised Catholic but no longer practices Catholicism, said to me once when we were having a philosophical discussion about answers not being immediately forthcoming, "When in doubt, wait." Those are wise words. But when my religious friends can't acknowledge even the *possibility* that God might not exist and wait for better evidence, that is an indication of a limiting precondition, the inability to wait for better evidence. It makes me wonder what the real reason is for their inability to acknowledge that God might not exist? Inexperience with questioning the dictates in their background? Unabashed (or even brazen) confidence in God's existence? Fear of potential retribution by God if they, even for a moment, thought the Deity might not exist? Potential abashedness at their own gullibility if they allowed themselves to acknowledge the merit of some of the convincing arguments against the existence of God? I'm really not sure.

In the spirit of encouraging both the intellect and the emotions, and to adopt for a moment a slightly mollifying and centrist posture, perhaps religious people and scientists are both right. Science has erred in the past by scoffing at anything that did not have an immediate physical explanation. This is a mistake, too. Science cannot assert or claim to know that everything in the universe is physical until it *proves* it so. There may indeed be dimensions that have some physical relationship to the universe but that are very different to other physical things around them. There may *be* a single intelligence made up of all the interconnecting molecules, protons, neutrons, neutrinos, particles, etc. that, together, make up the single "Intelligence" that religious people sense as *God*. This is definitely possible until proven incorrect. So to state that God does not exist is also premature because there is not enough detailed evidence to prove that conclusion.

In his book, *Broca's Brain,* Carl Sagan refers to God and the soul as hypotheses and stresses that people who raise questions about both are not all atheists. He says "An atheist is someone who is certain that God does not exist, someone who has compelling evidence against the existence of God. I know of no such compelling evidence." He states that to be certain of either are over-confident extremes, and that "…a questing, courageous and open mind seems to be the essential tool for narrowing the range of our collective ignorance on the subject of the existence of God." [13]

In the same book, in reference to God again as a hypothesis, Sagan writes, "The idea of God as a hypothesis rather than as an obvious truth is by and large a modern idea in the West…It is often considered that at least the origin of the universe requires a God—indeed an Aristotelian idea…First…it is perfectly possible that the universe is infinitely old and therefore requires no Creator…But secondly, let us consider the idea of a universe created somehow from nothing by God. The question naturally arises—and many ten-year-olds spontaneously think of it before being discouraged by their elders—where does God come from? If we answer that

God is infinitely old or present simultaneously in all epochs, we have solved nothing except perhaps verbally...A universe that is infinitely old and a God that is infinitely old are, I think, equally deep mysteries...I think it wise, when coming face to face with such profound mysteries, to feel a little humility...We simply do not know." [14] Clearly, humility and an open mind should be virtues for science and religion regardless of whether one considers the existence or non-existence of God an hypothesis, a theory, or a fact.

On the other hand, many scientists have not taken the possibility of a deity seriously yet because the matter and energy in the cosmos does not seem to be comprised of anything *except* physical forces. There is no evidence of anything other than physics, and no evidence for a separate divine entity. Yet. And since we are still discovering what the "intelligence" of the subatomic realm really means, it is also premature to conclude that any intelligence we observe in the subatomic realm is or is not divine. As Sagan put it, we simply don't know.

It is also important to know what is meant by *divine*. The only concise secular definitions in the Webster's Collegiate Dictionary are "superb" and "to perceive (or discover) intuitively; infer." Putting religion aside for a moment, when is it ever wise to come to a large conclusion only intuitively, without testing the conclusion logically and repeatedly to verify the intuition? Most of us would consider it very flimsy to conclude anything serious *only* on the basis of intuition. But referring again to my Catholic chaplain acquaintance's comment that religion is not an intellectual pursuit, this certainly supports my impression and experience that logic and the intellect are not encouraged on the subject of the divine. It also parallels my impression of the discouragement in religion of thinking logically about one's faith.

I think there could indeed be a God that exists separately from all the physical matter and energy in the cosmos. The evidence isn't conclusive, but it is still possible. It could also be true that the physical universe is all there is. Buy that isn't conclusive either. As in the preceding quoted passages from Sagan, one of my literary mentors, my encouragement is to continue the search keeping both and other possibilities open until more conclusive evidence is found. In the spirit of non-fundamentalism, when in doubt, wait.

Chapter 5

CREATION AND EVOLUTION

It was Charles Darwin who first understood that evolution is caused by natural selection, and that natural selection is death. Without death, life would never have become more complex than the simplest self-copying molecules. Death is the mother of structure. It took four billion years of death—a third of the age of the universe—for death to invent the human mind. Given another four billion years of death, or perhaps a hundred billion years of death, who can say that death will not create a mind so effective and subtle that it will reverse the fate of the universe and become God?

Richard Preston
The Cobra Event

*Tell ya the honest truth, I thought about it for five days,
and did the whole job in one.
I'm really best under pressure.*
God
Oh, God!
Warner Bros. Pictures

Similar to the seeming schism between science and religion is the continued clash between Creation and evolution. They are contradictory histories and explanations of the origin of the universe and life. There is also a stark contrast in their relative degrees of detail. The story of Creation contains evocative, but minimal detail. The history of evolution is abundantly rich in detail.

Unless interpreted as allegorical metaphor and pretty poetry, religion differs from science in proclaiming an external Creator, the verses of Creation as the Deity's direct dictum, and inerrant scripture. In addition, as many learned scholars have noted, its 6,000-year-old universe is in direct contradiction to the age of the universe that modern science and astronomy have strongly established: an approximately 13.799 billion-year-old universe. That is an *enormous* discrepancy, and one that should raise much more than an eyebrow. Furthermore, the text itself, and the fundamentalist adherence to it, do not do much to counter the impression many religions give of supporting, fostering, and promoting mythology.

Physicist and writer on the union of science and theology, Gerald L. Schroeder (who I will be writing about in more detail in Part II), offers an interesting perspective on this disparity between the timeframes of Creation and evolution. He attempts to bridge the incongruity rather than defend or refute either.

In his, *Genesis and the Big Bang*, he says that cosmology dates the creation of the universe at about 15 billion years ago (this figure predates the more recent estimate of 13.799 billion years, and certainly the *most recent* estimate of 12.5 billion years). Then he says that the Bible asserts the age of the universe as the six days of Genesis before Adam, plus the 57 centuries after Adam. He then states that the Bible speaks in the language of humans and rhetorically asks, "Can mankind comprehend billions of years? Not likely today and even less likely at the time of Moses." He continues referencing the General Theory (Law) of Relativity, "It took Einstein and the law of relativity to teach us that there is no absolute passage of time. It is as flexible as the possible differences in the force of gravity and the speed of motion across a boundary separating the observer from the observed...The passage of time on any one star could have been as different from the passage of time on another star as six days is different from 15 billion years…The duration of days or years or even billions of years is only a relative observation. It is only locally correct…" And encapsulating, "For the Creator and the created, the union of frames of reference occurred when mankind, represented by Adam and Eve, absorbed the image of God, some 5,700 years ago."

Though this is an interesting attempt at synthesizing the two, it strikes me as odd it two ways. First, I think it is somewhat presumptuous and insulting to assume that humankind (I dislike the term "*man*kind") cannot comprehend billions of years. The very implication of an inability to comprehend the universe (God) has often been a trademark of organized religion. Second, it sounds to me like an attempt to suggest that 13.799 billion and 6,000 are the same by the General Theory of Relativity. It is possible that this has some validity. The very fact of relativity negates, or at least challenges, any *one* perspective. But it also strikes me as trying to force a square into a round hole by *speculating* about relationships that might not exist. It reminds me of Cinderella's sisters desperately trying to squeeze their feet into her lone recovered slipper. It was pointless (their feet were way too large). Even allowing for relativity, so probably is trying to make 13.799 billion also mean 6,000. There's no comparison.

~~~

Isaac Asimov is most known as a prolific writer of science fiction, one of the "Big Three" science fiction writers with Arthur C. Clarke and Robert Heinlein. But he was also a professor of biochemistry at Boston University and an author of non-fiction books. Among his non-fiction works are a few mammoth reference tomes, including "guides" to the Bible, science, and Shakespeare.

Another of these is the impressive, massive, and thoroughly detailed compilation, *Chronology of the World: The History of the World from The Big Bang to Modern Times*. This magnificent undertaking—which covers the formation of the universe, Solar System, and nearly the entire span of human history—gives a detailed account of human global civilization divided into selected regions and/or countries. It ends in 1945,* but it begins where the book's title indicates—at the Big Bang.

As might be expected, Asimov includes the topic of the beginning of the universe, and touches on the concept of Creation. He says, "It might be interesting...to cast our eyes back to see how we got to where we are today...And I think it would be amusing to start at the very beginning, the time when the Universe began..." He says that since we can't physically travel back in time to witness the origin of the universe, we have to accept our ability to observe how the universe is now and, from those observations, make deductions about its origin. He states that the first suggestion of the universe originating from a single amount of matter (a "singularity") was given by the Belgian astronomer, George Edward Lemaître, in 1927. In 1948 the Russian-American physicist, George Gamow, coined the term for that initial explosion, the "Big Bang." He says that though the "Big Bang" is acknowledged by the scientific community as fact, it's actual occurrence in time is not know precisely. Then he poses the question that would naturally follow, "One question that everyone is bound to ask about the big bang is: Where did the original glob that exploded come from? Are we forced to say, at this point, that the only possible explanation is that it was created by some force or entity, that lies outside what we consider the laws of nature and is therefore, 'supernatural?' Not necessarily. In 1973, the American physicist, Edward P. Tryon, suggested that according to quantum theory (which is one of two basic, and so far entirely successful, theories for explaining the Universe), it is possible for the initial blob to have risen out of nothing more than a quantum fluctuation in the vacuum...Let us simply say that the Universe seems to have come into being 15,000,000,000 years ago through the operation of natural law [again, 15 billion is a former estimate]." [15]

I suppose one could argue that, "...a quantum fluctuation in the vacuum..." is also forcing a congruity from the incongruity of matter seemingly generating from nothing. However, Azimov did only write that it was "possible." Schroeder seemed to assert his contention with confident

---

* As if written as a companion to Asimov's tome, *A Concise History of the World Since 1945,* by W. M. Spellman spans from 1945-2004. Curiously, Spellman makes no mention of Azimov's book, clearly the greater undertaking. Spellman's work is, nevertheless, an important and necessary continuation and contribution.

certainty, a posture that I think is unwarranted when discussing relativity. Relativity is, by definition, *un*certain.

Clearly, the concept of Creation is dealt with quite differently by superb thinkers and writers of both religion and science. Asimov's angle is with history and physics supported by documented evidence. Schroeder's is perhaps more speculative but nevertheless intriguing. In keeping with healthy debate, these two perspectives are excellent examples of deep but divergent thinking on the subject of the creation of the cosmos.

~~~

Kenneth C. Davis states in his book, *Don't Know Much About The Bible: Everything You Need to Know About the Good Book but Never Learned*, "As many creationists like to point out, evolution is 'just a theory.' And that's true." [16] However, Carl Sagan, Isaac Asimov, and Richard Dawkins state quite the contrary, that evolution is a fact.

Sagan, in *Cosmos*, writes, "The genetic changes induced by domestication have occurred very rapidly. The rabbit was not domesticated until early medieval times (it was bred by French monks in the belief that new-born bunnies were fish and therefore exempt from the prohibitions against eating meat on certain days in the Church calendar); coffee in the fifteenth century; the sugar beet in the nineteenth century; and the mink is still in the early stages of domestication. In less than ten-thousand years, domestication has increased the weight of wool grown by sheep from less than one kilogram of rough hairs to ten or twenty kilograms of uniform, fine down; or the volume of milk given by cattle during a lactation period from a few hundred to a million cubic centimeters. If artificial selection can make such major changes in so short a period of time, what must natural selection, working over billions of years, be capable of ? The answer is all the beauty and diversity of the biological world. Evolution is a fact, not a theory." [17]

And Sagan in *The Dragons of Eden*, "Evolution is a fact amply demonstrated by the fossil record and by contemporary molecular biology. Natural selection is a successful theory devised to explain the fact of evolution." [18]

And Isaac Azimov, interviewed by Paul Kurtz in *Free Inquiry*, Spring 1982, "Certainly there are many arguments over the mechanism of evolution, but our knowledge about the evolutionary process is much greater than it was in Darwin's day. The present view of evolution is far more subtle and wide-ranging than Darwin's was or could have been. But it still is not firmly and finally settled. There remain many arguments over the exact mechanism of evolution, and furthermore there are many scientists who are dissatisfied with some aspects of evolution that most other scientists accept. There are always minority views among scientists in every respect, but virtually no scientist denies the fact of evolution. It is as though we were all arguing about just exactly what makes a car go even though nobody denies that cars go." [19]

And when referencing the "Pro Life" campaign (similar to the Sagans's argument I related in Chapter 3, and to my point about absolutes in the same chapter), Richard Dawkins writes in his book, *The God Delusion*, "Notice now that 'pro-life' doesn't exactly mean pro-*life* at all. It means pro-*human*-life. The granting of uniquely special rights to cells of the species *Homo sapiens* is hard to reconcile with the fact of evolution…The evolutionary point is very simple. The *humanness* of an embryo's cells cannot confer upon it any absolutely discontinuous moral status. It cannot, because of our evolutionary continuity with chimpanzees and, more distantly, with every species on the planet." [20]

So on what evidence does Kenneth Davis base his judgment when attempting to corroborate that evolution is "just a theory?" Since he does not offer more explanation, either Davis has not done quite enough research or Sagan and Asimov have jumped to a premature conclusion. Sagan taught to be unscrupulously skeptical, so are scientists being too hasty in calling evolution a fact? Or are Davis and the religious community not widely enough read? And on what argument does Davis base his corroboration that evolution is only a theory? Simply by the way some creationists habitually refer to the concept of evolution as it was originally presented by Darwin, as a theory, before more time and evidence has turned it from theory into fact (as Asimov's point above reminds)?

Evolution is often incorrectly defined as the transformation of apes into humans. However, the general principle of evolution applies to a much, much longer timespan. The concept and definition of evolution is really quite simple: complex life forms developed over billions of years from the simplest life forms. Put even more simply: *simplicity breeds complexity**; or the inverse, *complexity is bred (develops) from* simplicity (mathematically, the Reflexive Property of Equality (a = a)!)

This is because of natural selection,† the conclusion that Charles Darwin made after collecting, compiling, and studying a myriad of samples of species as a "naturalist" during his two-year voyage aboard the *HMS Beagle*. He discovered that in the struggle to adapt and survive, life forms had to *very gradually* acquire greater abilities/complexities in order to survive or their species would die, become extinct, as those which were less able to adapt indeed did.

Evolution does not mean that one species changes into another even in two or three generations in order to survive. The time needed for evolution by natural selection in nature is *billions* of years; not tens, hundreds, thousands, or even millions. Unlike artificial selection—in which humans impose the changes on life rather than nature—as Sagan pointed out, it was a much more slow and subtle process. But the evolution of life indicated by fossil records clearly shows that living organisms have not always been the same since the beginning of life on Earth. That is a direct and fundamental (not fundamentalist) contradiction of the story of Creation in Genesis, in which all life was created in its current, contemporary form immediately. With that in mind, can Davis demonstrate that the fossil record does not prove that simple forms of life evolved into more complex ones over billions of years, and that evolution is still, therefore, only a theory?

Based upon my reading and my impression of the degree of information and evidence put forth by Azimov, Dawkins, and Sagan, I would tend to

---

* Not to be confused with the principle of Ockham's Razor, or choosing the simplest solution among two or more complex choices (see page 198). Ockham's Razor is a later step in the process of the scientific method. Evolution is the principle and fact of the entire process and history of the universe and of life on Earth.

† In an article in the March, 2014 issue of Discover magazine, molecular evolutionary biologist and director of the Institute of Molecular Evolutionary Genetics at Pennsylvania University, Masatoshi Nei, asserts that Darwin's discovery of natural selection was actually never the "driving force" behind evolution. As evidenced by his book, *Mutation-Driven Evolution*, Nei believes that mutation is a stronger factor, a process that likely didn't even occur to Darwin from his observations. But then that is one of the beauties of science. Better and better knowledge is acquired over time, which is consistent with the entire principle and fact of evolution.

doubt that science has rushed to judgment in confirming that evolution is a fact in the cycle of life, although it's always possible. Short of not being versed enough in the current published scientific findings, it sounds to me more like many in the religious community are counting on the assumption that a "fact" means that *all* the pieces of the evolutionary puzzle need to be found before it can be acknowledged as correct, or at least the best and clearest explanation.

Using the above picture-puzzle as an example (and an imaginary and immense one!), if the puzzle indicates that it contains a billion pieces (since evolution occurs over billions of years) and you're only missing 25 pieces—but you can clearly make out the picture—it probably means that the remaining 25 pieces will not render the picture much different than it looks without the missing 25 pieces. But science has never said that were those 25 pieces to be found and the puzzle *did* look different, that science would cling to the old model. On the contrary. Nature would dictate otherwise and the fact would either change to another theory entirely or a different fact. Right now, the discovered pieces of the picture-puzzle of evolution by natural selection are more numerous than they are missing, showing the general evolutionary puzzle more complete than empty and painting a clear picture of the way life works and has evolved. Evolution can, therefore, be considered a fact until new, more compelling evidence refuting evolution is brought forth.

Conversely, the hypothesis of the non-existence of God—based upon the lack of physical evidence for God—cannot be considered fact yet either. Not having enough evidence to support a hypothesis is not the same thing as having the needed evidence to dismiss it confidently. (Sagan often said, "Absence of evidence is not evidence of absence.") Just like the demand to wait for physical (or, at least, more concrete) evidence to believe in a deity, so is evidence necessary in order to completely rule out a deity as well. That said, evolution was a theory as first proposed by Darwin. Since then, modern science has retrieved much more detailed corroborating evidence to support the theory, which has more likely enabled it to be comfortably changed from theory to fact.

I have another, imaginary (and slightly silly, but I hope illuminating) example. Suppose a child asked if *all* the various values of currency and coins of a nation looked the same? Would you have to summon the *entire* existing nation's monetary flow to be sure that all the different denominations did in fact have the same design? Of course not. You would only need to visit a few banks (perhaps different companies, too, for better objectivity) and ask the bank employees, and a few random people, to display their cash and coins to be convinced that all that nation's currency was in fact identical. In other words, just like the enormous, but imaginary, evolutionary picture-puzzle, you don't need to recall the entire currency of a nation to prove that the majority of currency that an individual has come across in a lifetime matches the rest of the currency flow. You no longer need as much faith to be sure because simple experiment and time provide the needed evidence. You have seen enough to know. The idea or proposition of any national currency all having essentially the same appearance is safely a fact and not a theory. It is the same for the principle/fact of evolution.

Darwin himself encountered enormous resistance to his early hypothesis of natural selection well before he wrote or published his book, *Origin of Species*. While aboard the *H.M.S. Beagle* he became a regular dining guest, and later a confidant, of the ship's Vice-Admiral Robert Fitzroy. In John Irving's, *The Origin*, in a conversation between Darwin and Fitzroy—in which Darwin explains his recent findings of the variety of feet webbing of the same type of bird on different islands in the Galápagos Islands—Darwin offers his tentative conclusion that the differences pointed to a change in the characteristics of the species over time rather than the species bodily characteristics remaining the same over time. To this, Fitzroy, a Christian, haughtily, stiffly, and defiantly declared that all life had remained unchanged since the beginning of Creation. Clearly this was not only a subject that Darwin could not attempt disagreement about with his superior, but it was a foreshadowing of what he would experience from much of the general public in reaction to his future research on evolution by natural selection and publication of his, *Origin of Species*. Vice-Admiral Fitzroy's attitude and response then was not at all uncommon. Sadly, nor is it still today.

It is really a great shame that any newfound knowledge is ever met with resistance or negativity. Knowledge is what makes intelligent beings grow and improve. It is more understandable though that Darwin's discoveries were rejected in his own time because they were so radically different (and new, and threatening) from the accepted teaching of Genesis. But it is doubly too bad that we are still resisting the idea now, after so many years in which further research and corroboration of fossil evidence have shown that Darwin was correct. By extension, it would be nice if stories like Genesis and Creation could be respectfully considered as significant, but ancient fables,* supplanted today by the ingenious discoveries of modern science and astronomy.

---

* A clever comparison between fact and fable is in this excerpt from the historical novel, *Raptor*, by Gary Jennings. The character, Wyrd (pronounced "Vord"), an elderly woodsman, is speaking to Thorn, the novel's protagonist (a youth at this point in the story), both fictitious. "The lynx is no magical mongrel fox-wolf. Look for yourself. You can see it is a greater cousin to the wildcat. Do not put your faith in fables, urchin, whether they are related by a booby or a bishop. Or even wise old me. Use your own eyes, your own experience, your own reason to determine the truth of things."

Chapter 6

SCIENTIFIC THOUGHT AND METHOD

Science is a way of thinking much more than it is a body of knowledge.
Its goal is to find out how the world works...
To penetrate into the heart of a thing—
even a little thing, a blade of grass, as Walt Whitman said—
is to experience a kind of exhilaration that, it may be,
only human beings of all the beings on this planet can feel.
We are an intelligent species and the use of our intelligence
quite properly gives us pleasure.
In this respect the brain is like a muscle. When we think well, we feel good.
Understanding is a kind of ecstasy.

Carl Sagan
Broca's Brain

"**P**erformance is the art of controlled ecstasy!" is the epitaph written on my mother, Elaine Lee Richey's gravestone. That was a quote from her, and my brothers and I chose it because both as a person and as an exquisitely beautiful virtuoso violinist and violin teacher, she championed the goal of experiencing deep emotional and intellectual understanding, and ecstasy in life and in performance. She died of pancreatic cancer[*] in September of 1997, only four months after she sighted comet Hale-Bopp.

She also said to me once when I asked her what her career might have been had she not been a musician and a violinist, that she would have been a scientist. She was fascinated by the integration of joy and the mechanical means of achieving it in whatever medium she took an interest. Her professional vehicle and voice was the violin, but she was also a prolific reader, an inventive carpenter (she made trundle beds for my brothers and me when we were children), an avid complex crossword puzzle-solver, made her own dresses, an excellent chef, loved her three sons, her work, her cats, and enjoyed fun, laughter, and great conversation and debate.

Many of my happiest memories are sitting around at night as a family, often with friends, discussing a wide variety of topics; the discussions were lively, insightful, and invigorating. She put deep thought and emotional care into everything she did. For her the two were inseparable. She once said of her own performing experience, "...the audience would be surprised by how much I'm thinking."

Thinking deeply about anything and how and why something works is the fundamental principle of the scientific method. But as Sagan and my mother both felt and said, scientific thinking also carries with it great ecstasy. It is both a tool and a process that works consistently well and

---

[*] If only someone like Jack Andraka had already been successful with finding an early detection for pancreas cancer, my mother and others like her might still be alive:
http://www.cbs.com/shows/60_minutes/video/RiQKqFPFfbNm2X9t2___Z_96zFT2AKno/boy-wonder-jack-andraka/.

produces deep joy. (One exception seems to be in quantum mechanics, the subatomic realm, where one part of the scientific method seems to be inapplicable. Experiments with them not only cannot be repeated with consistency, but subatomic particles seem to *know* they're being observed. They behave differently and randomly in repeated experiments seemingly *on purpose*!) This does not mean that, in the future, the scientific method could not be supplemented or even supplanted by something that works better. I hope that the scientific community, if and when it came to that point, would welcome that kind of discovery. It might be that the scientific method would still work well for most physical phenomena but less well for other, as yet undiscovered or extraphysical, phenomena.

I've heard it suggested that there might be areas of perception or dimensions that are sensed now, but have escaped measurement with our current scientific method and technology because they lie just beyond our ability to acquire physical evidence for them; the subject of metaphysics is an example. I think that's certainly possible. An excellent example, again, is the study of subatomic particles.

Subatomic particles often defy consistent repeated observation, not because they obviously emanate from a god (although they certainly might), but because their microscopic nature and random behavior appear to us as almost *intentionally* inconsistent. They don't behave predictably or consistently, in the ways that we're used to observing physical phenomena. They defy modern Newton/Einstein physics.

Other extra-physical phenomena include automatic writing, extrasensory perception, trance-channeling, fortune-telling, etc. But although we must remain open to every possibility, it would be very surprising to find something in the universe in which the scientific method could not at least be incorporated, because it has worked at helping us to understand the universe to the degree that it already has (gravity and centrifugal force seem to work the same everywhere in the known universe, for example). And while it is an obvious understatement to say that we have certainly not uncovered or come to know everything about the universe, we definitely comprehend the cosmos much better now than if we did not have science. We know an enormous amount for being such tiny intelligent creatures on a small planet.

My guess is that whatever the tools of discovery are that we have yet to stumble upon, they will likely relate to and be compatible with science and the scientific method. They will probably be an addition to science, not its replacement. Put another way, since the scientific method has worked for helping us learn so much about the universe already, it would be strange if there were portions of the universe that were not able to be perceived scientifically. But the opposite is certainly still possible. *Anything* is possible when approached by science, even that the scientific method itself could become obsolete. If new methods of discovery that worked well did not relate to science, the scientific community would need to be willing to put their prejudices aside and look at the new data just as I am suggesting that the religious community should be willing to put its prejudices aside when presented with compelling evidence that contradicts religious teaching.

It is therefore important for a religious believer and a scientific thinker to empathize with each other. The religious person needs to understand that believing in something as large and physically intangible as a Supreme Being is perfectly fine for them, but may be difficult to share with someone who needs physical evidence. If one shares their belief with someone who is skeptical, one needs to pay attention if the skeptic has trouble. The problem may not be with the skeptic. It could be possible that the details of one's faith are not entirely clear or the skeptic would be convinced more easily. If one can't make their point clear to someone who is intelligent but does not share their faith, there might be something wrong with the explanation. There could also be something in error about one's thinking. Put another way, something may be absent or omitted from an explanation but not necessarily wrong. All of our thoughts and feelings are there for a reason, but the details about our thoughts and feelings may lack clarity. The need for physical evidence, skepticism, and clarity are all fundamental to the scientific method.

In the same way—like the idea of a Supreme Being being difficult for a skeptic to accept or imagine—the idea that the universe evolved by its own natural law, without divine intervention, is hard for a religious person to accept or imagine. A religious person might acknowledge that a Supreme Being is an extension of human experience and therefore, in a way, easier to relate to, but that might not diminish their reality of the Deity. And it might also make the scientific method for them less attractive and compelling.

Both sensitivities are worthy of patience and respect.

We are all used to the fact that things (physical objects) are made by people or other living things. For example, wood is harvested by people from trees, which is used to build tables, chairs, houses, etc. Though humans didn't make or plant the first trees (trees have been around a lot longer than humans), it does take a human to fashion an object from a tree; humans can of course make trees now by planting and growing them, but the evolution of trees is of course a separate discussion from the evolution of intelligent life. Tree trunks are used by a beaver to build its dam; an ant hill built by ants; a hive by bees, and so forth. Objects with which we are familiar are made of physical matter and we are used to other living beings configuring and constructing that matter to make the objects. The idea or concept that a thing could *make itself* or have always existed *by itself* seems, from our perspective, to be disorienting and even preposterous. Things (objects) have to be *made* and *by something* or *by someone*.

The Earth and the universe obviously contain matter. Immense amounts of matter. The idea that all the matter in the universe could have created itself and therefore exists independently, *without* a living being to bring it into existence, by extension seems exponentially preposterous. It doesn't fit within our perspective for how something comes to exist. It also doesn't fall within our perceptions for something to have *always existed on its own*, infinitely. I would caution, however, that this is an example of where our perception is probably very limited to our own life experience, where we need to think further and have a wider perspective, "outside the box." Our lives are finite (at least the physical lives with which we are the most familiar). The universe (or God) may be infinite.

So what does it imply or mean to say that something *exists on its own*? Does it really mean that something (the universe as the prime example) has always been there? How does something come to exist if not by an "Instigator?" Or at least by some*thing* "causing" it to exist? This is a very interesting and legitimate question. But is the answer, if not readily available, by default a deity, a god? The healthiest (and, if you will, scientific) response should again be that we simply don't yet know. That, in my opinion, is where the discussion and/or conclusion of religious belief should patiently wait and join science in the continued search to better uncover the answer. Suspending conclusion until, by experiment, clear, unambiguous evidence is found that is satisfactory for both religious believers and scientific thinkers and skeptics.

Religion is skeptical of science, just as science can be skeptical of religion, and sometimes both have good reason. Science has made claims that were found to be erroneous, that it was reluctant to retract. Einstein's General Theory of Relativity, for example, is a universal maxim that has been shaken by Quantum Physics. I'm sure that there were some scientists who resisted the implied refutation of relativity. However, one major difference of science is that the scientific method itself is self-correcting, which discourages any reluctance to admit error. Religion needs to do the same: to be self-correcting, to admit error. The question of an Instigator, Entity, or God in personal form like us—but so profoundly powerful and perfect that it could make something as large and inordinately beautiful and complex as the universe—is a *huge* proposition, to say the least. And, although not dismissible (because it has so far not been proved or disproved), this proposition should certainly require the strictest evidence to be concluded as fact. Strict evidence is what a skeptic is missing and they have every right to demand the evidence. Once again, the temporary answer should be that if very strict evidence is not forthcoming, the idea should simply wait and be held as a *possibility* and not a *conclusion* until better evidence is found.

There is, however, much evidence of other "instigators." Instigators such as gravity, centrifugal and centripetal force, and inertia. Inertia, for example, is a force that seems to have had an indeterminate beginning or end—at least with the large celestial objects, like the objects in our solar system and in the known universe. Inertia is also a good example of a cause without a perceptible creator. The definition of inertia is either an object's permanent resting state or permanent and constant speed, provided it doesn't come into contact with another object or force. Universal inertia could have had no definite beginning. So it is with celestial objects. We haven't detected any *being* pushing the Moon around the Earth or propelling any other celestial or astronomical object in its orbit or motion (although the god, Atlas, of Greek mythology held the Earth on his back).

Another example of something existing on its own inertia with which we are very familiar, though involuntarily, is our heartbeat. I realize that it was a living being (usually a doctor, nurse, or mid-wife) who started the baby's heartbeat with an initial "spank." But maybe the "spank" that began the inertia of the universe is so far in the infinite past that we may never be able to detect it and therefore never know what or "who" gave the initial cosmic spank. Perhaps the instigator (the "spanker") of the initial inertia was an explosion caused by an earlier explosion, *ad infinitum*. The very concept of *ad infinitum* (infinity) is, itself, the idea of something occurring with no apparent beginning or end. This is certainly as much of a possibility as the possibility of God. In other words, God may have always existed or the universe may have infinitely existed. As Spinoza suggested, perhaps they mean the same thing.

Put another way, there can always be a prior cause. If God exists, who created God? And who created God's creator, etc., *ad infititum*. Or "What came before that? Before that? Before that? And before that? You get the idea. It verges on (or is) ridiculous.

John Allen Paulos poses exactly this question is his book, *irreligion: A Mathematician Explains Why The Arguments For God Just Don't Add Up.* He writes, "The absence of an answer to the question 'What caused, preceded, or created God?'...made...the existence of the latter...an unnecessary, antecedent mystery. Why introduce Him? Why postulate a...nonexplanatory...perplexity to...explain the already...perplexing and beautiful world?" [21]

Though questions are fundamentally valuable and necessary, at what point is there any point to the question of infinite regression, infinite pondering of a prior universal cause? The answer may be no point at all. In fact, this is probably the *exact* point of atheism: God, as the universal initial cause, is invisible, intangible, incorporeal, irrational to experiment, elusive to physical evidence, and therefore unnecessary and pointless.

Once again, I think we need to at least recognize that, in the absence of physical evidence for a deity, we could be superimposing our need to attach a "Maker" to the universe—like a chair, table, or house being made by a person (people) because, in our reality, those objects can't build themselves. It is hard for many people to imagine the grandeur of the universe always having been there with no beginning, no "Maker." However, this superimposing of our own manipulations to the physical world onto the origin of the cosmos may be what living, thinking beings do first by default. Perhaps it's difficult to avoid. We try to imagine how the universe came to be, and the first thing that occurs to us is our own beginnings. We know that we were created from two physical beings—male and female (sex between our parents)—so, by extension, our first thought might be that the universe must have to have a similar creator, in the form of at least one physical being.

As simple as it might at first sound, I think that this is a more enormous and supernatural proposition than the average religious believer realizes. I also think that the enormity is taken for granted by too many believers. (Again, for many skeptics, the proposition of a "Creator" of the cosmos is just too much like a fairy tale and can't be taken seriously). The believer often doesn't consider or even realize this dichotomy (simple and natural, yet *super*natural—a seeming contradiction). Maybe the missing evidence, once found, would point to the fact that God was a little different than we thought, but existent nonetheless. However, it is also possible that in our need to understand the universe in more simple terms and concepts, we're projecting onto it something that may be inapplicable to the universe or universes—the knowledge and experience of our *own* beginning.

In addition to acknowledging the possible mythology of God, organized religions should be open to employing the scientific method to attempt to discover physical evidence for their God. It might actually turn over some astonishing new findings which would educate both the scientific and religious communities. But it also might reveal a lot of errors and put to rest some old notions within religion. It might be discovered that God does indeed exist…in a dimension that was previously undetectable but sensed. That would be an incredible discovery! But it might be discovered that, like the Greek gods, our modern, monotheistic God is imaginary and mythological too. That would be a sober and profound discovery. Whatever the discovery, such a clarification would be monumental and a lesson in honesty and integrity.

The reader may be intrigued to know that I think the best scientists enjoy a religious sense. My perception is that the pursuit of religion generates from the emotions, our feelings. For example, upon beholding a particularly pretty sunset, my late Grandmother Richey (a Methodist) once said, "I don't see how someone could look at a sunset and not believe in God." I understood her feeling very much. Sunsets *are* beautiful! They make us feel beauty, wonder, and awe. They are also an example of one of the *most beautiful* phenomena of nature. But I don't think it follows that simply because my grandmother felt the existence of God when she beheld a sunset it means that God exists. It was her feeling, not a fact. There are clear explanations for sunsets in physics independent of potential divine causes. That said, the feeling of enjoyment in perceiving natural beauty and wondering what causes it (my mother's goal of experiencing ecstasy) is, I think, where both the religious and scientific experiences are born. A scientist is in awe of the universe just like a religious person is in awe of God—this is consistent with my perception of God as a term or metaphor for the cosmos, and, as Paul Tillich emphasized, not an actual *being*—so the awe of the scientist and the religious person may, in fact, be the same. Awe is awe (again, the reflexive property of equality!). Still, though awe is a wonderful feeling, it is only a feeling. What is needed with awe is deep and critical thought, and tangible and physical evidence.

Another example of how scientists have a religious experience is that scientists would like to *believe*, *trust*, or *feel* that life exists elsewhere in the universe. The odds seem to be in favor of us not being alone given the "building blocks," or matter and energy, necessary for life and the abundance of both in the universe, or perhaps at least in our own Milky Way galaxy.* But science does not "believe in" life on other worlds *yet*. Scientists only think it's *possible*. As I've emphasized, that is a difference with science. A proposition is not certainty. It is not confirmed ("believed") until very strong physical evidence is discovered or presented. The proposition of God, it seems to me, is at the same stage. Belief in God is equivalent to belief in life elsewhere in the universe (extraterrestrials). I think they are in the same category (and might, in fact, be the same thing).

If extraterrestrials do exist, they might strike us the same way God would if God were found to be evident. I'm sure they would be very difficult to understand. Perhaps, at first, incomprehensible. This might be where the proposed loss of free will in religion—the creation by God in humans with

---

* The Drake Equation is one example of an intriguing and specific mathematical proposal for the likelihood of extraterrestrial life, at least in the Milky Way galaxy. Without including it here, I encourage the reader to research Dr. Frank Drake's equation online. It is a fascinating computation. To many scientists, including Asimov, Drake, and Sagan, it was also a more plausible proposition than the popular suggested legitimacy that extraterrestrials have already visited the Earth (the suspicion and even conclusion of many people regarding UFOs), or that extraterrestrials are currently and clandestinely living among us (as depicted in the films, *Men In Black*)). For those and other scientists, the evidence confirming extraterrestrial visitation, their terrestrial habitation, or their abduction of humans is highly unsubstantiated. There is also the thought—to which I have already eluded—from some scientists that these latter proposals about extraterrestrials are simply a variation on the proposed existence of God.

the ability to choose for ourselves right from wrong (and, by extension, whether or not to believe in God)—could enter the discussion of extraterrestrials. Would we lose our free will to understand or comprehend ("believe in") extraterrestrials if we were to physically encounter one? Would some religious people invoke the danger of losing our free will to try to inhibit contact or communication with the extraterrestrials?

I think it highly unlikely that we would lose our free will by physically encountering an extraterrestrial, and I think it highly unlikely (and really a pointless and defeatist argument) that we would lose our free will by physically encountering God. Frankly, I think the surest way of losing our free will is not in the pursuit of, acquisition, and experience of knowledge, but in the ready and hasty acceptance of dogma with little physical evidence. I think our free will is a great survival mechanism. It makes us crave knowledge. Knowledge is our brains' food.

I think that our universal perspective would only increase if better evidence for God were pursued and found. It seems clear to me that the fear of losing one's free will by encountering physical evidence of God is an excuse in disguise for the lack of, and inability to present, concrete physical evidence for God.

It is not important to "believe in" a proposition derived from the results of scientific experiment either immediately or even at all, or at least until one has verified the results for themselves. "Believing" is not a goal of science. So, as Richard Dawkins emphasized, why is it important to "believe," either immediately or eventually, in a tenet of religion? Why can't God be an interesting hypothesis or metaphor requiring further study? Experiments with other phenomena (such as trance channeling, or out-of-body experiences) that are intriguing but have not been tested thoroughly enough are open to further study but not considered conclusive. So as well could be the goal for the propositions of religion.

Unwillingness to search for physical proof before announcing validity often results in what is called pseudo-science. As I mentioned earlier, "Don't reinvent the wheel" is a good example of a phrase derived from the use of the scientific method. (Someone made the initial discovery that a round object would have many uses like enabling faster speed than we can walk or run and carrying large loads great distances with relative ease. It's a wise thing not to reinvent.) Physical evidence is required cross-disciplinarily for a reason. We live in a physical world. Part of separating what works from what doesn't is separating the propositions that provide physical evidence from those which do not. Think of the multitude of discoveries that human beings have already made and the accomplishments that we have achieved as a result of physical evidence and the scientific method. Is there a comparable number derived from the use of religious practice alone? (I'm not concluding that the answer is no.) Perhaps religion can be thought of as a first step: The trust or awe that gives us the confidence that we can find the answer, by experiment and evidence, physical and sensory. All of our successful projects were accomplished first by romanticizing ("believing" it was *possible*), then considering all possibilities (*thinking*), and then applying the scientific method (separating what worked from what did not by experiment) in order to *know* and complete the project. In this view, religion might be considered the first part of the discovery process (the inspiration) followed by science.

As I have already suggested, the topic of a belief in a deity really seems to come down to matter of private personal perception. In many conversations I've had with religious friends, most examples I've thought of for the testability for God, or my suggestion that God might be an invention of the imagination, are met with the response that the Deity is beyond the scope of science or reasoning. The Deity, God, these religious friends say, not only created the universe and all of existence and is therefore *super*natural, but cannot thus be analyzed by the relatively elementary and natural (*non-super*natural) logic of the thought (science) of its creations. This reasoning is consistent with the impression most religions give of their deities, but it also raises problematic questions. First, the very concept that God is supernatural and all life is only natural implies a hierarchy that God is superior and humans are inferior. I question whether that is a necessary or healthy implication. It also suggests a separation similar to a caste system. And it implies that human thought is incompatible with the Deity, that God would be impregnable and immune to critical thinking.

But as I raised earlier, why would the Deity *create thought* in its creation if said deity was *inaccessible by thought*? This makes the least sense to me. Why would the Deity necessarily be perceived in a different way than its creations? And why would a Creator create creations that were inferior to itself? Do parents hope that their children will be less intelligent, be permanently dependent on them, and fare less well than themselves as a result? In both my hope and experience, the opposite is true. Most healthy and loving parents want their children to turn out better, be smarter, be better educated, and have a more fulfilling future than they did. Doesn't even the suggestion of God creating such potential disconnect as "original sin" and relatively inaccessible contact between itself and life imply a lack of respect on the part of the Creator for its creations? That disheartening disparity notwithstanding, isn't it also suspect that the central topic of divinity (the Deity itself) within all religions seems to be the one point that reason and the scientific method do not apply? Shouldn't we ask *why* it doesn't seem to apply and whether it *should*? If the Deity were really as clear and as real as believers say, why are there any skeptics or unbelievers at all, especially highly intelligent ones? If the Deity created the cosmos, life, and all natural laws, just as natural law is impossible to break so should natural selection have selected out unbelief from human beings as the natural law of God (if belief is indeed the fundamental for knowing God). In short, if God did, in fact, create humans, all life, and the universe, survival should be *dependent* on belief. It should not *work* to be an unbeliever. Or, a possible postulate: If God existed, then a non-believer would not.

In a long conversation years ago with a good friend of mine who is Lutheran, I told him that I thought humanity was lucky to be here, that we should be grateful for the existence of all life and our own lives. I told him that were it not for a probable cometary impact with the Earth (which is thought to have caused the extinction of the dinosaurs), we would likely not be here. We probably owe our lives to a comet.

He asked, "How do you know that the comet wasn't sent from God?"

I said I didn't know that it wasn't. But I countered, "Can you show me how you think it could have been sent from God as opposed to being a random event in the cosmos according to natural law?"

He said he could not.

I liked both of our admissions. But it revealed that there may simply be no physical evidence to support or refute God and that a belief in God comes down, as I have said before, to the individual *choosing* to believe in the absence of evidence. The late Christopher Reeve said as much in his book, *Still Me*. He said that believing in God felt better, so he chose to believe.

The only conclusion I reach from these examples is that, at this point, God is relegated to individual perception, "in the eye of the beholder," and neither exists nor is a fallacy until proven so, like everything else.

Regardless of the truth or falsehood of a deity, I don't think that there is any question that our need to believe in a secure and loving God is at least in part because human beings need to feel security and love and we are overwhelmingly small and vulnerable in the universe. In the secular view, the cosmos does not appear to provide love. We seem to be completely on our own. Love comes from within us and is (hopefully and naturally) given back to us by other life.

This is my feeling of what Barbara Brown Taylor meant in the introduction to her book, *An Altar in the World*, when she wrote, "No one longs for what he or she already has, and yet the accumulated insight of those wise about the spiritual life suggests that the reason so many of us cannot see the red X * that marks the spot is because we are standing on it. The treasure we seek requires no lengthy expedition, no expensive equipment, no superior aptitude or special company. All we lack is the willingness to imagine that we already have everything we need." [22] Simply put, we embody and exude love. It's the simplest "soul search" because love seems to be an inherent and independent universal force which permeates us and all living things. Like The Beatles sang in, "All You Need Is Love," perhaps love is an unsung natural law. It is very understandable, though, that rather than recognizing Taylor's red "X" of love radiating within, *inside us* and life, because we are physically and emotionally vulnerable, much of our effort at coexisting with the cosmos would be to seek for security *outside us* from the cosmos.

But imagining that there might be an entity who made us, loves us, and protect us in the expansiveness of the universe, and there actually being one are very different things. In other words, it's very different to have fun *imagining* that the universe was created by an entity or is an entity itself (like imagining pictures in clouds), than to take the idea that the cosmos was created by an entity *seriously and literally*. What is reassuring is that, along

---

* In his book, *When God Is Gone Everything Is Holy: The Making of a Religious Naturalist*, Chet Raymo shares this fun summary of the origin of "x" (used first by Descartes in his book on geometry in 1637) to represent anything not known or mysterious: "Spry little x, with its feet planted firmly on the ground and its arms uplifted in surprise, is our emissary to the unknown." Barbara Brown Taylor is suggesting that the X marking our spot (our inner being) is much more known than we think.

with the sobering realization of how tiny we are within the cosmos, we have the security of knowing that our intelligence has *enabled us to survive*. If that intelligence was given by a deity then maybe one day we'll know it for sure. But if our intelligence is only the result of our own efforts at survival over millions of years without a deity, then we'll hopefully come to know that, too. Dorothy expresses this realization to Glenda, the Good Witch of the North near the end of the film, *The Wizard of Oz*:

> Dorothy: Oh, *will* you help me? *Can* you help me?
> Glenda: You don't need to be helped any longer. You've always had the power to go back to Kansas.
> Dorothy: I *have*?!
> Scarecrow: Then why didn't you tell her before?
> Glenda: Because she wouldn't have believed me. She had to learn it for herself.
> Tin Man: What have you learned Dorothy?
> Dorothy: (*to Glenda*) Well...I think that it...wasn't enough just to wanna see Uncle Henry and Auntie Em...and if I ever go looking for my heart's desire again, I won't look any further'n my own backyard...because if it isn't there, I never really lost it to begin with. Is that right?
> Glenda: That's all it is!
> Scarecrow: But that's so *EASY*!! (*to Dorothy*) I should have thought of it for you!
> Tin Man: I should have felt it in my heart!
> Glenda: No, she had to find it out for herself.

In other words, the answers were not outside herself ("over the rainbow" or through a god), but within her and in her heart and mind all along (in her (our) own backyard). Maybe we humans have already proven our ability to survive without a deity through the evolution of our intelligence. It's a fact that we're still here, but there's still debate about whether a deity exists. Like Dorothy, maybe our "Creator" is *ourselves* and we, "...never really lost it to begin with!"

I would suggest that whether or not there is a living, supernatural entity responsible for all of what we observe and experience is not particularly important. What *is* important, I think, is that we live life together with love, honesty, flexibility, intellectual curiosity, emotional expression, religious reflection, and scientific thinking and passion. They are all our joyous ecstasies.

Chapter 7

FAITH

To one who has faith, no explanation is necessary. To one without faith, no explanation is possible.

St. Thomas Aquinas

Faith is the great cop-out, the great excuse to evade the need to think and evaluate evidence. Faith is belief in spite of, even perhaps because of, the lack of evidence.

Richard Dawkins
From his speech at the Edinburgh International Science Festival, April 15, 1992

*Sophie, every faith in the world is based on fabrication. That is the definition of faith—acceptance of that which we imagine to be true, that which we cannot prove. Every religion describes God through metaphor, allegory, and exaggeration, from the early Egyptians through modern Sunday school. Metaphors are a way to help our minds process the unpr ocessible.
The problems arise when we begin to believe literally in our own metaphors.*

Robert Langdon
The Da Vinci Code
Dan Brown

In addition to the words *God* and *believe* I think that the word *faith* is also not understood or explained specifically well. Similar to the varying definitions of the word believe, it is curious that a relatively unspecific word like faith is used as the primary *explanation* for believing in the relatively intangible concept of God. *Faith* for *believing* in *God.* One, twice, and thrice the confusion.

Faith is first defined by the Webster's Collegiate Dictionary as "allegiance to duty or a person: LOYALTY." The second definition is "belief and trust in and loyalty to God." The first definition is interesting in two ways. One, unlike for the word believe, the first definition is not the religious definition. And two, that the first definition includes a "person" as well as "duty." It is consistent with the tendency of many religions to borrow words and definitions in order to cast the deity both as a person and as the male proper pronoun, "He."

It is quite interesting that the two dictionary definitions do not begin with the faith of religious faith, but with faith as it is more generally and secularly used. Clearly, the kind of faith encouraged in religion is not acknowledged as the most important kind of faith to the editors of the dictionary, or it would probably be listed first. It is also interesting that the word faith (like the word believe) is adopted as a primary virtue by religions even though its meaning tends more toward the general and secular. Since the concept of God is extremely difficult to define clearly, it is surprising that two words that are sometimes defined more generally—belief and faith—are chosen as additional tools of focus for a topic that is itself quite devoid of specifics. The concept of God lacks clarity and so are two of the weightiest words used to gain a better understanding of the concept. It's a bit of a paradox. One would think that more specific words would be chosen as vehicles for understanding such a profoundly abstract concept.

Faith—or trust—is a very lovely, compassionate, noble, and honorable quality. But its application should be very dependent on the magnitude and clarity of the subject or object. We can trust in the repetition of physical and emotional experience because we can all experience the pattern of frequency in which those things occur on a daily basis. Repetition, or consistency with immediate physical and emotional experience, reinforces our ability to trust.

If the things we trusted stopped showing any physical evidence of existing we would stop trusting in those things very deeply. Examples of simple trust and faith might include faith that our hearts will continue to beat; faith that we will wake in the morning after being asleep; faith that our loved ones and pets will experience the same; faith that our loved ones will continue to love us; faith that our machines will work today because they worked yesterday, etc.

Alan W. Watts put the difference between faith and belief very insightfully is his book, *The Wisdom of Insecurity: A Message for an Age of Anxiety*, "We must...make a clear distinction between belief and faith...belief is almost the opposite of faith. Belief is the insistence that the truth is what one would "lief" or wish it to be. The believer will open his mind to the truth on the condition that it fits in with his preconceived ideas and wishes. Faith...is an unreserved opening of the mind to the truth, whatever it may turn out to be. Faith...is a plunge into the unknown. Belief clings, but faith lets go. Faith...is the essential virtue of science, and...of any religion that is not self-deception." [23] This is splendidly said and shines a more specific light on the practical benefit of faith. I think it also speaks directly to the deepest intention and goal of science: faith in the unbiased and unprejudiced search for knowledge (truth) and understanding.

The concept of God, though possible to imagine emotionally and deserving of a kind of metaphorically respectful trust, is less a candidate to warrant such an exceptional degree of trust—faith—as the creator of the universe and all of life. Therefore, in the absence of a more specific physical experience of God, why do believers use faith as one of their primary tools for believing that a "Supreme Being" really exists? Is it partly because it is simply easier psychologically to trust that a "Supreme Being" exists rather than to try to search harder for better physical evidence? If that is true, then it seems clear that religious faith is perhaps guilty of taking too easy a route, opting for ease over veracity. (I suppose some might counter that the struggle of faith in the absence of concrete evidence is harder, but also a more noble, humble, and worthy posture. But then there are those who would rebut that as a self-inflicted and unnecessary burden.) Or is it out of another kind of respect for the Deity, a kind of "benefit-of-the-doubt," especially if it cannot be proven false? In other words, if the deity does in fact exist, distrusting its existence would be disrespectful. Or worse, that it could have dire future repercussions for the non-believer.

The latter reason seems self-defeating. Sort of like the old negative adage, "Curiosity killed the cat," in which curiosity is not only implied as dangerous, but fatal, as if the search for better evidence might ignite the wrath of the Deity. We (the cat) should not be curious or we might get ourselves into not just mortal danger, but *eternal* danger. However, these examples imply that it is always too risky to be inquisitive, a notion that I think most of us would find silly and even demeaning.

Because the initial teaching of many religions is the emphasis on belief in its dogma and not as much on intellectually understanding the ideas, the necessity of faith, it seems to me, is largely due to that very omission of intellectual understanding. To use a quasi-biblical phrase, "one begets the other." Faith is viewed by the religious community as a virtue, one of respect and humility in the absence of strong evidence. But to the skeptic, it is also seen as a virtue of folly: an extreme, irrational, and anxious trust in the face of scant evidence. Respect and humility are obviously admirable virtues, but to what degree and/or extreme? Without skeptical questions about God, how can one really be sure that the strong faith is warranted? What if religion is indeed invented by humans and no God exists? On what, then, is the faith based? Really, even the possibility that this could be true stems from a question that comes from the intellect and should be an alarm bell of warning to withhold such unwavering trust (faith) until better evidence is provided.

The following extract from Jon Krakauer's, *Under the Banner of Heaven*, speaks to the phenomenon of faith. "All religious belief is a result of non-rational faith. And faith, by its very definition, tends to be impervious to intellectual argument or academic criticism. Polls routinely indicate, moreover, that nine out of ten Americans believe in God—most of us subscribe to one brand of religion or another. Those who would assail *The Book of Mormon* should bear in mind that its veracity is no more dubious than the veracity of the Bible, say, or the Qur'an, or the sacred texts of most other religions. The latter texts simply enjoy the considerable advantage of having made their public debut in the shadowy recesses of the ancient past, and are thus much harder to refute." [24] Clearly, this is correct. Many esteemed authors, scholars, and other academicians have stated essentially the same thing. But simply being hard to refute is only a partially compelling attribute. Indisputable, or nearly indisputable, evidence is more compelling. A larger question might be: What percentage of the above ratio of Americans are asking themselves what their faith in any kind of deity really means, by what is it motivated, and whether they regularly question its dictates? That, to me, is a very interesting psychological question.

I'm sure most of us are familiar with the phrase, "You want what you can't have." All of us would probably like to understand the universe more fully, know where we came from, why we are here, etc. Like the effect any new technological age creates in desiring instant gratification, the same tends to be true with questions about ourselves and our origins. We want the answer, and we want it *now*. If something is beyond our present understanding or comprehension, we are often impatient and want immediate understanding and comprehension all the more. Unfortunately, like the increase in speed that new technology regularly offers, humans are also prone to want to understand better *quickly*. This might have its roots in the basic instinct of survival. If one is attacked and one has to think too long about how to defend oneself, one could be dead. Therefore, wanting an immediate solution may be a natural survival instinct and response for all life, whether it's for physical survival or intellectual and emotional understanding. As a result of that natural instinct, when presented with something as seemingly incomprehensible as the universe, maybe we are prone to jumping or reaching too quickly for religious faith. It also points to a kind of *paralysis* or *intimidation* by the magnitude of nature and the universe. But resigning to any of those reactions seems like not only an abdication of curiosity, but an anxious, apologetic or even servile posture.

There is also an element of a preference for the intangible. Like wanting what we can't have, the intangible rouses our curiosity and desire to make it tangible. But instead of insisting on more clarity for what makes us curious, religion often teaches that the intangible is intangible by nature, almost like a carrot in front of a horse. (Of course, the more the horse tries to walk toward the carrot, the more the carrot remains just out of its reach, and the rider on the horse successfully gets where they're going. The ruse is very effective for the rider but completely lost on the innocent horse). Could the concept of God be our "carrot"—the intangible, imaginary being that will always remain just out of our reach?

An intangible, grand, unfathomable idea excites us into a sense of longing; again, we want what we can't have. But an intangible explanation is also a little like a photo or video that is just enough out-of-focus that you can't make out the detail, but you can see some approximations. There is some intrigue in an out-of-focus image. It is almost more titillating for it to remain out-of-focus. If it came into focus it might feel too ordinary. This is perhaps how the prospect of a physical explanation of God (or of the origin of the universe) might feel to many religious people. A clearer picture might suddenly feel disappointing, like one would want the picture to go slightly out of focus again because it would feel more "otherworldly" or "spooky" (maybe hence, "God-fearing"). We enjoy a "shudder" at the unknown. It's enticing and even exhilarating.

In his epic historical novel, *Aztec*, Gary Jennings illuminates the human desire for the "intangible" in a saga of the sculpting of the Sun Stone, perhaps the most venerable of all Aztec works of art. Jennings describes two immense stone sculptures—each wrought by one of two brothers and each weighing approximately 24 tons—which were transported on top of logs, rolled consecutively and continuously, to the Aztec city center: The Heart of the One World. While attempting to cross a river causeway, the first stone sculpture's immense weight collapsed the causeway, and that sculpture plunged to the river bottom. The sculpture in the rear, not yet on the causeway, was subsequently and safely transported by log raft to the Heart of the One World. It became known as the Sun Stone.

Perhaps unremarkably and predictably, but still dishearteningly, the lost sculpture became more revered and worshipped than the surviving Sun Stone. Through an elderly character describing the history of the two sculptures to the protagonist, Mixtli, and Mixtli's father, Jennings writes, "But the whole world will forever wonder…Might there be a work more sublime even than the Sun Stone lying beneath Lake Texcóco? In time, indeed, the myth-enhanced unknown came to be treasured more than the tangible reality. The lost sculpture came to be called In Huehuetótetl—The Most Venerable Stone—and the Sun Stone regarded as only a middling substitute." [25] In the following climactic scene, the sculptor brother who fashioned the surviving Sun Stone was thus regarded as a failure to the gods. To appease those gods (and presumably all Aztecs and humanity), he nobly offered *himself* for the venerable and honorable "Flowery Death": A public human sacrifice in which a priest deftly and swiftly extracts, with an obsidian blade, one's still-beating heart.

It is intriguing, and maybe even beguiling, that something inaccessible and intangible is often held in higher esteem and reverence than something accessible and tangible.

The exhilaration of the intangible is natural and normal. But focusing on the intangible should be temporary, not the end effect or goal. Isn't a scene in a movie that begins out-of-focus and then sharpens into focus very effective and satisfying exactly because the picture finally becomes focused with great clarity? And isn't the clear picture *more* gratifying?! (The photographic technique of making the subject in clear focus and the background out-of-focus works for exactly this reason.) Remaining with a slightly out-of-focus image is seldom preferable. It is interesting, then, that many religious people prefer not to persevere to bring the picture of God into better focus. Maybe the fear is that achieving a better focus will reveal a beautiful picture but absent what was presumed. Perhaps the clearer image would reveal a beautiful and tumultuous universe with more exquisite and explosive detail, but no God. Or maybe God would also be clearly evident. Either way, endeavoring to make the intangible tangible is probably highly advantageous and desirable.

What is it that makes some people prefer faith in the intangible as ultimate truth? I understand the search for things just beyond our grasp. That is problem-solving. But I don't understand using faith to *settle* on the intangible as truth, especially if it doesn't make physical or intellectual sense.

Putting the degree of faith aside for a moment, the only differences I've ever observed between a religious person and a non-religious person are family background, education, and experience. We are all products of our families, what we've been taught, and what we associate with that education based on what we experience and observe. If someone is told that God made the world/universe/cosmos, then every time that person sees a sunset, or a rainbow, or a brilliant, star-filled night sky they see evidence for God (like my late Grandmother Richey). But if the same person were never told that a deity created the universe, the concept might cross their mind as an interesting metaphor, but I don't know that they would conclude a deity on their own in the absence of physical evidence. After all, a sunset or rainbow are physical phenomena in nature and have explanations in physics. And if a person has had religious exposure in their upbringing, will they be more likely to experience physical phenomena from a religious association first and consider physical explanations last? This doesn't mean that a deity is not one possible explanation, but it does suggest that our family background, education, and experience play a large role in our perception of intangible concepts like God—of the way the universe works in general, and the degree to which we utilize faith.

Faith is not absent in the scientific method. It is faith that nature contains answers if you trust that the scientific method will help you uncover them. This could parallel prayer. If you have faith in God (nature), and do your part by praying (performing the scientific method), God (nature) will provide the answer. Don't these sound very similar with slightly different terminology? Curiously, I don't think the biggest difference in this instance is with the term God. *God* could easily be translated as *nature* and the *universe*. The biggest difference is between the respective processes of the scientific method and prayer. Both require thought and emotion, but the latter requires less in terms of *detailed* thought. Prayer is often viewed as a primarily emotional vehicle; less critical thinking and detail is sought (hence my Catholic chaplain friend's earlier comment about religion not being an intellectual pursuit). As I have noted before, in my experience religion does emphasize less intellectual and critical thinking.

A question for me then arises: Why would one search for significant answers to the cosmos/God without looking for deep detail and without using both the emotions *and* the intellect (my visceral connection)? Emotions are a very strong part of the religious experience (why else would God most often be equated with love?), but the intellect appears to be less important. In my view, religion uses less of the intellect than the emotions, thereby often making the mistake of *assuming* an absolute before obtaining enough detail about the absolute through critical intellectual thinking. Accepting an absolute (the Deity) emotionally prior to understanding with the intellect is not just a religious tendency, it is also a religious *encouragement*.

There is also no deity *per se* of science. Nature is not even a deity. The cosmos is the closest parallel to a deity but without the recognition of the cosmos as an entity or a being (the view of Einstein, Spinoza, and Tillich). The scientific method, or the thoughtful consideration of its steps, would be the closest parallel to prayer. But science and the scientific method are a process that humans *apply*, not an external entity (or even an additional entity) that is believed in, worshipped, prayed to, or considered responsible for, or the creator of, the cosmos.

~~~

Now a bigger leap: Is the need to reach for the "intangible" or "unattainable" a subconscious longing to breach other possible dimensions? Dimensions beyond the four we perceive—length, width, height, and time—are sensed to exist by scientists, but are simply beyond our physical ability yet to measure or perceive. Such is the case with the very recent concept of multiple universes, or a *multiverse*. These might be dimensions where our laws of physics would not apply. And isn't that akin to not being able to provide physical evidence for a deity?

In *God: The Evidence: The Reconciliation of Faith and Reason in a Postsecular World*, Patrick Glynn, whose philosophy I will be discussing in more detail in Part II, had the following to say about the concept of multiverses (it also references the anthropic principle and miracles): "The main strategy of the physicists for discounting the anthropic principle is to multiply imaginary universes. The reasoning behind this strategy is fairly simple: If there were an infinite number (or, in the late Carl Sagan's favorite phrase, 'billions and billions') of other universes, then the fact that ours hit on the right combination of physical laws to produce the miracle of life might not be such a miracle after all—or so the argument goes. Humanity would again become an "accident." [26]

This statement of his is an odd one because he offers no evidence to make his point. It seems more defensive than provocative. Unimpressively, it also misquotes Carl Sagan. Glynn references Sagan with an apocryphal phrase. Sagan himself humorously clarifies the title of his final book, *Billions and Billions*, and in the first sentence, "I never said it. Honest." He clarifies that he said the word, "billions," many times, but not the phrase, "billions and billions." (Apocryphas are evidence of one common human error. A specific word or phrase is connected with someone, verbatim, that they never said.) Sagan used the latter, misattributed phrase for the title of his last book, but as a joke: partly just to be funny, partly to set the record straight, and partly to educate the reader about apocryphas. Worse yet, Glynn's book postdates Sagan's by two years (Sagan's in 1997; Glynn's in 1999), which reveals poor research and writing by any author when quoting another author. But then the above excerpt from Glynn is not a very carefully crafted statement.

While it could be said in science that faith is needed for other dimensions, it does not matter in science whether there actually *are* other dimensions. It matters more that one strives to understand why we *perceive* that there might be. Perception and reality are not identical and are themselves somewhat word opposites, further exemplifying our current and limited understanding of the universe. Our perception of, or wondering about, other dimensions could prove to be something else altogether just like our perception/concept of God—at present (and maybe forever), impossible to experience physically. But if other dimensions do exist, it would be one explanation for our instinct for searching for the "intangible." It would also work with the theory that atoms and the subatomic realm might "communicate" with each other across vast cosmic distances. If so, who knows how far the communication can reach? Maybe the communication can cross dimensions. Even if so, perhaps like we occasionally experience with our cell phones, subatomic communication across dimensions gets poor or weak reception.

But even if other dimensions (or infinite dimensions) were detected and verified, it would not necessarily mean that the additional dimensions were in fact God or created by any god. Because it is much too soon to physically perceive these dimensions now, we can't know (and may never know) whether the other dimensions are, or are not, evidence of God. This might be an additional explanation as to why it has been impossible to prove or disprove the existence of God. But if this hypothesis is correct, both great scientists and great religious people may have *both been right* in their instincts. Science has been right in warning not to assume a conclusion before verifying with physical evidence, and religion has been correct to be frustrated with science's seeming unwillingness to penetrate beyond our perceived physical world, which other dimensions certainly are. (Unveiling a deity in another dimension, and/or responsible for all dimensions, *might indeed* be physical proof.). In any case, I think a joint effort is needed. If multi-dimensions were discovered, at least much closer conclusions could be drawn on the physical properties of those dimensions, hopefully revealing the accuracy of some of both of the disciplines of science and religion.

William Bramley made an interesting, although slightly fantastical proposal in his book, *The Gods of Eden*. He suggests that, unwittingly, we could be teaching religious faith and worship of God because "God" is actually aliens, extraterrestrials, tremendously more advanced than we. In the early evolution of Homo Sapiens, he posits, the extraterrestrials genetically engineered us to worship and serve them, to follow rather than lead, and to war more than love. According to Bramley's research (and he emphasized that he reluctantly followed what his research was steadily implying), humans were biologically engineered by their "breeders," the extraterrestrials (called by Bramley, "Custodians"), with little or no recollection of that process. This to keep humans ignorant, faithful, fearful, and warring with each other. In short, humans were bred to be the servile slave species of planet Earth. If this is true, then, dismally, the aliens have to a large extent succeeded. If it is wrong, since history is wracked with war, we bear sole responsibility. So, genetically bred by aliens or not, when we don't at least question our beliefs and rely too much on faith—succumbing to following more than leading—we are more likely to remain ignorant.

In, *The Demon-Haunted World*, Carl Sagan offered the following reasonable and rational rebuttal to the concept that aliens administered the genetic engineering of humans: "How could humans be the result of an alien breeding program if we share 99.6 percent of our active genes with the chimpanzees? We're more closely related to chimps than rats are to mice."[27]

However, Bramley offers this wise and supportive commentary at the end. "I hope that some of the above questions will provide good starting points for additional research…the important thing is to be flexible with ideas, and even to have a little fun with them. By sticking my neck out as I have done in this book, I hope that I will encourage other people to explore those topics about which they are curious, and to share what they find…do not base all your beliefs upon a mere handful of writers, teachers, ministers, or scientists. Learn from them, but also explore on your own…If your integrity says that something is a certain way, stick to it, regardless of any…criticisms. On the other hand, be ready to change if you discover…that you are wrong. Learning that one has erred is often a hard pill to swallow, but it is part of the learning process. The man [human] who pretends that he [or she] has always been right is either an egoist or a liar, and he does not learn much of anything either." [28]

These thoughts from Bramley are extremely impressive. Regardless of the truth or fallacy of his alien human breeding theory, it is heartening indeed to hear encouragement, support, and emphasis on humanity, humility, and a lifetime of learning.

As I've already suggested, relying on faith to the extent of reluctance or indifference to ask deep questions about the universe and the origin of life may be an intimidation and fear of facing the enormity of the universe. Failing to ask questions is a sure ticket to ignorance. Unflatteringly, many of us might desire too strongly to be provided with answers whether we're given enough details or not. As I've intimated before, it saves us the time and energy of thinking for ourselves. If Bramley is right, perhaps that is simply our alien-bred genetic engineering. However, and with complete respect to him, I have my strong doubts. Alien (extraterrestrial) bio-engineering of humans—to produce a terrestrial slave species—seems more like another easy excuse (masquerading as a horrifying alternative to human history) for avoiding thinking of more realistic plausibilities.

Though taught as a religious virtue, faith has even been acknowledged as one cause of problems for our reasoning by the Catholic Church. Pope John Paul II addressed this issue in his Encyclical, *Fides et Ratio* (*Faith and Reason*) of 1998. The two can obviously be in conflict. As I've mentioned, a deity, and the faith needed to perceive a deity, are not proposed by religion simply as concepts. They are taught as "truths" that the mind (our reason) then has to struggle to understand. Clearly, utilizing faith more than reason can be problematic. Part of the mind is being ignored (hence the Pope's motivation for his 1998 Encyclical).

Put harshly, favoring faith and avoiding reason with regard to deeply difficult questions resembles an addiction, an addiction of "needing to believe," of wanting provided answers, with those culpable reluctant to admit it; Ann Wilson Schaef's, *When Society Becomes An Addict* is a direct theoretical indictment of the general societal tendency toward addictive behavior. Regardless of whether the need to believe in a deity or have any religious faith is indicative of psychological addiction, we should certainly be more constructively critical and circumspect of ourselves, particularly knowing that we are a species of addicts in many other ways. Why would our thinking and emotions in terms of large questions be immune to avoidance through addiction (to quick-fix answers/solutions) when much of the rest of our biological make-up is prone to addiction? In any case, I think we should be open to examining our weaknesses whatever they are. The need for sobriety can exist in many forms.

I'm aware that people raised within, or converts to a religious faith feel strongly that they don't necessarily need physical evidence of God for their belief, and that they feel that they do indeed *know* that their faith is true. I will share in some detail my experience with the Mormon Church in Part III, but among my experiences visiting various churches as a teenager was witnessing Mormon congregants profess *knowledge* of their faith through their "Testimony." The Testimony is one of the rituals or "rites of passage" of all Mormon congregants, especially for young Mormons. The Testimony is a significant step for each Mormon, to deepen their faith and accept "The Truth" of the Mormon Church, The Church of Jesus Christ of Latter-Day Saints (LDS). Mormons are trained to verbally *recite* their Testimony at specified moments during the services or during special Testimony services. (To Mormons, one's personal Testimony is clear evidence of God's loving and active presence in their lives. To an atheist, and perhaps many other non-Mormons and non-religious people, the Testimony is probably clear evidence of religious indoctrination.) As I suggested in Chapter 1, religious rituals, like the Mormon "Testimony," seem to me to be mostly subjective knowledge. But they are also to be deeply respected. Indoctrinated or not, personal testimonies are private. Privacy is always to be respected, no matter the source, circumstance, or reason. Period. However, as I've also mentioned, when private feelings are made public, either voluntarily or inadvertently, one cannot presume public acceptance. Subjectivity does not always work objectively.

～～

An example of subjectivity clashing dysfunctionally, violently, and fatally with objectivity is the religious history of violence and bloodshed in the Middle East. Not unlike the Mormons, each of the predominant religious faiths in this region—the three monotheistic faiths: Christian, Islamic, and Jewish—believes that theirs is the truth and infallible. As a result, each faith is nearly wholly inflexible to compromise with the other two. If, instead, they respected each others' differences and made living together equitably and peacefully their primary focus, they might find that many of their problems would vanish. Sadly and tragically, the opposite is true. They don't get along with each other well at all. Each faith thinks that the other is completely or mostly in error. And each faith is convinced that their own people are entitled to stewardship of the same holy land, by divine decree.

Very unflatteringly, this resembles an elementary domestic situation. (In advance, I ask any Jewish, Islamic, or Christian reader to follow Don Miguel Ruiz's "Second Agreement" and not take this personally. The following analogy represents the general dysfunction in the Middle East, not any one particular citizen or individual in the Middle East nor any one individual anywhere.) It resembles three small children wanting the same toy and not aware yet of what it means to share. It doesn't occur to children that sharing doesn't mean complete loss. But children hopefully grow into much greater awareness and maturity as adults. In the case of the Middle East, each religious group insists that they are right and divinely sanctioned. But they can't all be right in every respect of their faiths. (No one on the planet is right about everything in every respect. This should go without saying.) And if they are each at least partly right, why couldn't each of them make more of an effort to learn from each other and share the land than to each insist on having it *all* to themselves? Isn't it obvious by the pattern of trouble that they have lived with for millennia that none of their approaches to sole sovereignty are working? In this case too, relying predominantly on faith to solve the trouble has never worked.

This situation *does* prove something to me, but not that there is a God. It proves to me that though humans are highly intelligent, we are also deeply fragile and vulnerable, and fundamentally self-centered in our struggle for survival. I do not translate that as concluding that we are all basically selfish (or "sinners" to use the religious term). But I do think that our individual vulnerability makes us focus on our own concerns and survival first.

Though I'm offering that we are biologically more self-*centered* than self*ish*, I'd like to draw a direct distinction between being self-centered and the concept of sin. The word *sin* means "an offense against religious or moral law." A "moral law" could certainly be translated both secularly and religiously as "The Golden Rule." I have observed that although humans are primarily aware of themselves first, we don't feel good when we deny the same right of self-awareness, self-concern, and self-survival to others. We know what it feels like to be discriminated against, to be denied our own feelings and rights. I propose that the real meaning of sin is denying someone else their right to self-preservation, their right and innate need to be healthily self-centered—their right to be themselves.

This empathy and respect for the self-preservation or self-centeredness of others is possibly a *sympathetic* fear of death, and fear of being left alone unwittingly. If we allow someone else to suffer and/or die, not only do we know that fear for ourselves, but we are also automatically left alone, more vulnerable to death. And since we know, or can imagine, what that feels like, we are able to know how it must feel to someone else. Consequently, the ones who are more sensitive to that tend to be the most empathetic, compromising, compassionate, helpful, and assisting. They compromise and cooperate their way to success. Coexistence becomes of paramount importance—the welfare of not just the individual, but of the family, community, city, state, country, continent, and global populace—not whether any single person or group is *right* or not. And even if one thinks they are right, being able to see that the other person also thinks they are right and allowing for that possibility—because they are a fellow human with as much right to their viewpoint as everyone else—is a trait with high survival value. Cooperation is a proven survival strategy. With this reasoning, faith, or one's point of view, should always be flexible, no matter how convinced one is of the validity of their own belief or viewpoint. One can always be wrong.* Humans are not infallible.

Using the analogy again of children playing, it's also as if part of the "toy" in the Middle East were invisible (their respective deities), which perhaps only heightens the anxiety of each faith. There may seem to be nothing tangible to share, nothing tangible with which to compromise (God, by any name, is not physically tangible). It would be nice, of course, if the motivation of sharing was not limited to physical objects, and inclusive of religious, spiritual, and secular thoughts, ideas, beliefs, writings, and traditions. But maybe the sharing of, or with one another's faith is a stickier wicket. As it still stands now, each of the faiths in the region thinks relinquishing any aspect of what they believe (along with the allowance of the belief of others) will mean the degradation and disintegration of their entire faith. The adage, "Give [the other faith] an inch, they'll take a mile"

---

* In an article in Newsweek on May 14, 2019, entitled, "Flat Earthers, and the Rise of Science Denial in America," Lee McEntire writes the following to encourage awareness of self-fallibility, "In scientific reasoning there's always a chance that your theory is wrong. What separates science deniers from actual scientists is how rigorously they pursue that possibility."

comes to mind. Regardless of the issue of divinity, it is no surprise to me that someone like Jesus Christ, a Middle Eastern Jewish man, courageously demonstrated and encouraged unconditional love in this region and was—by fanatic hatred and Levitical Law—resented, reviled, and executed by crucifixion.

This was much like the arms race during the Cold War. One specific fear of the United States during the Reagan administration was that if we backed off on the Strategic Defense Initiative (SDI, or "Star Wars") proposal, that the (then) Soviet Union (or some other rogue country) would not have taken similar disarmament action, potentially launching a nuclear warhead against us. Obviously, because if its extinction, the specter of the Union of Soviet Socialist Republics as a global usurper in some of our national imaginations was fallacious. On the other hand, rogue countries, extremist groups, and/or individuals with lethal intentions and power obviously do exist, as in the World Trade Center bombing of September 11, 2001. But those realities did not and still do not justify concepts like the SDI proposal nor any other exaggerated or extreme defense systems as solutions. Extreme solutions of any kind should be avoided until other, more sober solutions have been attempted, failed, and exhausted. Why couldn't we also be wrong, or at least extreme, about some of our belief systems?

In my view, there are three possible answers or scenarios regarding the question of which faith in the Middle East is correct: 1) They are all partially right in different ways. They do have the same God, but they are all slightly wrong on some of the details of each of their faiths. 2) Only one of them is exactly right. The other two have come close, but have made too many errors in interpretation. Those two would have to acknowledge their error. But acceptance of the correct answer, especially if the correct answer is not yours, is a mature human response of the highest degree. If even just *one* of the dominant monotheistic faiths were to demonstrate that kind of humble acknowledgment (about any aspect of their faith) it would be an admirable example of the greatest magnitude. As I offered in the Preface, admitting error can be far more impressive than claiming credit for being correct. 3) They are all wrong. None of them got it right. It is either a God in a different form or no God at all. There are historical facts, but they have been largely misinterpreted. And there is no God that was the initial cause of any of them. These three possibilities are my own, of course, but I think that they are examples of the scientific method applied to religion.

Another area where humans tend to use faith more and patient reasoning less is with the subject and attraction of technology. Technology is growing at an astonishingly rapid rate, particularly since the beginning of the 20th Century. And even though the public at large becomes irritated when technology doesn't work for them or they don't understand it, they don't like the alternative which is to demand that the speed of their procurement and use of the technology slow to allow time with which to better understand the technology.

What happens instead is that the public wants the latest, fastest, and best (new technology) *now* even if they don't understand it fully, and even if slightly slowing the speed of their purchase and use would help facilitate their fluency. They would rather trust (have faith in) someone else (the corporations and technical support) to deal with the problems of technology but receive the power and benefits of (believe in) that technology immediately. People tend not to want to wait patiently to understand better. They want to be gratified immediately and understand later. Avoidance of even an elementary (much less a fluent) knowledge of technology could be analogous to relying on faith for the avoidance of questions about religion, rudimentary or advanced. With technology, the companies, programmers, and technicians are the quasi-deities, and we put our faith in them too much sometimes because we want to own and use the intriguing and powerful products as quickly as possible.

I realize that this particular analogy is not entirely fair. There are many things about which we are not experts. It is noble and courageous to seek guidance from a trained professional, to instruct us in understanding the machine, instrument, or discipline with which we feel at least some degree of ignorance. But there is a difference between pursuing instruction in order to better understand a new piece of technology, and wanting to own and use the technology immediately without accepting the responsibility to patiently learn how to use it well. The same can be said for religious faith.

In fairness, too, many religious people feel emotionally (spiritually, if you will) and intellectually close to a belief or faith because they are sincerely motivated by a deep belief in God, by a deep interest in the historical significance of their faith. And, most importantly, they are motivated by a genuine and deep love for their fellow human being and living creature. They do not abdicate reason for faith, or they at least abdicate reason much less. Their faith enhances their reason, and visa-versa. This model of religious practice is wonderful and exemplary (and perhaps nearly proof of its divine validity!). Too often, though, some people are driven to faith because they feel the need to trust someone or something else to provide their solutions and happiness. In that perspective, the desire for a "God" and the allure of and desire for rapidly advancing technology are not very different at all.

I think that faith is a quality and state of mind that one freely determines for themselves but is not useful or productive to impose on others. The reason is that if faith is employed privately and it doesn't work, the only one affected is the individual. But if it is imposed on a group and doesn't work, then the dysfunction affects many. The problem and scourge of religious unrest and violence in the Middle East is a prime example. It is an example of *imposition* of ideas on others rather than *sharing* of ideas with others. I submit that, regardless of one's religious belief or scientific focus, sharing, respecting, and loving are always beautiful qualities in which to believe and have faith.

Chapter 8

MIRACLES

Come out, come out, wherever you are, and meet the young lady,
who fell from a star.
She fell from the sky, she fell very far, and Kansas, she says,
is the name of the star.
She brings you good news, or haven't you heard...when she fell out of
Kansas,
a miracle occurred!

Glenda, the Good Witch of the North

It really was no miracle, what happened was just this...
Dorothy

The Wizard of Oz
Metro-Goldwyn-Mayer

I don't do miracles. They're too flashy.
And they upset the natural balance.
I'm not sure how this whole miracle business started...
the idea that anything connected with me has to be a miracle.
Personally, I'm sorry that it did—
makes the distance between us even greater.

God
Oh, God!
Warner Bros.

My brother, Craig Johnson Richey, was bitten by a copperhead snake when he was three years old. He was incredibly sick, but he survived. While still in the hospital but feeling nearly well enough to go home, when his doctor came to see him, Craig leaned up and—to the doctor's startled surprise—kissed him on the cheek! Craig innately sensed that he had suffered a brush with death.

In fact, he had. What none of us knew at the time, but came to realize, was that my brother's survival from that snake bite was nothing short of a miracle.

When Craig first cried out in pain from our backyard in Davidson, N.C., and managed to hobble over to where my dad and I were sitting on the back carport, we could see two small red dots on the top of his foot. I noticed, even at the time, that one dot was smaller and lighter than the other. Craig had been bitten by a baby copperhead snake and only one of its fangs had fully penetrated, which released only half the snake's normal venom.

We learned later that baby copperhead snakes are more venomous than adults. It is a trait of natural selection that more greatly ensures the survival of the babies in the event that they are separated from their parents. Had both fangs embedded into Craig's foot, the entire venom of that baby copperhead snake's bite would have entered his body and he most certainly would have died. Like all siblings, Craig and I have had our brotherly differences over the years, but when I think that I might have lost him at only three years old, it makes me thank the universe for the miracle that deflected the baby copperhead's second fang.

To be clear, when I say *miracle* I mean the word in its original sense, from the Latin, *miraculum*, meaning "a wonder" or "marvel." The word miracle also has a divine meaning, which, according to the Merriam Webster Dictionary, is "an extraordinary event manifesting divine intervention in human affairs." Or, at Dictionary.com, "an effect or extraordinary event in the physical world that surpasses all known human or natural powers and is ascribed to supernatural causes," and "such an effect or event manifesting or considered as a work of God." Curiously, the latter two definitions appear first in most dictionary sources. Though the original Latin meaning of the word—which I advocate—does not carry supernatural implications, the word clearly implies a supernatural cause to many people in contemporary society or those definitions would not appear first.

I could certainly choose to believe (or at least consider the possibility) that the snake that bit Craig was prevented from inserting both its fangs into his foot by God, and was thus a divine miracle. But I also know enough about biology and evolution to understand that natural phenomena don't necessarily require divine intervention, and that the concepts of divine intervention and/or miracles in nature are themselves debatable.

In Lorraine Hansberry's, *A Raisin in the Sun,* the character, Beneatha, expresses this to her mother. "Mamma, you don't understand. It's all a matter of ideas, and God is just one idea I don't accept. It's not important. I am not going to be immoral or commit crimes because I don't believe in God. I don't even think about it. It's just that I get tired of hearing Him getting credit for all the things the human race achieves through its own stubborn effort. There simply is no blasted God—there is only man and it is *he* who makes miracles!" [29]

I'm inclined to think that Craig simply stepped too near, or even on that baby copperhead, and either his stepping on the snake prevented it from fully extending its fangs to bite him, or Craig was lucky and the snake was not, and the snake missed slightly with its strike. Regardless, and because we have no video of the snake biting Craig, what actually prevented both the snake's fangs from fully impaling his foot will be a mystery forever. But it really doesn't matter. My brother survived and is living a full, healthy, and happy life, and I and the world are the incredibly more fortunate for that fateful luck. I hope that the snake also grew to be an adult and enjoyed a comfortable existence, but without harming any other human in the process!

I have experienced other forms of miracles in my life as well, but none that I would necessarily attribute to supernatural or divine cause. However, like the original Latin definition, they *have* given me great cause for wonder and marvel.

～～～

Not long after my father, David Frank Richey (warmly sensitive person, pianist, composer, and teacher), died of a malignant brain tumor in 1977 at the much too young age of 49, both my brothers and I began experiencing (and continue to experience) the uncanny recurrence of the numbers 111 or 1111.*

It happened to Craig, then my brother, Evan, and then to me. One of us spontaneously wondered what time it was and, turning to look at an available digital clock (which had not been in our field of view), saw that it was either exactly 1:11 or 11:11 (a.m. or p.m. didn't seem to matter).

It also happened to me with my *car's* digital clock. Occasionally, I would arrive at work or home from work, or just on an outing, and when I pulled into my parking space and stopped, the time on the digital clock would be one of those two times. It didn't happen every day, but it happened with at least some consistency and without my thinking about it at all. It felt so unusual that I often found myself bursting out laughing at the sheer bizarre frequency of the phenomenon. I did fancy a few times that it might actually be my deceased father somehow channeling himself and "messaging" me through the digital clock. After all, I had two brothers (which, including me, made three boys, or the number 111). And my brothers and I, together with our dad, watched the 1960s television program, *My Three Sons*, when we were young. That made four males, 1111, watching four other males, 1111. I've imagined with fun that the strange occurrences of these numbers on a digital clock is my dad's way of saying "hello."

Of course, it could certainly be my subconscious motivating me to leave and arrive in my car with enough of the same daily rhythm that I indeed arrived at my destination (whether at work or back home) close to the same time each time so that, periodically, I arrived at exactly 1:11 or 11:11. I simply didn't notice the other times when I arrived at, say, 11:02, 10:59, or 11:16.

But it has also happened on my car *odometer*. With two different cars, I have managed to notice (and photograph!) when the odometer turned to all ones, 111,111 miles! Seeing the inevitable number approaching, I slowed, pulled off to the shoulder or curb, stopped when the odometer read all ones, and got out my camera. Granted, in both instances I could see the odometer directly in front of me on the dashboard, so unlike digital clocks in the house beyond my peripheral vision, the element of complete surprise with my

---

* I also know that we are not alone with this curious and amusing experience. Ellen Degeneres has a record label named "ElevenEleven" after her similar experiences with these numbers.

odometer was prevented. But I did notice the change of the numbers coming and took pictures. I can also say with surety that I have seen no pictures of other peoples' odometers showing that mileage marker. It is not a common observation or documentation. I noticed in time, both times, and took pictures. Was it my dad's spiritual influence that I was lucky enough to notice the series of ones on the odometer *twice* and get pictures? Not one but *two miracles*? Probably not, but who's to say?!

~~~

I own the 50th Anniversary DVD/BluRay of *Ben-Hur*. It is an incredible classic film and I enjoy it even more now. I had forgotten that it was subtitled "A Tale of the Christ." It certainly does include portions of the life of Jesus Christ and his crucifixion, but it is primarily about two old, boon childhood friends, Judah Ben-Hur (Charlton Heston) and Messala (Stephen Boyd), who become complete opposite personalities as adults. Ben-Hur, a compassionate and courageous defender of his Jewish people, and Messala, now the Tribune of Rome, a zealot of its conquering and murdering manifesto against the Jews. Boyhood friends turned tragic enemies: One a noble, proud Jewish leader. The other an arrogant anti-Semite.

What I had not remembered was how beautifully presented the idea of a divine miracle is in this film. Due to a simple accident by Ben-Hur's sister, Tirzah (Cathy O'Donnell), which caused the injury of a Roman dignitary, his mother, Miriam (Martha Scott) and sister are cruelly imprisoned by Messala early in the film. Ben-Hur is sentenced to servility on a slave ship. After Ben-Hur saves the life of his slave ship captain, Quintus Arrius (Jack Hawkins) when the ship is sunk, he is rewarded by the captain as the latter's honorary adopted son. Although deeply touched and humbled by the gesture, Ben-Hur declines the adoption and returns to Jerusalem to search for his mother and sister, who he fears have been executed. Only after being defeated by Ben-Hur, and fatally injured, in the famed chariot race does Messala reveal to Ben-Hur that his mother and sister are not dead. They were moved from prison to the "Land of the Lepers" (because they caught the disease in prison). With his wife Esther's (Haya Harareet) help, Ben-Hur finds them and rescues them.

During their passage home, they encounter Christ's pre-crucifixion procession. Earlier in the film, a man brought Ben-Hur water when he was being transported to the slave labor ship. Though it's unclear at that moment whether Ben-Hur realizes that the man offering him water is Jesus Christ, when he later witnesses Christ being tortured in the crucifixion procession, he does remember and tries to offer Christ water in return.

Both moments of the offerings of water are pivotal to the film. While Christ is dying on the cross, a thunderstorm erupts. Esther, his sister, and his mother seek shelter from the storm in a cave. This time, there is no doubt that the thunderstorm is God's sorrow (and possible rage) over Christ's death. However, because Ben-Hur tried to help Christ by offering him water, when Esther and the two women dying from leprosy are able to see themselves in the flashes of lightning from the storm, Esther cries out with joy because the hideous scars on both the other women's faces and hands have vanished. They have received a divine miracle cure of their leprosy. (It also occurred to me that, like the religious rituals of baptism and anointing, and the necessity of water for life, wellness with water is a central theme in this film: Jesus Christ offering water to Ben-Hur; Ben-Hur offering water to Christ in return; the water of God's thunderstorm as the miraculous cure of leprosy.)

For me, this ending scene is the most beautiful moment in the film. I find myself tearful both rewatching or thinking about it even though I don't take the idea of a divine or supernatural miracle seriously. I don't think it's necessary to think of miracles as divinely caused. In reality, most people at that time died of leprosy. Few survived. But I don't think it follows that those who did survive were necessarily the recipients of miracles from a deity. In modern times, leprosy is much less common. The reason is less likely due to divine miracles. It is more likely because of the excellent medical treatment that sufferers of leprosy receive due to the advances of medical science. On the other hand, I think it's pure fun and emotional exhilaration to enjoy the fancy that a God or other supernatural force or deity could actually perform the kind of beautiful miracle as presented in *Ben-Hur*—particularly as a way of rewarding the return of love and kindness from a stranger.

Chapter 9

PROOF AND FREE WILL

The interest I have to believe a thing is no proof that such a thing exists

Voltaire

Faith is a knowledge within the heart, beyond the reach of proof

Kahlil Gibran

*If I hadn't spent so much time studying Earthlings,
I wouldn't have any idea what was meant by 'free will.'
I've visited thirty-one inhabited planets in the universe,
and I have studied reports on one hundred more.
Only on Earth is there any talk of free will.*

The Tralfamadorian
Kurt Vonnegut
Slaughterhouse-Five

Proof for verification is required or sought in almost every serious endeavor or proposal. It is a *chose normale à faire*: a normal thing to do. A standard final test.

I was first introduced to the discipline of proofs in my high school geometry class. I find it amusing now to think that I feared proofs before I took the class because I was intimidated by the idea. But I got lucky. It was in my senior year of high school at the [now University of] North Carolina School of the Arts, and it was the best math class I ever experienced. The teacher was Mrs. Judy Land, and she was one of the finest academic teachers I've ever had. It helped that the class was quite small, only about eight students. The textbook was also one of the best textbooks I've ever used. It was called simply, *Geometry*, by Harold Jacobs (W.H. Freeman & Company; 1st edition, September 1974). One unique and delightful feature of this book is that inserted throughout its pages (and in most of its editions) are selected cartoons of B.C. and Peanuts, and M.C. Escher prints. Impressively, the cartoons and Escher drawings pertain exactly to the topic of the chapter and mathematical example in which they appear. It is a superb textbook. It made learning the principles of geometry much more accessible, interesting, and fun.

Proofs, I quickly learned, were not so intimidating. They are simply an organized way of using individual and simple principles of geometry to demonstrate, or "prove," how and why two measurements—whose relationship is neither adjacent nor immediately apparent—are related or equal. The proof depended on the logical application of the smaller principles, in a series of sequential steps, to prove the relationship of the first measurement to the last. Proofs are an excellent example of the scientific method employed in math.

Significantly, solutions to mathematical proofs are never that one must primarily have faith that the two measurements are related *before* applying the smaller principals to solve them. The relationship of the measurements is proven only *after* the steps taken with the smaller principals are demonstrated. No "cart before the horse" with proofs. Plus, the solution can be attained or accomplished readily and repeatedly. One only has to learn the smaller principles (theorems and postulates) that apply to individual angles and geometric shapes, and show how they are related to other angles and shapes; a kind of interrelated community of mathematical objects.

Proofs not only show the relationship of these shapes, but, as I noted above, they are exercises in the scientific method: reaffirming remote relationships (measurements), by proceeding step-by-step using previously tested and proven smaller principles. The individual principles used consecutively to solve proofs are also simple to understand and remember. The only requirement is that one has to learn and use them. Thus, if you learn the smaller principles, using them to tie the relationship of the first fact to the last fact is a cinch!

This procedure can be applied to most any problem solving, and usually is. It is also called "deductive reasoning." A "proof" is just one calculated formula of deductive reasoning: combining small facts successively to prove larger, more complicated or remote facts.

If the procedure of proving something can be applied to anything, why should a religious idea or proposition not utilize the proof process, especially when the claim or concept is extremely large, larger than most mathematical proofs? Shouldn't the need for the clarity of proof be proportional to the concept. Shouldn't proof be particularly required of a *very large* idea?

Another, although hypothetical, example. If someone unknown applying for a job asked the employer to accept their qualifications without proof (without the prerequisites of qualification; with no résumé; no interview; completely on faith), they would very likely not be hired. Even someone hired with immediate tenure, and so on a kind of faith, often has a clear record of years of experience and the experience of working with others (recommendations) as evidence for the employer.

So *consideration* of a beautiful but deeply debatable idea is one thing. But forming a deep, personal *belief*, much less a belief *system*, from a beautiful but debatable idea—especially an enormous one, without enough rigorous physical evidence—is, to me, not only not dispensing with the requisite process of proof, but it is really going "blind." (Hence the phrase often used in criticism of religious faith, "blind faith" or "blind following"; the 1968 blues/rock group Blind Faith adopted the name in parody of that syndrome.) It is very tenuous and therefore highly unwarranted. It should actually be embarrassing to purport something as truth without rock-solid evidence of as many kinds as possible. Wouldn't one want to be taken seriously by a greater number of people, and especially those most skeptical?

What an honor to the purported idea if it passed the test of the most credulous *and* the most skeptical.

One less-than-compelling offer of proof that I have heard mentioned of religious validity and truth is simply the billions of people who have accepted religious faith. I suppose this is akin to the phrase, "strength in numbers." Unfortunately, this is not strong enough evidence, much less proof. It's a start but not a conclusion. There could be many reasons why people accept an idea on faith. How many of those who believe or converted were previously strong skeptics? What were the specific reasons for their conversions and what was the evidence that convinced them? That evidence should be available for other skeptics to study and should be very clear and compelling, and much less debatable.

Another offer of proof that I have heard for religious conversion is the experience of an epiphany: a strong sense, or a feeling defined as "God." Epiphanies are very personally compelling. However, no matter how real and sincere personal epiphanies can be, they are not easy to test. They are only an individual's personal (and therefore, subjective) perception and feeling, and thus not adequate as strong evidence. There are other reasons and causes for personal feelings than the existence of a god. (Again, if held privately, enjoying a "feeling" for God is perfectly fine, a non-issue, and not the focus of this book; though I would still be curious to hear the reasons for this perspective.)

Since personal feelings and testimony are considered only a start to a proposal with most other subjects, why should as large a proposition as the existence of a deity rest almost exclusively on personal testimony, or the personal testimony (dictation) of a leader or leaders in history? Personal testimony alone, though genuinely felt, is not infallible from anyone. To be most effective, personal testimony or conviction needs to be reinforced, "backed up," with strong arguments and strong evidence. Proof. Or as close to proof as possible. For example, successfully and unambiguously converting the majority of skeptics and publishing the strong, clear, and unambiguous evidence that converted them would be an example of both compelling evidence and proof.

There is another curiosity about personal testimony. In many personal religious epiphanies, people experience the god or religious symbol of a familiar religion, one that is already known to them. It's quite interesting that some people experience the exact deity that their particular religion of choice professes. Why wouldn't more people experience hearing from the deity of another faith, like a "cold call" or radio interference? (This begs the question of whether one God represents all faiths, just under different names. But that would likely be blasphemous to most believers of differing faiths who each feel that *their* God is the sole and true God.) Too often, candidates for conversion conveniently hear from the deity to which (or to whom) they're introduced. This is not always true of course. There are many converts to religions that are not native to their locality or even their country: Christian to Islam; Hindu to Mormon; Catholic to Judaism; Protestant to Jehovah's Witness, etc. Less often, Agnostic, Buddhist, or Atheist to any religion. But even if convenient conversion is somewhat consistent, why wouldn't, once in a while, an omnipotent God voluntarily (and unambiguously) contact one or more skeptics, without any effort from the skeptics, and video-record the contact?

This is exactly the premise of the film, *Oh, God!* God (George Burns) contacts Jerry Landers (John Denver), a non-believer, by a typed letter and invites Landers to interview God (I avoided the male personal pronoun "him" deliberately.). Landers had not prayed to God requesting the interview. God's invitation was direct, unsolicited, and physically evident. However, being the skeptic he was, Landers tore up the invitation letter from God twice thinking it was another prank by his friend, Artie Coogan. But Burns's "God" is persistent and physically restores the letter each time, replacing it first under Jerry's pillow in his bed and, the next day, within a head of romaine lettuce that Jerry was trimming at the grocery store, where he was manager. This final time, Landers is so shaken and baffled that he feels compelled to at least satisfy his curiosity and end the likely prank. He drives to the indicated address to "meet" God.

When he arrives for the interview he discovers that it is not a prank. One piece of uncanny evidence finally convinces Landers that it is definitely not Artie Coogan and, as impossible as it seems, likely God: To guarantee privacy for their interview, God has "miraculously" added a 27th floor to an office building that has only 20 floors. The meeting room is on the 27th floor. As an added imaginary touch of proof, God suggests that Jerry get on the hotel elevator again and take it to any floor. After initially going down to the lobby to ask if there is a 27th floor (which an hotel employee humorously replies that he would need a giant can opener to create), when

Jerry rides the elevator back up, every floor he presses then opens onto the 27th floor!

In this imaginary scenario, God makes the initial contact, persists until Jerry shows up for their interview, and provides at least powerfully persuasive visual evidence that would be extraordinarily difficult to fake: a non-existent office-building floor level. God offers and delivers other fun physical evidence to Landers as the film progresses (including rain *inside* Jerry's car).

Curiously, however, in this film there was one method of obtaining evidence of God that was impossible to perform or acquire. The Deity could not be audio-recorded (the film was made before video-recording was common consumer technology). This, to me, was the only slightly weak part of the otherwise extremely clever movie. It implied that God was exclusive when it came to talking directly with humans, an hypothesis that I hope, if there is a God, would not be true. (The God of the Bible, for example, is, of course, exclusive. Moses, Abraham, and later Jesus Christ, are the conduits, and Christ the sole prophet and resurrected human/deity. In Islam, though Muhammad is the prophet, Allah requires no intermediary deity and is, therefore, more accessible and less exclusive.) At least, though, it was a nod in support of the religious idea that the Deity's existence has to be taken on faith.

The examples of evidence and proof of God offered in the film, *Oh God!* are imaginative and fun, but they are, of course, fiction. However, they also cause one to think about the kinds of evidence that might be needed to be more convincing as proof of God to a skeptic.

I think it can be fairly said that the burden of proof rests with the one making the claim. So it should be with proof of the existence of God (or of any deity). Proof of God rests with those who believe in God. A religious believer may not feel that they need proof. Many of the religious people I have talked to say that proof is not part of their faith. It is not a requirement, or even useful or necessary for them. Privately, this is perfectly fine. But once one attempts to share their belief—and who of us doesn't want to share something that feels deeply emotional?—proof seems to be demanded by at least a substantial segment of the population (including me). That desired proof is physical evidence. The argument that humans and everything physical in the universe *are* the physical evidence for God is not enough proof because there are other possible explanations for the origin of the universe and life than just God.

One fundamental principle of science is that a conclusion, especially of enormous magnitude, can only be reached when most all other possibilities have been rejected. Other possible explanations of the origin of the universe, in addition to God, have not been rejected and/or are quite plausible: an infinitely old universe, an infinitely expanding universe, multiple universes, and/or a universe created by itself from its own energy. All of these hypotheses and theories could require either no god or God. Furthermore, these alternative explanations are as clear to those who think of them as the clarity of the concept of God is to those who believe in God. Proof helps tip the scales.

~~~

There is a religious response to the argument for the need for proof of God that says the following: that if the Deity provided clear, unambiguous evidence, proof of its existence, it would negate the Deity's test of our "Free Will" ("Free Agency" of the Mormon Church), our freedom to *choose* between good and evil, between God and Satan (the fallen Angel). By extension, proof of God, and the resultant loss of free will, would mean not only losing our freedom to decide whether to be good or bad, but also the freedom to decide for ourselves whether to believe in the purported *source* of the good. The Deity, God.[*]

Perhaps. But first let me make a respectful but firm point. There are many non-religious people who feel strongly that they do not need any assistance from religion or theological belief to know right from wrong, or good from evil. They (myself included) feel incredulous at the notion that the only way to know how to be moral is to learn it through religion and God. I feel, as many others non-religious do, that morality and goodness are probably an additional product of evolution. If that is true, then they emanate naturally from within us reinforced by our formative family years, not from a supernatural source like an external entity, whether the jury is still out on proof of a deity or not. The notion of the *necessity* of God for morality or the

---

[*] Put another way, proof of God would make the test of "Free Will" obsolete. That, metaphorically, is what occurred when Toto exposed the Wizard.

evolution of the universe and life feels, to me and many non-believers, demeaning and insulting to the equal possibility of the autonomy of the universe, life, intelligence, and humanity.

But let's look at the potential loss of free will by the scientific method and eliminate possibilities. First, let's assume that the loss of our free will would happen. That is, if one witnessed clear, physical evidence of God they would lose their ability to make a free and clear choice to be moral and believe in God.

First, it implies that choice is negated by proof. Though proof is the most substantial evidence that I am aware of and much more difficult to dismiss, one always has or can make a choice whether to acknowledge or refute the proof. In other words, proof does not negate choice.

Second, this could imply that *anything* proven—shown to be extremely, abundantly, and unmistakably clear by physical evidence—would have the same effect. I think there is little credence to choice or free will being lost when strong physical evidence corroborates something not previously known. I have not experienced it personally, nor do I know of anyone who has had that experience. My experience has been the opposite. Rather than negating my free will or choice to acknowledge the proving evidence, proof provides me with enough of the missing information to *more freely* make a choice.

As I have indicated already, it seems to me that this suggestion of the loss of the free will to choose our morality—by providing physical evidence of the existence of God—is a subterfuge for *avoiding* the search for physical evidence for a deity. It also implies concern from those who are religious about the possibility that physical evidence for a deity might not exist. And if one is warned about losing their free will by finding physical evidence for God, and consequently has that fear, one might be more apt to stop looking.

In my experience that is exactly what I have found to be true of many in the religious community. But just because someone has stopped looking for physical evidence for God (whatever the reason), it neither means that the physical evidence doesn't exist, nor that their free will would be lost if one were to discover evidence for God. For some, the acceptance of fear of the loss of free will provides one satisfactory reason to end the quest for physical evidence for a deity. For others, it only skirts the question.

Another argument used for ceasing the search for better evidence for God is that, since we are so small and insignificant compared to the cosmos, how could we possibly expect to understand God and the engineering of said God's creation? And since God purportedly created the universe, it would follow logically that God is larger than the universe, and therefore perhaps ultimately impossible to understand. Attempting to understand would utterly overwhelm us, and in being thus overwhelmed we might also lose our free will. But when is it ever unproductive or unprogressive to have *more* information? (I'm not referring to cases of "TMI"!) Doesn't this imply that faith and belief are a choice based on *less* knowledge, that more knowledge is harmful and robs us of the freedom to will and to choose? Is free will in this context a euphemism, a decoy for accepting and following in ignorance?

Further in line with scientific inquiry, how do we know that we would lose our free will if that assumed proclamation by God has never been *tested*? Is there an account of someone or many who witnessed the Deity physically and whose free will to be moral and believe in the Deity was subsequently eliminated? (The story of Doubting Thomas may be the closest to physical evidence for God, but I will elaborate more on that in a moment.) Even if there are any such stories, we would need to determine the validity of their encounter(s) and why their ability to choose loving morality and to believe in the Deity—their "Free Will"—was lost. This is, for better or worse, an experiment that is likely impossible to test. If untestable, it may also be pointless and not an argument or concern worth paying much heed. Once again, I suspect that the concern for the loss of free will in searching for physical evidence for God is a veiled excuse for avoiding the search.

~~~

The story of "Doubting Thomas" is an example both of one person's experience with physical evidence of God, and offered as proof of the divinity and resurrection of Jesus Christ. Jesus invites the disciple, Thomas, to insert his finger into the wound caused by one of the nails that held Jesus to the cross. According to the story, Thomas inserts his finger into Christ's wound and is thus convinced of Christ's resurrection. This would appear to be an example of *physical* evidence for this story.

As with any account, however, there are questions and problems with the story. First, it is a story that cannot be repeated. Second, there are many causes of flesh wounds. How did Christ demonstrate to Thomas that the wound was from a nail, and a nail embedded in wood, the very wooden cross upon which Christ had been crucified and died? Did Jesus intend that his mere physical presence in front of Thomas was the obvious evidence that he was alive again, resurrected—so undeniable proof that he, Christ, was the Son of God? Was the skin surrounding the wound stretched upward as Christ's body was pulled downward by gravity? And what was Thomas's physical condition when he inserted his finger into Christ's apparent wound? Could he have been hallucinating? Drunk? Drugged? Was he sleep deprived, even purposely so? Could Christ's wounds have been faked?

These questions are, of course, my own and may seem frivolous, micromanaging, and obsessive, especially to the religious believer. But scientific inquiry is very much about asking questions, even to the degree of micromanaging and obsessive. Better to err on the side of obsessive than uncomprehensive. It could also be said that detailed questions only look frivolous, micromanaging, and obsessive to those who (regardless of the reason) ask fewer questions.

Perhaps a missing point to the story is that Thomas actually didn't doubt for long enough. Maybe he should have asked *more* questions. Maybe Thomas was too gullible. Or, maybe he tried to be skeptical but relented under pressure, or his many questions were not included in the account. On the other hand, maybe the account is accurate and he indeed saw and felt the open physical wound from the nail in the resurrected Jesus Christ. Maybe Thomas was telling the truth about what he was astonished and aghast to see. In any case, a temporary conclusion in this case, too, is that there is simply not enough information about this story to conclude one way or the other, so judgment about the divinity of Jesus should be reserved.

Regardless of the validity of this and other religious references, there is a disappointing implication about the reluctance to think critically to search for corroborating proof. Acceptance is easier. Thinking critically is more difficult. Granted, one can think compulsively (obsessively) which can be as much of an addictive tendency as any other addiction. But to avoid necessary thinking robs humanity of the reward of the *process* of thought: striving to sift fiction from fact. It can certainly be a difficult and tedious process to think critically. But if thinking is patiently persevered, finding an answer that works more accurately is worth the time and enhances rather than detracts from the solution.

Another interesting consideration (that I touched upon earlier) is that religion might not only be offering an already-solved solution to the universe (the existence and divinity of God), but also delivery from death. Not only is there great momentary relief and comfort in provided answers, but we are all innately fearful of being reminded that we are mortal. One opportunity offered by faith in God is the prospect of eternal life. What better remedy to the Darwinian "Survival of the Fittest" than the promise of being *one of the fittest* just by "believing in" the Deity, thereby escaping eternal death. In scientific, and even Buddhist terms (reincarnation), it is the implication of infinity and the infinity of life.*

Regarding the fear of death, in the MGM film, *Moonstruck*, Rose Castorini (Olympia Dukakis) asks Johnny Cammareri (Danny Aiello) why men chase women. (Rose suspects, correctly, that her husband, Cosmo Castorini (Vincent Gardenia), is having an affair.) Johnny first speculates that since God removed a rib from Adam to create Eve, men constantly seek other women to refill the hole left by Adam's lost rib. Rose thinks for a moment and then asks a slightly different question, "Why would a man need more than one woman?" Johnny considers for a moment more and answers, though somewhat tentatively and questioningly, "I don't know...maybe because he *fears death*?" Rose's eyes widen and she exclaims, "That's it!! That's the reason!" Moments later, when Cosmo returns home she calmly but pointedly inquires, "Where you been?" He says sourly, "I don't know, Rose. I don't know where I've been or where I'm going, alright?" After a moment, she replies with soft resolve, "I just want you to know, no matter what you do you're gonna' die, just like everybody else."

This scene from *Moonstruck* is tender, thought-provoking, and poignant. And though it's specifically about men and their fear of death, it speaks to the fear of death in all of us. Few of us looks forward to dying, but it's obviously a part of life that none of us will avoid. Is it possible that in our avoidance of acknowledging our inevitable death, some of us are steered toward the embracing promise and reassurance of eternal/infinite life in religion?

Another point or perspective on proof of God's existence or non-existence regards an obviously concise concept. I find it curious that, while many religions have been continuously vehement in denouncing Darwinian

---

* In fact, life on Earth has already been infinite to a degree. It has been an unbroken phenomenon since the emergence of the first microbe and single cell organism, and will continue infinitely until, or if, all life on Earth becomes extinct.

evolution, within the variety of the world's religious history there has been an obvious evolution of a different, and opposite, kind. Scientific evolution is from simple to complex. This religious evolution is unequivocally from complex to simple (again, like the Order of Operations). It is the evolution from the worship of plural deities, *polytheism*, to the worship of a single deity, *monotheism*. From many gods, to one.

Without considering Jesus Christ or any other intermediary or Messiah, monotheism is clearly the opposite of polytheism—the difference in God and any gods of mythology is singular versus plural, respectively. It is trading complexity for simplicity. (The danger is overlooking the interest of existing complexity in an effort to be simple.) And besides implying simplicity, monotheism is also more specific than polytheism; a single cause for the universe and nature is more specific than many causes. It seems to satisfy, at least on the surface, the same need as science for simplicity, specificity, and clarity. (Hidden subliminally with all those is the implication of the sole and absolute authority of God.) However, specificity and clarity are not always congruent. Though more specific than plural gods, is the concept of a monotheistic God really much clearer than the gods of mythology?

For example, most of us have no trouble agreeing that some of the Greeks of antiquity were limited in their understanding of nature. This is evident by their invention of gods for almost every natural phenomenon. Those gods, of course, have been rendered extinct by physics. Is it not possible that the entire universe is more economically and conveniently represented by the singular God of any monotheistic religion? Humans are vulnerable and fallible. Isn't it possible that we have unwittingly (and maybe even consciously) replaced the complexity of polytheism with the simplicity of monotheism from a reluctance to abandon gods altogether?

It is also intriguing that any monotheistic Deity is referred to cross-culturally and cross-denominationally as *God*, albeit in different languages and dialects of course. Do all monotheistic religions believe in the same God? The historical and documented source materials are, in many cases, quite different. If they are not the same God, are there as many monotheistic gods as there are monotheistic religions? And if there are many monotheistic gods, why do many religions use essentially the same term, implying only one? And what is the difference between many monotheistic gods and polytheism? Or if all religions have the *same* God, why are so many religions convinced that *their* specific God/faith/religious history is the truth and all others false? Is the same God dictating different truths? A belief in God is not as simple, economical, or efficient as it's often made to sound.

Clearly, many modern humans have discovered, through science, that there are other explanations for the natural phenomenon on Earth and in the universe than explanations involving gods. Is it perhaps easier to dismiss the ancient Greek gods because many of those gods represented specific *terrestrial* phenomena which have been efficiently, clearly, and accurately explained by modern science? A monotheistic God is not only credited for all terrestrial phenomena, but for *universal* phenomena, so the problem of inefficiency in completely eliminated. However, constellations are not terrestrial, and most of us have no trouble acknowledging now that the characters in the constellations of antiquity are mythical. But we don't treat the creation of the universe, the Solar System, and life on our planet the same way. We still ascribe one god as their creator. (It's a curious separation or compromise that I don't pretend to fully understand). In other words, the polytheistic gods of the Greeks and other ancient civilizations are regarded and taught as mythology, but any monotheistic god is taught seriously by religions as fact.

Unsurprisingly, a single, monotheistic God and the ancient, polytheistic gods bear much similarity: they are both incorporeal (perhaps because they were all invented in our collective imaginations); they are both credited as the cause for natural phenomena; they are both immensely more powerful (and omnipotent) than humans; and they both have the capacity for great love and great wrath. Tellingly, it was proof through the discovery of clear, physical evidence that ushered ancient gods to extinction. We (humanity) outgrew them with our intellectual searching and understanding. Might we eventually, through continued scientific understanding and spiritual awareness, also outgrow our collective, modern, monotheistic God?

To give a somewhat silly (but I think appropriate) analogy, if the fear of losing our free will should be taken seriously, maybe the Hubble telescope should never have been built or deployed (and later successfully repaired). Could utilizing the telescope have robbed us of our free will by potentially photographing clear evidence for the Deity? Would verifying the Deity's existence not have helped us understand the origin of the universe more deeply? Is the fear of the loss of free will concern that humanity would not be able to emotionally or intellectually process the evidence (and maybe verification) for God?

Once again, fear of negating our free will in this example seems synonymous with remaining ignorant, an excuse to distract from the lack of convincing evidence for a deity. We certainly don't seem to have lost our free will to understand the universe by seeing far more deeply into space through the Hubble telescope. It has been entirely and exquisitely the opposite. It was the free will of scientists that brilliantly built, deployed, repaired, and utilized the Hubble Telescope, which has dazzled humanity with breathtakingly beautiful images of our universe, even to its youth.

The warning that we will lose our free will if we understand and comprehend God by physics—as opposed to *choosing* to believe in God by faith with less physical evidence—again seems to me to be self-defeating. Applied generally, what does one decide are questions, searches, and answers about physical evidence that *won't* destroy our free will? Is pondering the existence of God the only hazardous one to our free will? Ironically, whether one is comfortable or not with thinking and scrutiny, the question of which questions are possible to answer or which ones would negate our free will are themselves questions that take some thinking to decide. Are *any* thoughts and considerations free will loss contributors?

Centuries ago, building the Hubble telescope and using it successfully would have been beyond our capability. Plus, the mere notion would have been considered by some beyond our ability to understand, and probably even blasphemous. Surely, though, it would not be argued that we should not have built and deployed the Hubble telescope (in order to avoid our vanity that we could come to better understand the cosmos, or that it might destroy our free will)? But if the analogy can be made that God might simply be a term or metaphor for the cosmos, then we have, beyond a doubt, already "seen" God much more clearly *with* the Hubble Telescope. That conception of God is of course not what religions tend to mean by God, but it is a plausibility.

Now a very specific example. What if scientists were to say that a pulsar was a sign of an extraterrestrial civilization? And suppose that scientists said they *believed* and had *faith* that there were civilizations there but that they couldn't offer proof. They just "felt" it was so. (Some may have prayed and their prayers had been answered confirming extraterrestrials.) Suppose scientists seriously asserted that? Would the religious community accept this news from scientists with no other evidence? Maybe some, but most probably not. Wouldn't much of the religious community need more evidence, physical evidence, proof that there really *were* extraterrestrials there and not trust the belief and faith of the scientists? I think the answer is, most likely, of course. A religious person would likely *demand* proof of the extraterrestrials and not be ready to accept the scientists' word for it on faith, just as a skeptic about religion needs physical evidence and proof for God. (It's very easy to see the error and folly of others, but much more difficult to see the same in ourselves.) On the other hand, I suspect that even if some scientists were to actually say this, there would be some people who would believe it very quickly, in the same way that belief in a deity is often accepted quickly and without evidence. Like Mr. Spock said, "Humans have the distinct tendency in believing that which they choose and excluding that which is painful."

I strongly suspect that the idea of a supernatural God (just as concluding extraterrestrial habitation around a pulsar) might be a "quick-fix" explanation of the origin of the universe and life. It is outside the realm of physical testing and is therefore safely immune to disproof, skepticism, and inquiry. It can't be refuted because it is real for the believer and nearly impossible to test (like my trying to prove or disprove my earlier analogies: an elf, a fairy, Santa Claus, the Easter Bunny, or the Tooth Fairy, etc.). If someone believes in God or any of the above fictitious characters deeply enough, proof is unnecessary and immaterial. Practical, logical, rational, reasonable arguments are irrelevant. There is no physical evidence *for* a fairy and there is no physical evidence *against* one. There is no physical evidence yet *for* God, but neither is there physical evidence so far *against* God. They are both true for those who believe them. Maybe that is the one thing that is definitely true about God: Like, "Beauty is in the eye of the beholder," God is real, true, and exists for the one who believes in God.

~~~

Considering any of these possibilities takes courage, wonderment, and the willingness to ask difficult and penetrating questions. It also requires the rigorous demand for hard evidence. The scientific method is a successfully tested tool. Our sense of wonder (awe, religion) and our brains (thought and perseverance) are the conduits for that tool.

Following the scientific method, in order to know with much more certainty whether free will would be lost by providing physical evidence for God, it would have to be thoroughly and repeatedly tested. But other than the story of Doubting Thomas that I referenced already, is there an unambiguous example of someone who has lost their free will by witnessing physical evidence of God? This is really a paradox of a question because the answer depends partly on the premise that there is already physical evidence for God and that someone lost their free will in the discovery. To my knowledge, such evidence does not yet exist. But if it did (or does) and the test could be performed and free will *was* lost, this would be distinct evidence that we would have learned the limit of our comprehension and why, and that the loss of our free will was the consequence.

But let's suppose that it might not be true, that we might not lose our free will if indisputable physical evidence for God were to be shown. That would have to be tested too. If the tests were performed and passed and free will was not lost, we would have a gained a deep new understanding of what God really meant while simultaneously overcoming our fear of the loss of free will.

Unfortunately, once again, both of these tests are, very likely, impossible to perform. In the absence of the ready ability to perform either of these tests, one conclusion might be that since God doesn't seem to exist within the realm of testability either way, the concept of God could be relegated to the domain of deep, *personal* experience without the need to insist on the Deity's *factual* existence. It would then certainly seem appropriate to suggest that God might exist only in the imagination—or as a metaphor for the source of all existence—but not necessary to proffer (as Paul Tillich held) as a living entity or being.

An adorable analogy of why God might only be in our imagination was offered by Richard Dawkins in his book, *The God Delusion*. To explore his point, Dawkins chose the poignant poem, "Binker," from the second of A.A. Milne's classic collection of poems, *Now We Are Six* (published in 1927). The poem is about Christopher Robin's imaginary friend, Binker. As Dawkins states, Binker is even more imaginary than Winnie The Pooh or any of the other familiar Milne characters. Unlike Pooh, Piglet, Eore, or Owl, this imaginary character has no form at all. In this sense, Binker is very much like the concept of God.

This analogy of Dawkins also struck me immediately and emotionally in a very personal way. *Now We Are Six* and its earlier companion, *When We Were Very Young* (published in 1924), were books that my parents read to my brothers and me, when *we* were very young. These books were among my favorites and first reading lessons. Curiously, the poem Binker never particularly moved me as much as most of the other poems in those two books, possibly because the concept of an *invisible* imaginary friend did not resonate with me or interest my imagination, even at that age. But I agree completely with Dawkins's hypothesis.

Of course, the poem does not specifically reference any deity, much less the Deity, God. But Dawkins's analogy is clear and apt. One question that naturally follows is what really *is* the difference between Christopher Robin's friend Binker and God? Dawkins asks a similar question: "Is the imaginary-friend phenomenon a higher illusion, in a different category from ordinary childhood make-believe?…I suspect that the Binker phenomenon of childhood may be a good model for understanding theistic belief in adults. I do not know whether psychologists have studied it from this point of view, but it would be a worthwhile piece of research. Companion or confidant, a Binker for life: that is surely the role that God plays—one gap that might be left if God were to go." [30] Whether or not Dawkins is correct, I think that his analogy is both appropriate and a reasonable hypothesis.

Another interesting interpretation of the concept of God emanating from and communicating through the imagination was offered from Neale Donald Walsch in the following extract from his 1995 book, *Conversations with God: An Uncommon Dialogue*:

God: "My messages will come in a hundred forms, at a thousand moments, across a million years. You cannot miss them if you truly listen. You cannot ignore them once truly heard. Thus will our communication begin in earnest."

Walsch: "How can I know this communication is from God? How do I know this is not my imagination?"

God: "What would be the difference? Do you not see that I could just as easily work through your imagination as anything else? I will bring you the *exact* right thoughts, words, or feelings, at any given moment, suited precisely to the purpose at hand, using one device, or several. You will know these words are from Me because you, of your own accord, have never spoken so clearly. Had you already spoken so clearly on these questions, you would not be asking them."

God speaking to us through our imaginations may seem like a serene, sweet, and simple solution to the problem of proof of God. But it also seems to me a simplistic and inadequate explanation. *Imagination* is the general term for the gamut of our psyche, so is not, in itself, a specific explanation. And the interpretation of imagination is as subjective and diverse as the perception and interpretation of belief and faith in God.

For example, how many people of clearly questionable mental stability have claimed that God was a voice "talking" to them in their imaginations? How many mentally unstable people have committed murder following God's directive in their imaginations? Should their testimony of God's existence be trustworthy? And even for a very rational and mentally stable person, is that explanation sufficient or satisfactory?[*] Is the human imagination by definition *only* an inner megaphone for the Deity? And if so in some moments and not in others, how can one know which inner voices we hear are God and which are our own?

It seems clear to me that every concept we perceive begins in the imagination (whether the concepts actually exist or not). But it is not at all clear that the imagination is simply a divine lighting rod. Therefore, there needs to be a much more obvious distinction of evidence for God than simply the "voices" of our imagination, or even the healthiest and wisest of those voices.

---

[*] Joy Behar, a panelist on the television talk show, *The View*, questioned Vice-President Mike Pence's intimation that, when he prays, Jesus talks to him. Behar remarked, "It's one thing to talk to Jesus. It's another thing when Jesus talks to you…that's called mental illness…hearing voices." Understandably, her comment drew rapid reproach from Pence and other devout Christians demanding an apology. Behar retracted insisting that she was only joking. Whether she was joking or not, I think her comment raises a valid question about the meaning of the imagination, prayer, divinity, and God.

But the question that Walsch raises to God in his book is very legitimate. How *can* one tell whether a voice in our imagination that is giving us an extremely positive thought or direction is the voice of God and not just our own healthy inner voice? For indisputable evidence of God, I think that the voice of God in our imagination would have to be profoundly and distinctively different from our own (whatever "our own" means). For example, as Carl Sagan and Ann Druyan noted on the abortion debate, brain waves can be recorded. Would not the voice of God in our imagination generate spectacularly larger, or at least more distinctive brain waves than our own? I know of no such phenomenal and documented recorded brain waves.*

One clear example in physics of something we know to exist but that we cannot perceive directly by any of our five senses is radio waves. We can see and hear the *result* of radio waves when we listen to the radio or watch television, but we cannot physically experience radio waves as they pass through the air. This could, of course, be an analogy for the religious believer supporting the existence of God.

To the believer, though God is not measurable by physics, the result of God is detectable *emotionally*. The common descriptions are feelings of peace, tranquility, well-being, joy, happiness, and, of course, love. These feelings are as real and as strong evidence for the believer as experiencing radio and television broadcasts are evidence of radio waves for the scientifically minded. The fact that feelings—the emotions—are less compelling scientific evidence than radio waves is unimportant to the religious experience.

Another, perhaps better analogy to God in physics of something that cannot be perceived directly by the human senses, but is known to exist by its effects, is the reality of dark matter. Since physics is comprised of matter and energy, matter is definitely physical evidence. Dark matter gets its name for a very simple and practical reason. Dark is the opposite of light, implying

---

* Ann Druyan's brain waves were recorded and preserved on the Voyager Interstellar Record. As she noted in the companion book, *Murmurs of Earth*, her brain waves (her thoughts and meditations) were recorded and printed as a pictured graph. She did not, however, attribute her brain waves to God. Regardless, those recorded brain waves are less compelling evidence for God than they are a testament to the phenomenon, evolution, intricacy, and beauty of the human brain.

difficult or impossible to see. Matter is not only physical material, but by definition, has gravity. Therefore, dark matter is physical material that cannot be seen but has gravitational force. It attracts other matter to itself (the gravitation of dark matter is thought to be one culprit of comets[*]).

There is actually more dark matter in the universe than there is visible matter. Does that sound similar to a description of God? It seems to me only a slight step away from saying that something invisible and incorporeal dominates, is in control of, or maybe even created the universe. The differences are that the effects of gravity can be *seen* as well as felt and divine intelligence is generally not attributed to gravity. The question that arises for me, once again, is: Why the need to ascribe divine intelligence to the universe? Why the need for emotional comfort from the cosmos? Can it not, as Stephen Hawking has suggested, just *be*?

I propose that belief in God might stem from an unconscious awareness of just this kind of cosmic phenomena. Invisible but powerful forces. The discovery and confirmation of dark matter proves that invisible things can have physical effects. But they are not necessarily of supernatural nature.

∼∼∼

When NASA sent the rovers *Spirit* and *Opportunity* to Mars, the primary goal was to find any evidence of one element that is responsible for life as we know it on Earth: Water. That search proved fruitful and I think it is now a fact that while water may not exist on Mars now, remnants of the existence of water have been found, proving at least that water *used to exist* on Mars. That in itself is a remarkable and significant and profound discovery! The question of water (and possible life) on Mars was of course part of a larger question about the existence of life elsewhere in the universe. Intriguingly, maybe we have *already* found more life in the universe and we have just not yet realized the source.

At the quantum level, the smallest unit of matter is the particle. This is the realm of the subatomic. Atoms were formerly the smallest discovered known matter, but particles are smaller than atoms, hence the word *sub*atomic. The word quantum means "the least quantity of evidence," which

---

[*] **http://www.sciencefriday.com/segments/did-dark-matter-doom-the-dinosaurs/**

is consistent with the size of a particle. An underlying and mysterious principle of quantum physics—the microscopic—is that not only is the activity of a particle difficult to observe or predict, but that the observer seems to actually affect the outcome of experiments with particles. At the normal level of physics—the macroscopic—the outcome of an observed phenomenon doesn't seem to be affected by our observation. A given experiment can be repeated many, many times and the same result occurs. Not so at the quantum level. In experiments with particles, they can behave one way in a given experiment, but sporadically and seemingly at random when the same experiment is repeated. The particles move as if they *know* they're being observed. They seem to "behave" differently *on purpose*!

Scientists don't yet understand why particles do this. Some logical questions that follow might be: "If the particles know that they're being observed and purposely change their behavior (perhaps to confuse the observer), *how* do they know?" And, "If they do know, does that mean that particles are *intelligent*?" And, "If they are intelligent, does that mean that particles are *alive*?"

If the answer turns out to be that particles have intelligence and are, in fact, alive, then perhaps we already have proof that intelligent life is *abundant* in the universe. It's just not quite the kind of intelligent life that we were expecting.

~~~

Concerning the burden of proof once again, I would like to restate a simple requirement of religion regarding proof: that the burden of proof of the existence of God lies with the one who believes in God. In William C. Placher's compilation, *Essentials of Christian Theology*, theologian, philosopher, and environmentalist, John B. Cobb, gave this concise assessment of the burden of proof in a chapter entitled, "Does It Make Sense To Talk About God?": "In the contemporary intellectual world, the burden of proof is placed on the one who claims that the answer is yes."[31] In science, the burden of proof always lies with the person making the claim. It is a very fair requirement. It is one clear and tough principle that better ensures the separation of a spurious or specious proposition from one that is extremely well conceived and supported.

Russell's Teapot is an excellent analogy in the argument of the burden of proof. It is also an obvious example of an intangible, immaterial, and probably pointless concept. Formulated by Bertrand Russell, the analogy essentially states that if a person claimed to see a teapot orbiting the Sun, the burden of proof would rest on the one making the claim, not on anyone who would question the idea. If the one questioning the existence of the teapot were chastised or ridiculed as blasphemous, the ridicule should be considered nonsense and irrational. In 1952, Russell was commissioned by Illustrated magazine to write an article. Though it was never published, he entitled it, "Is There a God?" In the following excerpt of the article, he discusses his "teapot" analogy and adds an indictment against fundamentalist (he refers to it as "dogmatist") religious teaching. "Many orthodox people speak as though it were the business of skeptics to disprove received dogmas rather than of dogmatists to prove them. This is, of course, a mistake. If I were to suggest that between the Earth and Mars there is a china teapot revolving about the sun in an elliptical orbit, nobody would be able to disprove my assertion provided I were careful to add that the teapot is too small to be revealed even by our most powerful telescopes. But if I were to go on to say that, since my assertion cannot be disproved, it is an intolerable presumption on the part of human reason to doubt it, I should rightly be thought to be talking nonsense. If, however, the existence of such a teapot were affirmed in ancient books, taught as the sacred truth every Sunday, and instilled into the minds of children at school, hesitation to believe in its existence would become a mark of eccentricity and entitle the doubter to the attentions of the psychiatrist in an enlightened age or of the Inquisitor in an earlier time."

Few people, philosophies, or religious faiths subscribe to the notion of a teapot in any cosmic orbit. But, like the concept of God, if one imagines it keenly enough how can anyone demonstrate disproof? Against all logic and evidence, the teapot exists in that person's mind. But what would be the reason for adhering to that imagination, that intangibility? Perhaps the answer is only known to the one imagining the teapot. As with belief in God, any intangible idea may be solely in the eyes of the beholder, in the perception of the believer.

But if one who believes in God desires not only to share their belief, but to convince others of the validity of their belief, they need strong arguments, and stronger arguments than personal feelings. They need solid, physical evidence, which is the fundamental basis of proof. This holds true for an atheist as well as a religious believer. An atheist, or a non-believer, must be able to prove that God does not exist. (As you will see in Part II, Stephen Hawking attempted to do this.) Allan W. Watts also spoke to the issue of the bearer of the burden of proof in his book, *The Wisdom of Insecurity: A Message for an Age of Anxiety.* "What science has said...is this: We do not, and in all probability cannot, know whether God exists...All the arguments which claim to prove his existence are...without logical meaning. There is nothing...to prove there is no God, but the burden of proof rests with those who propose the idea. If, the scientists would say, you believe in God, you must do so on purely emotional grounds, without basis in logic or fact. Practically...this may amount to atheism. Theoretically, it is simple agnosticism. For it is...the essence of scientific honesty that you do not pretend to know what you do not know, and...the essence of scientific method that you do not employ hypotheses which cannot be tested." The last sentence is, I think, a very reasonable and fair point. It makes common and sound sense. What is the reason for asserting *any* knowledge or faith without logical basis? That makes almost no sense. The reason probably hinges on an individual choice of the importance of logic.

On the other hand, an atheist's inability to test or prove that God does not exist neither confirms nor refutes a believer's faith. It only means two things: that physical evidence for or against the existence of God is unavailable, *and* that faith in God is still only right for the one who believes in God, or until such time as either the atheist or believer could prove their respective arguments. In the absence of indisputable physical evidence and proof, this is true, of course, for everything.

Except for religious privacy, why should proof also be necessary for organized religion? Because any knowledge that has survived the rigor and test of time has had to undergo severe scrutiny and repeated demonstration of validity...of proof. It is a tough but necessary test. Things that don't stand up to proof undergo *continued* serious scrutiny because the same questions about them continue to arise. The knowledge that survives the scrutiny and test of time does so because enough proof is eventually provided.

Some of my religious friends have used as evidence (and proof) the assertion that religious texts, though transcribed by men, were dictated to those men by God. It is very grand assertion. So can a religious person *prove* that religious texts believed to be the word of the Deity were *not* simply the writing of the transcribers? Can a religious person *prove* that the words originated directly from the Deity? This seems like a very reasonable question and requirement. Religious texts are almost always considered to be the "Word of God." It is actually considered insulting and even blasphemous to suggest that the scribes surmised the words themselves and then *attributed them* to God. In my humble opinion, if the answer to this question is that it *cannot be proven* that the written text came directly from the Deity, then it is impossible to conclude with certainty that the religious texts, in and of themselves, are evidence and proof of the existence of God.

I have a two-fold assessment about faith and belief, which might temporarily alleviate the need for proof of God and even the fear of the loss of free will in discovering evidence for God: First, that believing in or having faith in anything is fine, a personal choice, and a human right. And second, that it would be healthy for those who "believe" or have "faith" in God to acknowledge that they have enough evidence for themselves but perhaps not enough for everyone else. Those acknowledgments would put the issue back into the domain of privacy where, in my view, religious belief belongs.[*]

By the same token, I think scientists need to be open to the idea that supernatural phenomena may be possible to prove at some point in the future. I think science needs to be able to acknowledge that science itself could be limited by its own tool, the scientific method; that other tools (maybe similar to science or religion) might be necessary to uncover and reveal extra-physical phenomena (like ghosts, automatic writing, trance channelers, God, etc.). Regardless, until those alternative tools for discovering them are found, and the tools themselves are tested, the concept of God's meaning, existence, or non-existence should remain a concept but not a conclusion, no matter how beautiful and real the perception of God may be to the believer. It would be nice if both viewpoints could coexist in more tentative flexibly.

Referencing imagination again, I have one possible proposition from my own imagination (my own instinct or faith) about the meaning of God. Though it is not proof, it is very similar to what Einstein and Spinoza suggested (it is also an "If...then..." statement): If the Hubble telescope has

---

[*] The late George Carlin said it simply and brilliantly in his comic revision of the Ten Commandments. After boiling the ten down to two, he added a third (another kind of trinity): "Thou shalt keep thy religion to thyself!"

already helped us to see God, then God could be defined as the *observed physical universe*. As Paul Tillich proposed, it is possible that there is no *being* God, no Entity, only the phenomenon of the cosmos. God can be a metaphor for the cosmos. God is also beauty and love, in metaphor. God is a *term* we have invented, and use, to refer to the vastness of the universe, exactly like any gods in history, only singular, monotheistic. Instead of multiple gods for aspects of nature that we didn't understand, we have "graduated" to one god as creator of the entire universe.

In a sense, the monotheistic God is a solution similar to one the scientific method seeks, Ockham's Razor, or the simplest of two or more potentially workable solutions. The difference between Ockham's Razor and a simpler, monotheistic God is that the simpler solution of Ockham's Razor is still based on solid, physical evidence. The problem with God as an Ockham's Razor solution is that there is not enough physical evidence to support the idea of an entity *external* to the cosmos, so the simplicity of the monotheistic deity is insufficient. It's actually the opposite extreme from the scientifically complex. It's *too* simple. It's so simple that it's simplistic, elementary. It is also too abrupt a conclusion. Ockham's Razor is not employed abruptly.

There is abundant evidence and proof for almost everything that we experience: Many well-written books on a nearly infinite variety of subjects; testable facts that took years of painstaking experiment to establish; many wonderful human beings and other living things leading enriched and productive lives, often with no assistance from religion. But humans are also vulnerable, mortal, and addictive, and it can be difficult, frightening, and sobering to replace the traditionally and dogmatically accepted with the progressive, practical, and thought-provoking.

I propose that our biggest error is a lack of self-trust and critical thinking and the education to pass on that combination. Just as in my example of our desire to enjoy the use of technology without a deeper individual understanding of the technology, our tendency in life in general is to feel that we need to trust someone else instead of ourselves. Trusting someone else is of course basic nature for infants, and normal for children. But it should be much less true for adults.

Sadly, many of us have also been taught that to trust oneself is selfish. Indeed the avoidance of trusting *oneself* is at the heart of the religious principle that humans are innately "sinful." This is the reason for the Genesis story of God punishing Adam and Eve with expulsion from Eden. Adam and

Eve were curious (enticed by the snake) so trusted themselves to gain knowledge (from the tree of knowledge). But the Genesis God did not want Adam and Eve to gain knowledge or trust themselves more than God. The message of the story is apparent and demeaning: not only do we not have the *capacity* to trust ourselves, but that trusting ourselves is anathema, *sacrilegious*, to trusting (having faith in) God.

Another problematic thought: If God is accepted as perfect and does not make mistakes, how could God create any life that was sinful? I made this point before, but I want to emphasize it again. Wouldn't *any* creation of God be perfect, free from sin? Water, for example, can't naturally and unaided flow uphill. Shouldn't God be unable to produce sinful creatures? Doesn't the emphasized and punished sin in humans imply that God botched the recipe? Isn't the concept of free will—the freedom to choose between good and evil, right from wrong, to believe in God—an excuse to cover for God's foible, for failing to create perfection in the first humans? And if sin in humans was not God's error but God's intention and test, what was God's desire in creating humans? That they be like God and hopefully better (like most parents want for their children), or that they have the stupidity to make bad choices (what no parent should want for their child)? Why would a perfect God create imperfect life, especially *deliberately*? And if the answer is that some Old Testament stories are not literal but allegory, which ones? Adam and Eve, the first humans? Human original sin? Abraham, the common ancestor of humanity? What about New Testament stories? The Resurrection? Jesus turning loaves into fishes? Jesus walking on water? All of them? None? The culprit of the confusion, or "the buck stops here," it seems to me, is the Deity, God. The confusion about divinity and the inconsistent results of God's work—imperfection in life created by a divine and perfect Creator—are not only a poor reflection on God, but makes the concepts of divinity and God themselves highly suspect.

So how could we trust ourselves if, according to Genesis, we are basically untrustworthy, riddled with error from the start, and sinful as a result? Is it any wonder, then, that so many of us don't trust ourselves and our own thinking? I submit that, regardless of how it's taught, equating knowledge with sin is erroneous and a tragedy. In addition to love, knowledge is our lifeblood. It is what enables the progression from ignorance to insight. (I've already offered what I think is the only meaning of the word *sin:* denying someone the right to be themselves, as long as being oneself does not deny anyone else the same right.)

Though we should trust ourselves, humans are, of course, not perfect. Nothing is perfect, not even the universe (I've joked that the musical interval terms, *perfect fourth* and *perfect fifth* are half-misnomers.). We can't know everything. We are intelligent, but we are not omniscient. We are tiny and vulnerable. Even the magnificence of the universe (or multiverses), and our Solar System within it, are vulnerable. Our Solar System and we have been the recipients of cosmological violence in many forms: cometary and asteroidal impact; cancer from the Sun's radiation; tidal waves from the Moon's gravitation; geological tsunamis and earthquakes; viral infections like the COVID-19 pandemic. All of those are examples of imperfection, but they are also the normal forces of nature and physics. Imperfection is normal in the universe. Humans have evolved intelligently to coexist with the imperfections of nature, both in our ability to better protect ourselves from their occasional annihilating forces, and in our ability to accomplish wonderful physical and mental feats in spite of them. Our species would not have survived had we not succeeded with both. (I don't think it's as arguable that humans have survived primarily on belief and faith.)

Although we are not perfect, we certainly have plenty of reason to trust ourselves. Religion and science are both our inventions. We should be proud of ourselves and those accomplishments, of our sacred and secular ingenuity and productivity. Too often, though, we forget the distinction between extreme selfishness—no regard for other forms of life or other ideas—and simply feeling wonderful about ourselves and others, and striving to understand more about ourselves, each other, and the cosmos.

Religion is obviously adhered to by a great many people and is a testament to the fact that we all have deep feelings and want peace with those feelings, both internally and externally. But focusing on our drawbacks (sins) has not been the primary answer to our success and survival; I would strongly argue that the opposite is true.

Therefore, in our continued search for validation and proof, and exploring the meaning of free will, if we choose to harbor faith and belief in a god (whether a proper noun or not), let us first have faith in ourselves, other living things, and our collective ability to live together peacefully in this vast universe—my personal trinity—whatever our inner definition of it may be.

PART II

A SAMPLING OF

NOTED AUTHORS

In this section, I will be examining writings and arguments from both scientists and theologians, comparing them, and offering my own opinions. My choices of authors were subjective, based on my own reading and research, and were not intended to purposely exclude any specific author. Some of the authors' books in these chapters are less current than others. The authors I chose presented points and propositions that I found particularly interesting, intriguing, and/or compelling.

Chapter 1

C.S. LEWIS

I was introduced to the creative writing of C.S. Lewis, as many children were, through *The Chronicles of Narnia*. I wish I could say that I read all seven of the books, but I blush to confess that I did not. However, when I was 12 years old I did attempt, *The Voyage of the Dawn Treader*. And, perhaps a year later, I was cast as the lion in an adapted play of *The Lion, the Witch, and the Wardrobe*—one of many plays performed annually by the Children's Drama Workshop, under the direction of Constance Debear Welsh, in Davidson, North Carolina. I loved everything about being in the play, including the wonderful fantasy of the story.

It was years later that I learned that C.S. Lewis was also an author on the subject of religion, specifically Christianity. His book, *Mere Christianity*, is probably the most known and notable. Based on and adapted from BBC radio talks given by him (at the invitation of then Director of Religious Broadcasting, James Welch) between 1942 and 1944, and presented in three parts—*The Case for Christianity* (1942), *Christian Behavior* (1943), and *Beyond Personality* (1944)—the book is a serious and scholarly effort at providing clarity and evidence for the existence of God. Although also about a supernatural subject, unlike his *Chronicles of Narnia*, *Mere Christianity* is not intended as fun fantasy.

In the latter book, Lewis expounds on what he considers the source of human morality, our sense of right and wrong. The source of that morality, he proffers, comes from something outside ourselves rather than internal or biological. He introduces what he calls the Law of *Human* Nature. This is similar to the "Golden Rule," and Immanuel Kant's "Good Will" and "Categorical Imperative." But it is distinguished from Newton's, Laws of Nature.

According to Lewis, we don't obey this Law of Human Nature, emanating through us but not from us, even though we know that we *ought* to. He uses the word, ought, to describe our inner ethical sense—like our free will—and explains that this sense, motivation, or "voice" originates from an *external* source, a "Mind" that is telling humans how to behave. It predates but resembles "*Intelligent* Design." Lewis says regarding this externally driven inner voice that we either choose to listen or choose not to listen. (His proposition is also somewhat of a contradiction in terms: that our *inner* voice originates from an *external* source.)

Since we can *choose* whether or not to listen, Lewis separates this Law of Human Nature from the Newtonian, Laws of Nature. In Newtonian physics, objects appear to have no choice about obeying the Laws of Nature; most of us would consider it a preposterous proposition, for example, to suggest that objects are only pulled by gravity *willingly* instead of *forcefully*. So objects seem to obey the Laws of Nature involuntarily, whether they want to or not. There is no volition with the Laws of Nature. But Lewis points out that humans have a choice when it comes to *behavior*. We can choose how we want to behave.

His point is that if our morals were part of the Newtonian, Laws of Nature we would have *no choice* but to obey them. We would obey them *in*voluntarily. He states further that we know how we should behave, what we ought to do, and we simply choose not to in some situations, even though we know that we probably should.[*] Like other theological authors, C.S. Lewis calls the source of this ought voice in us "God" and offers the theory that though the source is *outside ourselves*, the only place we can find that source is *inside ourselves*—because our behavior begins with an *internal* decision we make to follow, or not to follow, a directive from an *external* source.

Although this is somewhat contradictory, it is not entirely implausible. Many external forces affect us internally, so his hypothesis would be hard to disprove. However, the sense of an ought voice may also have nothing to do with an external source telling us how to behave. It could simply be another part of our biology, our psyche. Given the difficulty of testing for the source of the ought voice inside ourselves, biological physics seems to me equally plausible.

---

[*] Who knows whether mass murderers or terrorists ever hear that voice of what they *ought* to do? If so, do they ignore it or just misinterpret the voice? Maybe their brains are so genetically damaged that they do hear the ought voice in their minds, but their minds can't distinguish the humane from the heinous. And if they do hear the voice of *ought*, is it necessarily God (the possibility that it is the Devil is equally dubious)? If so, it would appear that God is powerless to a certain degree; at least, perhaps, against human mental madness.

So without concrete physical evidence for this external source, Lewis's point may be only an interesting speculation, hypothesis, or theory, but not knowledge or fact. It is another interpretation or perception of the meaning of God. In other words, it is possible that our inner voice that Lewis refers to *is* God. But it is just as possible that this inner voice is just a part of our brain, biology, genes, and innate instinct—our DNA—not external or divine.

~~~

Regarding our inner voice, in Chapter 3 of the book, *Varieties of Anomalous Experience*, psychologist, Richard P. Bentall, of the University of Manchester reported an interesting finding. He cited neurologist, Vilayanur Ramachandran's theory in 1997 that the religious experience may be a wholly neural phenomenon. Those initial results revealed that religious feelings might stem from stimulation of the temporal lobes, an area of the brain also called Broca's Area which is responsible for speech perception. As a result, he suggests that some religious people misinterpret their imagination as an external voice. As Bentall notes, "One experience common to many spiritual states is hearing the voice of God. It seems to arise when you misattribute inner speech (the "little voice" in your head that you know you generate yourself) to something outside yourself." In such instances, he says, the brain's Broca's area[*] is triggered. "Most people interpret their inner voice speaking as part of their imagination. But during meditation or prayer, when the brain's senses are restricted, people are [as Ramachandran says], 'more likely to misattribute internally generated thoughts to an external source.' "[32]

In her article, "Religion and the Brain," in the May 6, 2001 issue of *Newsweek*, Sharon Begley offered a response to Bentall. Though she credits scientists for, "...tentative success...in their search for the biological bases of religious, spiritual, and mystical experience...," she emphasizes that one mystery will probably remain elusive. "They may trace a sense of transcendence to this bulge in our gray matter. And they may trace a feeling of the divine to that one. But it is likely that they will never resolve the greatest question of all—namely, whether our brain wiring creates God, or

---

[*] One of Carl Sagan's early books (from which I have drawn quotes for this book) is titled, *Broca's Brain*, in admiration of the late physician/surgeon/anatomist.

whether God created our brain wiring. Which you believe is, in the end, a matter of faith." [33] Begley may be entirely correct. It certainly may be that regardless of attempts to analyze meditation or prayer scientifically, our "inner voice" will always be defined subjectively.

~~~

Lewis also takes issue with an alternative term for God. He derides the phrase, "Life-Force" and substitutes it with the word, "Mind." He finds "Life Force" to be a non-committal term verging on cowardice. He clearly does not admire the substitution. He describes the phrase as, "…all the thrills of religion and none of the cost. Is the Life-Force the greatest achievement of wishful thinking the world has yet seen?" [34] For me, the problem is not that one would wish for a more convenient or more accessible term for a potential Designer. The problem is a need for more concrete physical evidence of a Designer.

Lewis then draws a universal but practical perspective of God by comparing God to an architect. He says that God cannot be found as a fact within, or "inside" the universe any more than an architect could be a wall or staircase or fireplace inside the house. God can only be found, Lewis asserts, as an incorporeal energy within us, just as the components of the house are evidence of the architect's design but not the architect. However, rather than this just being evidence of God, to Lewis our minds are reflective products of the deity, manifested in our internal moral sense.

This is an interesting and imaginative proposal. It is not dissimilar to the fact that we are comprised internally of the atoms from stars. What is interesting, though, is that Lewis does not seem to notice a contradiction in his own analogy. He holds that God cannot be found as a fact inside the universe (because God is the creating "Mind" of the universe, outside or external to the universe), and yet he allows that God *can* be found inside us. But we are also a fact in the universe, as are stars. So, if we are a fact in the universe, and God can be a fact within us, why can God not also be a fact within the universe? (This is, once again, applying the Transitive Property of Equality.) Or if associating God with a scientific *fact* is the stumbler, how and why is God able to exist in us at all but not *in* the universe? If God is inside us in any way, isn't God *also* inside the universe? My continued point, of course, is that the concept of God as a supernatural entity external to the universe is always going to be a problematic premise for want of proof.

Subjectivity and proof aside, in my view Lewis is mixing metaphor and physical example. He is clearly correct in his analogy that the architect of a building cannot physically be a part of the building. That is a physical impossibility. But it does not immediately follow, and is not immediately or obviously correct, to suggest that our inner ethical voice is God. That may be physically impossible too, or at best, improbable. At the very least it cannot be scientifically tested or corroborated. Lewis is essentially beginning with the assumption that God already exists, and on that basing his comparison and definition.

Unfortunately, my feeling is that the comparison is erroneous since it begins with a familiar and standard assumption: the existence of God. Lewis also does not offer any physical evidence to prove that the "command" we hear inside ourselves is anything other than our own ethical instinct and education. It is very reasonable that his proposition might make us *wonder* whether the inner voice or command was actually God speaking to us. But wonder and knowledge are very different.

I have suggested that one would more likely imagine and define our inner voice being God if one has been raised to believe in a Deity. Since I was never taught that, I have consequently never taken it seriously that my inner voice might be God. (The possibility that I might not be taking that seriously because I could be listening inside myself more to the voice of the Devil than to God seems to me equally speculative and spurious. It also seems silly, and a negative notion. With utmost respect to all religions, God *and* the Devil are, too me, equal and opposite supernatural extremes, so similarly suspect. They both fall in the category of, and as candidates for, modern mythology.) I was not raised to take *anything* supernatural seriously, or at least not at face value, without solid physical evidence. My own inner voice, whatever its definition, feels like a memory of my parents, siblings, friends, and all my other life experience. I do not imagine or feel the presence of any deity or devil, polytheistic or monotheistic. I think the reason is because I was not taught to believe in deities or demons, so I don't think of or imagine my inner voice or voices in that way.

But a thought occurs to me about C.S. Lewis's argument. It centers on his use of the word, *ought*, which carries a connotation of obedience to authority. It seems plausible to me that C.S. Lewis's personality had authoritative tendencies or he wouldn't have written this book about an authority figure, one that judged how one ought to behave. He was attracted to the idea of an "authority" of life and the universe. It's the way he thought. As I offered in the Introduction, I aver that the way each of us was raised and continue to think is the reason we all arrive at our belief systems. Our belief systems may not necessarily be based on actual reality but on an extension of our own thinking. To quote the late, Robin Williams, "Reality, what a concept!" In that Einsteinian, or *relatively* real sense, I think our subjective reality is where all our own thoughts originate—our own thinking and perceptions and how they are reflected back to us through the feelings and perceptions of others.

Where I agree with Lewis is that I think that *one* source for answers to questions is indeed internal, within each of us. Where I disagree is that the source of our internal voice *has to be* God rather than just us, our brains. Again, I think he is jumping to the conclusion that the "voice" *within us* is emanating from an *external* source, a "God."

Pertaining to this external source, he then adds a rather extreme thought, one that gives only two choices. He says that either the universe exists for no reason or that there is a power behind the universe. He holds that, if that external power exists, the power would not manifest itself as a fact within the universe but, "...a reality which makes them...no mere observation of facts can find it." [35]

He also gives further details about his Law of Human Nature. "We do not merely observe men, we *are* men. In this case we have, so to speak, inside information; we are in the know." [36] Besides his gender bias being a reflection of his time, he is saying that because we are in the horse's mouth we have the advantage of not just observing ourselves but of *being ourselves*. To Lewis, not only can we observe the Law of Human Nature in others, but we can listen to the Law of Human Nature in ourselves. Put another way, according to Lewis, God infused us with the Law of Human Nature so that we can be our own moral monitors.

As simple as this scenario might seem, it also carries negative connotations. It casts God as a universal cyber-dictator or the Orwellian, "Big Brother," fashioning and installing the human brain as a dependent and undependable computer program. By extension, it portrays humans as little more than moral machines, incapable of evolving our own intelligence. Both are not flattering on the résumé of God or of God's purported Creation of humanity.

Lewis takes the posture of assuming that because we sense a moral absolute which we know we should follow and don't always, that the source for that moral absolute must be external to us or we would all behave morally all the time. To a certain extent, I agree with Lewis's point, that our moral goodness may be more voluntary than involuntary (I wish being kind and good *was* more involuntary!). However, I think Lewis is oversimplifying the source of morality and of the creation of the universe, while simultaneously undervaluing the degree of intelligence and brilliant complexity of humans and all of the various forms of life. His proposition of God is really quite demeaning to our intelligence and all of life. While I sadly agree that mature morality is probably not wholly involuntary, I nevertheless feel that my sense of morals/ethics *originate* internally, not externally as Lewis proposes.

As I have stated, I feel clear and confident that I do not need religion or God to distinguish ethical right from wrong, my free will. That awareness for me feels biologically and neurologically natural—inherited. Conversely, though I sense that morality originates internally, that does not nullify a possible external source of morality. It only means that I don't *perceive* an external source, not that I have concrete physical evidence to refute or disprove that contention. I simply and strongly sense (though I certainly don't know) that the moral choices we all make are generated autonomously, by our inner instinct and life experience, not by a deity, imagined or real.

So what evidence did Lewis have that morality is *not* part of our genes? Granted, we probably did not decide one day to make up a moral law by which to live, but the knowledge of how to behave well in order to survive might be hardwired into our brains as we gradually learned behavior from what worked and what did not. In other words, morality may have evolved just like everything else has evolved. Morality may have developed largely because of humanity's discovery that treating each other well more times than treating each other badly leads to the strongest survival sum of our species and all other life, and we needed a way to communicate that survival value to others—the birth of "The Golden Rule." In that perspective, morality has been another evolved and experiential survival tool.

Later Lewis moves from the origin of human morality and discusses the origin of the universe. In his view, the universe is either purposely created by an immense external power, or it exists for no reason. There is no middle ground. He references what he concludes are two differing views of the universe. The first he calls the *materialist* view, or the perception that, "...matter and space just happen to exist, and always have existed, nobody knows why; and that the matter, behaving in certain fixed ways, has just happened, by a sort of fluke, to produce creatures like ourselves who are able to think..." This is where he puts science. The second view, he says, is the religious view, or the perception that, "...what is behind the universe is more like a mind than it is like anything else we know. That is to say, it is conscious, and has purposes, and prefers one thing to another. And on this view it made the universe, partly for purposes we do not know, but partly, at any rate, in order to produce creatures like itself—I mean, like itself to the extent of having minds..." [37] This is where he puts Christianity (and probably all monotheistic religions).

He refers to science as materialist because he thinks that science only experiments, observes, and makes conclusions about physical phenomena. *Why* physics works as it does he does not consider a scientific question. He states, "Science works by experiments. It watches how things behave...But why anything came to be there at all, and whether there is anything behind the things science observes—something of a different kind—this is not a scientific question. If there is 'Something Behind,' then either it will have to remain altogether unknown to men or else make itself known in some different way." He feels that the vastness and immensity of the universe is beyond mere physical observation, that it is naive to think that it exists with no apparent purpose. He thinks that the grandeur of the universe is, itself, the proof of the purpose of its Creator, God. Then he makes a leap of an assessment of science. He says, "Supposing science ever became complete so that it knew every single thing in the whole universe. Is it not plain that the questions, 'Why is there a universe?' 'Why does it go on as it does?' 'Has it any meaning?' would remain just as they were?" [38] These are very interesting perceptions of science, but I think his conclusions are not as obvious as he implies.

First, when he refers to the scientific view as the "materialist" view, he is technically correct in using a form of the word "material." Science does indeed study the material of matter and energy which are the two fundamental physical building blocks in the universe. But he uses the adjective form, "materialist," which can connote a superficial interest in physical matter or possessions and/or a disregard for any emotional connection to an observation of physics. In my experience with science, observing the activity and physics of the universe is anything but superficial and unemotional. Quite the contrary. Observing the magnificence and beauty of the physical reality of the universe is joyously emotional, whether one imagines it caused by a deity or caused by its own natural law.

Second, he states that according to this materialist or scientific viewpoint that matter and space just "happen to exist...always have existed." And "...nobody knows why...by a sort of fluke...By one chance in a thousand...By another thousandth chance...by a very long series of chances...to produce creatures like ourselves who are able to think." [39] This is a common argument of frustration among some religious thinkers/believers: The feeling that it seems almost disrespectful to suggest that the enormous beauty of the cosmos would be due to a random series of "blunders" or *chance*. The universe appears to some to be too beautiful to be an accident. Perhaps. But maybe the problem is in our perception of an accident. Maybe accidents on a cosmic scale happen all the time (as most astronomers would almost certainly say). Maybe an accident can be an unpredictable event, including the possibility that the origin of the cosmos, if any at all, was an unpredictable event. Without concrete physical evidence and proof that a separate entity, God, *physically made* the universe, then the universe existing by chance is still a possibility. It might feel like an unappealing or disappointing possibility and one that might not suit our desire or perception, but the fact that we might have that feeling is neither a reason to dismiss nor assume that the universe originated by either chance or by God. Both possibilities remain open until stronger evidence is presented.

Third, he presumes science's inability to pose and/or answer larger questions. With the statements, "...why anything came to be there at all, and whether there is anything behind the things science observes—something of a different kind—this is not a scientific question," and, "statements that science can't make." [40] That is simply untrue. Science has been probing the large questions—which Lewis asserts that science cannot address—since science was invented in The Enlightenment. Contemplating the origin of the universe—how and why it came to be—are areas in which science has made tremendous strides and contributions in the most recent past. The theory of the Big Bang, and the provocative question of whether the universe will ultimately die (as a result of its own matter speedily receding from itself with insufficient gravitation pull to retract) or prove to be an infinite cycle of explosions and implosions (an infinitely expanding and contracting universe or set of universes), are certainly examples of the type of questions Lewis is suggesting that science does not ask.

Fourth, to my knowledge the scientific community has never had the faintest fancy or audacity to think that it was possible for science (or anyone) to know, as Lewis states, "...every single thing in the whole universe." [41] It is too silly a thought to express much less contemplate.

Fifth, the question above that science perhaps acknowledges, but certainly considers less relevant, is the last hypothetical query he proposes: "Has it [the universe] any meaning?" Speaking as an amateur scientist (but perhaps for other scientists as well), the question of *meaning* to the universe is a puzzling one. I have always felt, to some extent, that meaning is automatic once something is understood clearly. I think a good example is the invention of the dictionary. A dictionary is the tool for understanding the specific *meaning* of words. That is the dictionary's *function*. But the dictionary does not necessarily need to have its own meaning or "reason-for-being" apart from that function. Similarly, the universe may not need a reason-for-being. The cosmos may be an autonomous and independent collective mass of matter, energy, and dark matter characterized by both beauty and chaos. The reason-for-being of life on *this* beautiful ball of matter and energy (planet Earth) is, I hope, to survive and evolve to become better and more beautiful and loving forms of life. From my human perspective, aside from the possibly of its *own* survival, the universe does not appear to have, or to *need to have*, a purpose or meaning apart from simply existing. Its meaning may be superfluous. It is even debatable as to whether the universe has a *function*. Maybe, in a Buddhist sense, it is enough for the universe to simply *be* and have *always been*. Ascribing meaning, function, purpose, or a "reason-for-being" to the universe might be completely unnecessary, and possibly another attempt at assigning human perception and human conditions to the cosmos. In another sense, assigning "purpose" to the universe could be our unconscious need to feel in control of its magnitude.

Finally, Lewis returns to his proposal of a Law of Human Nature. He suggests that naming the forces that act upon physical objects as the Laws of Nature is limited to terminology and missing reality. He says, "The so-called laws [of nature] may not be anything real—anything above and beyond the actual facts which we observe. But in the case of Man, we saw that this will not do. The Law of Human Nature or Right and Wrong, must be something above and beyond the actual facts of human behavior. In this case, beside the actual facts, you have something else—a real law which we did not invent and which we know we ought to obey." [42]

I'd like to comment first on his use of the words *may*, *must* and *real*. He says, "The so-called laws [of nature] *may* not be anything real…" But he says that, "The Law of Human Nature or Right or Wrong, *must* be something above and beyond the actual facts of human behavior…you have something else—a *real* law which we did not invent…" Whether Lewis is right or wrong in his assessment here is beside the point to me. What is illuminating are his choices of words for emphasis. By using the word *may* referencing the Laws of Nature, but the words *must* and *real* for his Law of Human Nature, he is assuming that the Newtonian Laws of Nature do not fully constitute reality, but that the Law of Human Nature—which he feels is emanating from outside of us, and therefore a separate existence or entity (God) guiding us—is apparently and obviously real. In my view, since he has no physical evidence that this "Law of Human Nature" exists outside of ourselves, its apparentness or obviousness cannot be concluded. But his assumption of a Law of Human Nature is consistent with his emphasis on moral obedience to a divine entity.

In his book, *The Pagan Christ*, though referencing another of Lewis's books, *Miracles*, Tom Harpur observes the following irony and error from C.S. Lewis which augments my observations about Lewis's views on religion and Christianity: "C.S. Lewis struggled manfully to justify the Gospel miracles in rational terms, but he ended in a sad failure on philosophical and other grounds. His basic error was in treating as history what was never history—and indeed was prefigured at least five millennia earlier in the Egyptian mythology." In other words, borrowing from Egyptian (and other) myth has produced a fallaciously historical divine Christ. It turned the man and ethicist, Jesus, into something he was most likely not—a fictional and supernatural entity. The Son of God and God.

C.S. Lewis was a learned scholar and a renowned author of both adventure fantasy and theology. In addition to the beloved children's series, *The Chronicles of Narnia*, his perspective and questions on the existence of God and human morality are worthy of deep respect and consideration. Equal consideration needs to be paid, however, to the possibility that his theological viewpoints might have been influenced by his own religious background: obedience to the entity and authority of the Anglican Communion and the Church of England.

Chapter 2

———⊰⋅⋅⋅⋅⋅⊱———

SHELDON VAUNAUKEN

I read Sheldon Vaunauken's, *A Severe Mercy*, in 1984. The book illuminates an additional angle of the perspective of religion and conversion to religion, influenced by the Christianity of C.S. Lewis.

The book is autobiographical and tells the deeply happy and deeply sad story of the couple Sheldon Vaunauken and Jean Davis ("Davy"). Their life together ends with Davy's untimely death at the age of 40. Years prior to Davy's death, the couple meet and become close friends with C.S. Lewis. The author comes to learn, through his wife's death and Lewis's guidance, that not only does God exist and is the creator of the universe, but that God's intention and plan for all humans is that they love God first above all other life, particularly above any other human being they come to love deeply. The author chose the title of the book from a letter written to him by C.S. Lewis not long after Davy's death. In the letter, Lewis asserts that Davy's death was a necessary divine decision to turn Vaunauken's love away from his wife and closer to God, what Lewis refers to as "a severe mercy." To me, the phrase essentially means "an extreme relief or lesson."

Vaunauken and his wife Davy were deeply in love for many years, before and after their marriage. They referred to their love as the "Shining Barrier." Though the author does not directly define that phrase, I surmise it to mean, "radiantly impenetrable." What the author does specify is that their barrier of love went to the extent of choosing not to have children, lest the children infringe on their love. They had also been agnostics. When they met C.S. Lewis they explored Christianity. Not long after, Davy converted to Christianity, but Vaunauken resisted.

The premise of the book, again, is that to enable Vaunauken to come to accept and love God, God had to remove the deep human love in his life that was "distracting" him from loving God, his wife. By causing the untimely death of his wife, God left Vaunauken free and undistracted to completely love God, hence the "severe mercy." The clear message of the book is that the love humans have for God must be stronger and deeper than the love humans have for each other and all of life.

The 2007 best-selling novel, *The Shack*, by William P. Young, implies a similar premise. For those who have not read the story, this is not a "spoiler alert." I will be purposely vague. The protagonist, Mackenzie Allen Phillips

("Mack"), is uncommitted religiously. His wife, Nannette (Nan) is a committed Christian. Some years after the death of someone he loves (which occurred before the story begins), Mack receives a letter in the mail from God inviting Mack to meet with "Him." The meeting pertains to the person's death. Though it is not specifically stated as in Vaunauken's book, the implication of Lewis's severe mercy seems evident to me in Young's novel. The death of someone close to him spurs Mack to realize and experience the reality of God. Commendably, the strongest premise and principle emphasized is that of forgiveness, even for murder. Any deity aside, the ability to forgive is always admirable. More than implied, the author seems to be a clear devotee of C.S. Lewis. An epigraphic quote of Lewis precedes Chapter 7: *Let us pray that the human race never escapes Earth to spread its iniquity elsewhere.* The purpose of the quote's reference is unclear, but I dislike it very much. Regardless of one's perspective of the meaning and existence of God, the statement is very negative and derogatory towards humanity. It sounds like God's reason for the Expulsion from the Garden of Eden and The Great Flood—the result of the religious concept of sin, which I find primitive, insulting of humans, and authoritatively controlling. To me, the quote reflects more disappointingly on Lewis than humanity. I also find a "severe mercy" poorly reflective of God. It more implies "severe (and "supreme") jealousy."

    I must say that though I respected the author's honesty and conviction, I found the premise distasteful and disturbing. It is not only suggestive of a jealous and vindictive God, but eerily close to the "Big Brother" of George Orwell's, *1984*. (Orwell was, thankfully (and I hope permanently), wrong in his prediction.) The couple's love in *1984* is also destroyed, although much more savagely than Vaunauken and his wife experienced. Nevertheless, the imagery and similarity in the stories are, I think, evident. Both tell the stories of a human couple in love whose love is ended by an authority figure—because they expressed their love to each other more strongly than they did to the authority figure: in *1984*, "Big Brother;" in *A Severe Mercy,* God.

    As I've indicated, I certainly don't pretend to know whether God does or does not exist, and my thoughts and opinions are strictly subjective. But I find it hard to imagine that, if there is a God, the Entity would be so insecurely self-centered. It smacks of a Supreme *Ego*[*] rather than a Supreme *Being*. I would like to think that if there is a purpose to the universe (or at least to life), that it is to produce goodness in the form of life and love for itself and each other, which then proliferates itself with more goodness and more love. I hope that life simply continues to propagate more good and love for life itself, not for an Entity who *requires* adulation and accolades for and from its creation. In other words, not a Being that wants its "ego stroked." That would be a sad revelation about God.

Vaunauken's book chronicles his transformation from being an agnostic to becoming a Christian. He expresses that his central criterion was the question of the validity of the Christian claim that Jesus Christ was the only Messiah, the one true Son of God. He does acknowledge that there is no evidence for God, but also correctly observes that there is also no evidence against God. Though the apostles, through the four gospels, witness that Christ was the Messiah, Vaunauken was not certain that this was enough evidence to warrant his conversion from agnosticism to Christianity (he at least demonstrated some minimal but healthy skepticism). But Vaunauken also struggled with another inward dilemma. He did not feel secure rejecting the idea either. For him, if God did not exist and Christ was not the Son of God, he was none the worse for believing in fiction. However, if God *did* exist and Christ *was* God's only Son, Vaunauken would be rejecting a universal truth. He was, therefore, motivated not by evidence, but by trepidation. Fear. He wrote, "Perhaps the leap to acceptance was a horrifying gamble—but what of the leap to rejection? If I were to accept, I might and probably would face the thought through the years: 'Perhaps, after all, it's a lie; I've been had!' But if I were to reject, I would certainly face the haunting, terrible thought: 'Perhaps it's true—and I've *rejected my God!* This was not to be borne. I could not reject Jesus. There was only one thing to do, once I had seen the gap behind me. I turned away and flung myself over the gap towards Jesus." [43]

---

[*] A rather unusual and amusing thing was pointed out to me hidden in the word, supreme. It denotes the ego and sounds like a synonym of supreme, simultaneously. If you switch the letter "r" and the first letter "e," the new order of the letters hides a two-word phrase that describes someone who is brazenly egotistical, arrogant, and narcissistic: superme, or "super me." (President Donald J. Trump?!) Perhaps "super me" is the undocumented etymology of "supreme!"

When his wife, Davy, dies of a terminal disease, he writes to C.S. Lewis and shares many details of his and Davy's love relationship. He describes their "Shining Barrier" and their decision not to have children. He also shares that he and his wife had planned what they called, "The Last Long Dive." In a poem entitled, "If This Be All," Vaunauken and Davy imagined a joint suicide so that neither of them would have to endure life without the other. Their specific plan was to build a yacht and, with both of them on board and sailing, deliberately sink it so that they could die together. All this was to sustain what they referred to as "inloveness." Clearly, Vaunauken and Davy were deeply in love. But their "Shining Barrier" and plan for dual suicide was probably on the side of extreme.

When Lewis writes back, he expresses sympathy and understanding, but unequivocal admonishment for their impenetrable love, as well as asserting the cause of Davy's death. As Vaunauken explains in the book (and I already offered as a brief synopsis), the focal point of Lewis's reply was the origin of the book's title. Lewis states that Davy's death was divinely determined and delivered. It was the inevitable result of misdirected love. According to Lewis, since the universe and life are God's creation, life happiness is only achieved through love for God. All other love is a symbiotic but secondary reflection of divinity. Lewis wrote, "Perpetual springtime is not allowed. You were not cutting the wood of life according to the grain. You have been treated with a severe mercy. You have been brought to see (how true and how frequent this is!) that you were jealous of God. So from *US* you have been led back to US AND GOD; it remains to go on to GOD AND US. She was further on than you, and she can help you more where she is now than she could have done on Earth. You must go on." [44]

Lewis's perspective is a curious one. It is at least specific. However, as well-intentioned as he undoubtedly was to Vaunauken, his explanation seems as extreme as the extremity he sees in Vaunauken's and Davy's love. It also resembles a fallacious conservative political ideology which Democrats refer to as "trickle down economics." Bolster the powerful and the powerless inherit the residual. The weak reap the king's spoils. The dog gets the bone. Love of God supersedes love for all. In Orwellian speak, love only "Big Brother." An autocracy.

Vaunauken's book and story are an interesting view of love and Christianity. In his transformation from an agnostic to a Christian, he offers perspectives of both a non-believer and a believer. I also find it intriguing that, in his letter to Vaunauken, it is C.S. Lewis who suggests the reason for Vaunauken's wife's death which became the book's title, *A Severe Mercy*. Vaunauken might not have come to the same conclusion on his own. (But then, it could be argued that seeking the wisdom of others is simply soliciting healthy feedback. One can always choose what to do with that feedback. Lewis was of profound influence, but not wholly responsible for Vaunauken's decision to become a Christian. Vaunauken made his own choice.) I have already discussed C.S. Lewis, but his response to Vaunauken in this book is consistent with my impression of Lewis's view about Christianity: the assumed authority of Christianity over other beliefs and philosophies.

It is also interesting to me that Lewis would assert that, in their "Shining Barrier," Vaunauken and his wife were "jealous of God." As I offered before, I think the implication is precisely the opposite: Lewis's God was jealous of *them*. It strikes me that, if the God Lewis describes does exist and dealt the couple "a severe mercy" for the reason Lewis stated, it reveals God not only as jealous, childish, egotistical, narcissistic, and cruel, but as an executioner. That would hardly befit a perfectly loving God.

Another thing that struck me was when Vaunauken writes that he *chose* to believe. He shared this feeling, "...choosing to believe *is* believing. It's all I can do: choose. I confess my doubts and ask my Lord Christ to enter my life. I do not *know* God is, I do but say: Be it unto me according to Thy will. I do not affirm that I am without doubt, I do but ask for help, having chosen, to overcome it. I do but say: Lord, I believe—help Thou mine unbelief....Then I...committed my ways to God." [45] He did not offer specific points about Christianity, nor did he point to specific biblical verses that convinced him of the truth of the faith (albeit Mark 9:24). The only thing he offered was his intuitive inability to reject Jesus (as the Divine Son of God). However, this was based on his feeling of anxiety about rejecting Jesus rather than on specific evidence affirming the divinity of Jesus, "...if I were to reject [Jesus], I would certainly face the haunting, terrible thought: 'Perhaps it's true—and I've *rejected my God!*...I *could not* reject Jesus." [46]

On the other hand, I have heard a few Christian friends admit that it has occurred to them to wonder if perhaps the entirety (or at least a great portion) of the Christian religion—and by extension, possibly all religions—is a sham, a hoax perpetrated by the authorities of the early Church to control the mass populace. The sardonic phrase, "The greatest story ever *sold* " in obvious parody of the phrase, "The greatest story ever told" was coined from the suspicion of just such a hoax. Though it did not stop his choice to convert to Christianity, Vaunauken had a glimmer of this when he wrote in the same book, "If I were to accept, I might and probably would face the thought through the years: 'Perhaps, after all, it's a lie; I've been had!' " Maybe his credulity was greater than his skepticism.

This same hoax scenario was touched on by Dan Brown in his bestselling book, *The Da Vinci Code*, in a conversation between the characters Leigh Teabing and Robert Langdon: Teabing says, "In my experience…men go to far greater lengths to avoid what they fear than to obtain what they desire. I sense a desperation in this assault on the Priory." Langdon counters that the argument is paradoxical. "Why would members of the Catholic clergy *murder* Priory members in an effort to find and destroy documents they believe are false testimony anyway?" Then Teabing replies wryly. "Yes, the clergy in Rome are blessed with potent faith, and because of this, their beliefs can weather any storm, including documents that contradict everything they hold dear. But what about those who are not blessed with absolute certainty? What about those who look at the cruelty in the world and say, where is God today? Those who look at the Church scandals and ask, who are these men who claim to speak the truth about Christ and yet lie to cover up the sexual abuse of children by their own priests?…What happens to *those* people, Robert, if persuasive scientific evidence comes out that the Church's version of the Christ story is inaccurate. And that the greatest story ever told is, in fact, the greatest story ever *sold*." [47]

If true, that grim scenario is a damning indictment on the credulous in society. But the possibility is worth considering and stems from unquestioned dogma. If any dogmatic directive is suspected to be a hoax and one does nothing to challenge the dogma, how can one be sure of its validity? What does that say about the credulity or skepticism of the believers? When is it ever healthy to ignore or suppress a serious question? And what does it say about any dogma, individual, belief, and/or organization that is accepted with little or no questioning, or worse, accepted through anxiety or even coercion? Questioning any authority—literal or metaphoric—always takes courage. I argue that questioning is not only mentally healthy but fundamentally necessary.

The title of the final chapter in Sagan's book, *The Demon-Haunted World*, Real Patriots Ask Questions, speaks exactly to this point. Questions are a vital brain exercise in any study. Authorities, almost by definition, tend to inhibit and restrict questioning and enforce obedience. It is the emphasis on obedience to the authority of God and Christianity over human reason and love that I sense from C.S. Lewis and Sheldon Vaunauken.

If Vaunauken's conversion to Christianity was motivated primarily by the anxiety or fear of rejecting God's authority and less by substantial evidence, how convincing does that make his conversion? Anxiety is a form of fear and fear is never a healthy motivator for critical decision-making in the long-term. Fear is obviously healthy and necessary in the short-term (to escape predators or other imminent danger), but that may be the *only* way that fear is healthy. Vaunauken's conversion reminds me of the principle of Pascal's Wager: the formulation by Blaise Pascal in which betting that God exists is less risky than the opposite. If one chooses not to believe in God and God does exist, the price of skepticism and unbelief would be the loss of God's reward of salvation in Heaven, an eternity in Hell. But this is an example of extremes. It seems to me, again, a choice motivated by anxiety and fear rather than by evidence.

Though I think acronym use has become excessive in much modern writing,[*] I learned an acronym not long ago that is very apropos to Vaunauken's testimonial. It is easy to remember because this acronym is also a word, and a word that means the same as the phrase formed by the words each letter represents. The acronym is FEAR. The words corresponding to the letters are: False Evidence Appearing Real. This is one of the simplest and most practical acronyms I know. The phrase is also very wise. It means that fear often makes something seem real when it is not.[†]

---

[*] Too frequently, acronyms are used for even simple phrases that don't necessitate abbreviation. Part of being skillful and fluent with any language is knowing when to use complete words and when to abbreviate. I have a funny T-shirt that reads, "AAAAA—American Association Against Acronym Abuse." (AAAAA could also stand for American Association Against *Alliteration* Abuse!) Excessive or unnecessary use of acronyms can cause one to frequently forget the words that the letters represent.

[†] In Season 1, Episode 6, "Moaning Lisa," of *The Simpsons*, Marge Simpson uncharacteristically exhibits irrational, prejudiced, and unnecessary fear toward "Bleeding Gums" Murphy, a large, bearded, middle-aged African-American saxophone player. Lisa Simpson has been depressed by life in general during the whole episode. Unable to sleep one night, she suddenly hears Murphy playing somewhere in the distance. Yearning for some consolation, she sneaks out into the night with her saxophone following his sound. After

Fear causes this because it is fueled by adrenaline, which in turn creates a heightened or exaggerated response in comparison to our other senses. But the function of fear, that heightened reaction, is short-term and is too anxious a state to be in regularly. It is not an efficient, productive, or reliable response for long-term decisions. A quote that I read feels apropos to the encouragement of functioning less from our fears and more from love. It comes from the philosopher and priest, John O'Donohue:

> May all that is unforgiven in you be released
> May all your fears yield their deepest tranquilities
> May all that is unloved in you blossom into a future graced with love.

It is also noble, admirable, self-preserving, and life-saving to overcome unproductive or paralyzing fear. In Robert Lewis Stevenson's novel, *Kidnapped*, the young protagonist, David Balfour, demonstrates this in a harrowing moment of the story. While being pursued by a posse, he comes upon raging river rapids. His choices are either to cross or be caught. Realizing he has only one choice, he crosses by hopping on a series of exposed but water-soaked boulders in the river to the opposite bank. He had momentarily hesitated—fearing that he would lose his footing on one of the slippery boulders and fall to his death—but overcame his fear when it was clear that, had he not risked crossing, he would certainly have been captured or killed by the posse. His sense of self-respect, worth, and preservation—all strong character and survival traits—became larger than his fear.

Once he was safely on the other side, his friend, guide, and mentor, Scotsman, Alan Breck (who preceded him hopping across the same wet boulders), exclaims to him in genial admiration, "To be feared of a thing and yet do it is what makes the prettiest kind of man."[48] I was deeply moved by that line. I was moved both by its wisdom, and by the lilting Scottish wording and loving personality of Breck's character. And it was refreshing and lovely (even though fiction) to hear a man referred to warmly and unabashedly as

---

finding him playing on a bridge under a street light, she and Murphy play a saxophone duet. They have just finished when Marge, out looking for her, suddenly drives up.
Marge: "Lisa! Get away from that jazz man!"
Lisa: "But, mom! Can't I just stay a little longer?"
Marge: "Come on. Come on. We're worried about you. [*then to "Bleeding Gums" Murphy*] Nothing personal. I just fear the unfamiliar."

"pretty"—and by another man, in a culture clearly less dominated by machismo. Like David Balfour and Alan Breck, would that we all might have the consistent courage to overcome our own anxieties and fears, or at least be less motivated by them.

Making a serious decision—whether philosophical, religious, scientific, or some other complex subject—should be based on long-term thinking, consideration, and courage, not on anxiety or fear. Anxiety and fear about the rejection of religious authority is my impression of the writing, and the conversion to Christianity, of Sheldon Vaunauken.

Chapter 3

TENZIN GYATSO

Though his birth name, Lhamo Thondup, and his religious name above are seldom used, the Fourteenth Dalai Lama needs no introduction. He is an advocate for love, compassion, and human rights, and is, in the world of spirituality and Buddhism, the equivalent of the "Pope." However, contrasted with many popes, he has clarified many times that he is only a man; not a god, prophet, or saint. In this he is unique among the so-called religious figures of contemporary society. He is a highly exemplary leader for ethics, spirituality, religion, faith, compassion, empathy, human rights, and, in fact, science.

I had the marvelous fortune to see the Dalai Lama speak live in 1998 in Madison, Wisconsin, both at a convocation in his honor and at my doctoral graduation the next day. He was extremely impressive and eloquent with his commentary at the convocation. I enjoyed everything he had to say about compassion and love. He was also quite the striking figure the following day onstage with the other dignitaries at the graduation ceremony. It was wonderful to behold him at closer proximity that day from my vantage point on the floor nearer the stage.

I did not know that he was also a scientific thinker until I happened to be browsing in a store one day several years later and came across his book, *The Universe in a Single Atom: A Convergence of Science and Spirituality*. It is a fascinating book. I was struck and surprised by his interest and enjoyment of science, and extremely impressed by his command and skill as a writer. Granted, every author has editors and proofreaders, but unless an assisting writer is given credit on a book's front cover, a book's content can be trusted to be primarily the work of the author. His prose flows easily and eloquently and offers many insightful perspectives about the potential for a symbiotic relationship between science and spirituality.

He is also refreshingly critical of both science and his own faith. In short, he holds no dogmas. He feels that if one has a contention, regardless of the subject, that one must offer evidence to support that contention. But he also suggests that science may have a thing or two to learn from the realm of the spiritual. He further adds that there should be no authority sources, including a didactic deity. Each individual must search for his or her own knowledge and spiritual guidance.

He said essentially the same thing during the convocation I attended. After emphasizing love and compassion and other homilies of sentience, he added (and I'm paraphrasing, but very little), "If these things mean something to you, fine. If not, then fine, too." In fact, I later learned from a friend of mine also in attendance—who gave my then girlfriend our two free tickets—that her husband turned to her after hearing that phrase and said, "You would never hear the Pope say that." With the exception of possibly the current Pope, I have to agree with him. The Catholic Church is an example of a very dogmatic religion that does not emphasize the same flexibility with its own beliefs. As with any church, the Catholic Church has done much to promote and accomplish beauty in the world. However, like many other religions, flexibility with its own beliefs is not one of its stronger characteristics. The Fourteenth Dalai Lama clearly emphasizes love, compassion, and flexibility with one's thinking above dogma. In my view, this is central to a healthy mindset, whether one is deeply religious or primarily scientific, or somewhere in the middle.

In the aforementioned book, The Dalai Lama reflects, "Who has not felt that sense of awe while looking deep into the skies lit with countless stars on a clear night? Who has failed to wonder whether there is an intelligence behind the cosmos? Who has not asked themselves if ours is the only planet to support living creatures? One of the great achievements of modern science is that it seems to have brought us closer than ever to an understanding of the conditions and complicated processes underlying the origins of our cosmos."[49] This lovely and emotional expression is extremely similar to the feeling and writing of the scientists I've read (Carl Sagan, Timothy Ferris, Frank Drake, Ann Druyan, and Neil deGrasse Tyson, for example) who feel awe, and even reverence when beholding the night sky or peering through a microscope. The universe is profoundly and deeply complex, and interwoven with both beauty and chaos. One need only look up at the stars on a clear night, as the Dalai Lama shares, to feel some of that beauty.

One of the central tenets of Buddhism, as the Dalai Lama emphasizes, is the concept of consciousness. Similarly to faith, consciousness is a term that is not readily understood. Like his feeling of awe with the cosmos, he relates deep human emotions with consciousness. He muses, "The joy of meeting someone you love, the sadness of losing a close friend, the richness of a vivid dream, the serenity of a walk through a garden on a spring day, the total absorption of a deep meditative state—these things and others like them constitute the reality of experience with consciousness...Any experience of consciousness—from the most mundane to the most elevated—has a certain coherence and...a high degree of privacy...The experience of consciousness is entirely subjective." [50] However, he acknowledges a paradox. Despite the obvious beauty we can experience through our subjective reality which feels highly conscious, because of its very subjective nature there is, he says, a lack of consensus on the meaning of consciousness (similar, in my view, to the confusion of the meaning of God). With that subjective nature of consciousness, plus the rigorous demand of science for non-subjective (objective) evidence, he notes, "Science...has made strikingly little headway in this understanding." [51] Clearly, he feels that science might dismiss some evidence of consciousness because it doesn't necessarily lend itself to objective experiment.

However, his lovely examples of experiences of consciousness above neither need the corroboration of experiment nor an external entity. They involve basking in the beauty of physical and emotional reality instead of focusing on a non-physical, abstract deity. I suggest that Buddhism is more naturally accessible and less of a mental struggle for this reason. Moreover, in this book the Dalai Lama suggests that consciousness may be a reality and state of mind that science has taken a bit for granted, or has at least underestimated. I think it is quite accurate for him to point out that consciousness is entirely subjective. As I have expressed a few times, I think that the same is even more true of religious belief. Religious faith and belief are a deeply subjective and personal matter, and one that should both be respected and remain subjective. What I like about the Dalai Lama's focus is that it relegates any religious or spiritual expression or concept—consciousness in this case, or faith, or spirituality—to the realm of the private ("...high degree of privacy...") which is where I feel religious belief and practice should remain: in private thought, prayer, buildings of worship, temporary holiday displays, unlimited and unconditional assistance and charity, and in any other way or anywhere else that is not public property or policy.

The Dalai Lama also discusses science and spirituality/religion specifically. He points to Einstein's General and Special Theory of Relativity and adds that it demonstrates that the universe is neither static nor eternal, but evolving and expanding. This, though challenging to many religious doctrines, is compatible with Buddhist cosmologists who also view the universe as evolving and expanding. To support this compatibility, he draws attention to the larger red shift in light emitted from distant galaxies as compared with the smaller red shift in light emitted by neighboring galaxies, both clearly indicating that the universe is curved and expanding. These observations are specifically and deeply scientifically aware.

And he emphasizes the similarity between science and Buddhism in placing primary importance on concrete evidence before scriptural and official authority. He states, "...in Buddhism scriptural authority cannot outweigh an understanding based on reason and experience. In fact, Buddha himself...undermines the scriptural authority of his own words when he exhorts his followers not to accept the validity of his teaching simply on the basis of reverence to him." [52] Just as in science, if new and compelling evidence is found which clearly contradicts a traditional Buddhist tenant, he says it is the Buddhist tenant that must change rather than adjusting the evidence to fit the ancient tenant. "If a [scientific] hypothesis is tested and found to be true, we must accept it. Likewise, Buddhism must accept the facts—whether found by science or found by contemplative insights. If, when we investigate something, we find there is reason and proof for it, we must acknowledge that as a reality—even if it is in contradiction with a literal scriptural explanation that has held sway for many centuries or with a deeply held opinion or view." [53] His perspective is very much in keeping with the progress and evolution of intelligence, and as he stresses, is applicable to both religion and science. It is also what I have been advocating: the marriage of the intuition and the intellect.

These ideas of his go the farthest in finding common ground between science and religion/spirituality. He specifically encourages both scientific thinkers and members of his own faith to investigate, with a healthy and open mind, *all* ideas, regardless of where they originate. He also encourages the avoidance of any dogma, scriptural *or* scientific. These, in my experience, are healthy principles in any thinking.

Thus, an openness to and skepticism of all ideas, coupled with emphasis on love and compassion, are the essence of the spiritual philosophy of the Fourteenth Dalai Lama.

Chapter 4

STEPHEN HAWKING

In the Introduction to Hawking's, *A Brief History of Time: From the Big Bang to Black Holes*, Carl Sagan related that in 1974, while on a coffee break from a meeting he was attending at the Royal Society of London presenting progress in the search for extraterrestrial life, he happened upon a larger meeting across the hall. That meeting was introducing new fellows into the Royal Society of London. He noted that, "In the front row a young man in a wheelchair was, very slowly, signing his name in a book that bore on its earliest pages the signature of Isaac Newton. When at last he finished, there was a stirring ovation. Stephen Hawking was a legend even then."

Hawking offers a very interesting proposition in his above book. After reviewing Einstein's General Theory of Relativity and the current theory of Quantum Mechanics, he shares that the scientific community is now searching for a *unified theory* [*] to explain the entire universe and how and why it came to exist. As one would expect, the question of the existence of God comes up frequently in Hawking's narrative; a unified theory of the universe obviously includes its origin. The reason for the search is simple, is compatible with both scientific and religious thinking, and is the definition of its prefix, *uni*. It is an attempt to offer *one* explanation for the entire universe.

Though there clearly appears to be two conflicting and opposing explanations for the origin and existence of the universe—for religion, it's the explanation of Creation by God, and for science, it's a search for one explanation by physics—Hawking and other scientists see little sense that the universe would also be conflicted by two opposing *scientific* theories. Hawking calls them "partial theories": General and Special Relativity, and Quantum Mechanics. Similarly to religion and science, these two scientific theories tend to blatantly contradict one another. So a "marrying" of the two theories is the goal.

Einstein's General Theory of Relativity deals with energy and the universe on the *macroscopic* level, what can be seen with the naked eye and

---

[*] This theory and Hawking are brilliantly portrayed in the Universal Pictures, Academy Award-winning film, *The Theory of Everything*, starring Eddie Redmayne as Stephen Hawking.

telescopes (as Neil deGrasse Tyson states, "The theory of the large." [54]). Einstein's famous equation is $E = mc^2$: Energy is equal to gravity (mass) multiplied by the square of the constant (the cosmic speed limit: light), and how energy is perceived relative to each individual human perception, hence "relativity."

Quantum Mechanics (and Special Relativity) deals with the subatomic realm, the universe on the *microscopic* level, what can only be seen with a microscope or other microscopically viewable or perceptible instrument. (what Neil deGrasse Tyson describes as, "The theory of the small." [55]). This is the realm of the action, motion, or "behavior" of subatomic waves and particles, and how they are perceived by, but also defy, human perception.

Because the *micro*scopic is, by definition, infinitesimally smaller than the *macro*scopic, it is much more elusive to observation. They are essentially opposites. And since Quantum Mechanics does not conform to Einstein's General Theory of Relativity, Quantum Mechanics is a special and significant theoretical discovery. In fact, it often utterly defies General Relativity. However, rather than treating General Relativity as inalterable truth and being threatened by or denying the existence of Quantum Mechanics (it's more like scientists feel confounded and confused) and attempting to force it to conform with General Relativity, like the Dalai Lama encourages of Buddhism, scientists have both acknowledged and are fascinated by the difference, and continue to accumulate and analyze the data that experiments with General Relativity and Quantum Mechanics reveal. Scientists are being very careful to avoid dogma, both by not stubbornly clinging to General Relativity and by not prematurely announcing a sloppy or weakly formulated unified theory.

Since gravity is common to both the scientific theories, the working term for this as yet elusive unified theory is called, practically enough, the Quantum Theory of Gravity. Hawking refers to the two theories—the General Theory of Relativity and Quantum Mechanics—as, "... the great intellectual achievements of the first half of this [the 20th] century." [56] But he also calls them both "partial theories" and proposes a "complete unified theory." He explains that the General Theory of Relativity is, "...the force of gravity and the large-scale structures of the universe...on scale from only a few miles to as large as a million, million, million, million (1 with twenty-four zeros after it) miles, the size of the observable universe." [57] Quantum Mechanics (Special Relativity), he says, is the opposite, and is,

"...phenomena on extremely small scale, such as a millionth of a millionth of an inch." [58] The problem, he points out, is that these two theories are inconsistent with each other. They conflict, so they cannot both be entirely correct. The challenge for scientists is to find a new theory in physics that will work for both. The goal, he says, "...is nothing less than a complete description of the universe we live in." [59]

Then he directly discusses a deity. To date, science has discovered natural laws that are consistent everywhere in the observable universe. These laws have remained consistent with the passage of time. He says, "These laws may have been decreed by God." [60] But then he proposes the question of a "...boundary condition at the beginning of time." [61] This means that *if* there was a beginning of time, was there or has there ever been a boundary to the universe? Or was it, is it, or has it ever been infinite? Those are certainly similar questions asked in religion, except that that the immediate answer is usually that those, and any questions like them, are beyond our comprehension because the universe is the work of God. Since God is beyond our comprehension, so is God's creation of the universe. Hawking poses, "One possible answer is to say that God chose the initial configuration of the universe for reasons that we cannot hope to understand. This would certainly have been within the power of an omnipotent being, but if he [God] had started it off in such an incomprehensible way, why did he [God] choose to let it evolve according to laws that we could understand?" [62] Because the laws of nature are consistent everywhere in the universe, he asserts, "It would be only natural to suppose that this order should apply not only to the laws, but also to the conditions at the boundary of space-time that specify the initial state of the universe...There ought to be some principle that picks out one initial state, and hence one model, to represent our universe." [63] Thus the motivation for the search for a unified theory; perhaps a Quantum Theory of Gravity.

He then questions the necessity of a deity. He suggests that since the Quantum Theory of Gravity might not require a boundary to space or time, behavior or original cause at the boundary would be rendered irrelevant and obsolete. There might be no need of a specified point in time, a designated threshold to allow for the universe's creation by an entity external to the universe. The universe may have been its own creator. He remarks, " 'The boundary condition of the universe is that it has no boundary.' The universe would be completely self-contained and not affected by anything outside itself. It would neither be created nor destroyed. It would just BE." [64*]

In his subsequent book, *The Grand Design*, Hawking and physicist, Leonard Mlodinow, proffer that though one can't prove that God doesn't exist, science essentially renders God unnecessary. In it, Hawking writes, "Because there is a law such as gravity, the universe can and will create itself from nothing. Spontaneous creation is the reason there is something rather than nothing, why the universe exists, why we exist. It is not necessary to invoke God to light the blue torch paper and set the universe going." [65]

~~~

I was visiting a friend one evening in mid-August, 2011, and he shared with me, among other fun and interesting television programs that he had recorded, the episode of Hawking's *Curiosity* series on PBS, "Did God Create the Universe?" It was most interesting to hear Hawking's deductive theory about why he thinks God *doesn't* exist. I had never seen it attempted as a physical/mathematical proof: adding the matter and energy and space together in the universe leaves no remainder for anything, including time. Therefore, since there is no remainder—nothing or no one else in the universe to do anything, and no time in which to do anything even if there was any*thing* or any*one* to do it—there can be no additional entity, no God. It is an interesting suggestion for proving that God does not exist. But it is only an attempt. It still falls under the category of the phrase, absence of evidence is not evidence of absence.

To Hawking's credit, his logic above *is* a quasi-proof of his theory mathematically. But the operative words are "quasi" and "theory." My friend who showed me the program asked, "Why couldn't a 'God' exist outside of the mathematical proof he proposes? Just because time seems to stop in a black hole doesn't mean God couldn't exist separately, *outside* the black hole." I think Hawking would admit that my friend posed an

---

[*] In his article, "Math Made Flesh," in the December, 2013 issue of *Discover* magazine (p. 44), Max Tegmark made a similar observation, but specifically about mathematics: "Our universe is not only well-described by mathematics; it may in fact *be* mathematics."

interesting question. But Hawking would probably also say (as would I), "What's the point?" In other words, like my earlier analogy of asking who or what created God, and then who or what created God's creator, one can always imagine something "outside" (akin to the view of C.S. Lewis), whatever one is describing, which may or may not be there. But, again, without physical evidence for an idea, one could keep imagining, inventing, conjuring (fearing?) something external and immaterial forever, *ad infinitum*. Again, it begs the question: And the point is...?

This is similar to an approach of defining God apophatically, or apophatic theology. The opposite of cataphatic (affirmative statement theology), apophatic means an argument through negation, or describing what God *is not* rather than what God is. This method is also referred to by the Latin term, *via negativa,* or "by or through the negative or opposite." It is a curious thought, like trying to reveal material hidden in the immaterial by turning the immaterial upside down—negating the immaterial. But it also seems indicative of straining to make sense of the senseless. I suggest that it points to an attempt of desperation, or reaching from the pointless to the *more pointless*.

Thomas Jefferson referred to the immaterial (the intangible), including God, as talking about "nothings." In a letter to John Adams on August 15, 1820, Thomas Jefferson remarked:

> To talk of immaterial existences is to talk of nothings. To say that the human soul, angels, God, are immaterial, is to say they are nothings, or that there is no God, no angels, no soul. I cannot reason otherwise…

Romeo says essentially the same to Mercutio (Act I, Scene IV) after the latter has ranted maniacally about dreams of Queen Mab:

> Romeo: Peace, peace, Mercutio…peace! Thou talk'st…of nothing.
> Mercutio: True, I talk of dreams,
> > Which are the children of an idle brain,
> > Begot of nothing but vain fantasy,
> > Which is as thin of substance as the air,
> > And more inconstant than the wind.

Imagination is wonderful, but I think focusing on something intangible or immaterial to the degree of doctrine and dogma is similar to talking of "nothings" and to my analogies of a child imagining a bogeyman, or a cat chasing its tail, or us trying to catch our own shadow. They are all in the realm of the imaginary, impossible, and probably pointless.

In the absence of more substantial physical evidence for God, we probably need to at least acknowledge that our ancient ancestors' focus on plural deities and our more modern focus on a single deity may indeed be us trying to catch our own shadow: external fictitious and mythological apparitions, like any god in human history. Perhaps, instead, we should trust ourselves and our minds to be just fine (and perhaps better off) without the comfort or necessity of any external entities, or a "God." A great many people/minds have already done exceedingly well without such a need.* Like Pierre-Simon de Laplace said to Napoléon Bonaparte, when the latter remarked that he saw no physical representation of God in Laplace's model of the Solar System, "Sire, I have no need of that hypothesis." And George Carlin compared God to Humpty Dumpty. Humpty Dumpty, said Carlin, couldn't be "...put back together again...," because (like God) he doesn't exist. Stephen Hawking would probably agree.

---

* This, as I proposed in Part 1, Chapter 5 should be far less possible, or even impossible. If God exists and created our minds, it should not *work* to think without believing in God. Why would a God create in life the *possibility* of not believing in that God if believing in said God was the intended focus/maxim for survival and peace? It makes very little sense. In other words, if God did indeed create the universe and life, perhaps God's existence should be obvious. But then, advocates for "Free Will" would likely weigh in again.

Chapter 5

GERALD L. SCHROEDER

That God exists separately from, or outside the known universe is also proffered by physicist, professor of Bible studies, and author, Gerald L. Schroeder. In his book, *The Science of God: The Convergence of Scientific and Biblical Wisdom*, he proposes that God is not simply the totality of the laws of nature but the intelligence responsible for them. Like Alan W. Watts, he acknowledges the concept of pantheism as seeing the universe as, "...a unity operating through the diverse laws of nature." [66] But he also sees pantheism as stopping short, "...of the crucial final step." [67] Pantheism posits that the universe, the laws of nature, and God are all synonymous, one-and-the same. Schroeder advocates that pantheism is missing the biblical blanket within which pantheism is wrapped. He states, "...the laws of nature are understood as a projected manifestation of an infinite wisdom that transcends the physical universe, within which the physical universe dwells, and of which the physical universe is composed."[68]

He also makes an argument against the idea of "chance" occurrences in the universe. The idea is that if God created the universe, all the physical matter and energy that we observe in the universe is operating according to God's initial direction, not independently by its own natural law. He says events like cometary collisions can give the feeling that life is, "...a game of chance...," [69] that life as, "...a dice game...," [70] is one conclusion. But he reminds that it was mammals who survived 65 million years ago, not the dinosaurs. "Perhaps," he offers, "instead of fortuity, we have discovered a cosmic tuning to the flow of life. Rather than chance, the fossils that mark the demise of the dinosaurs may be evidence for a teleology." [71] This is certainly a possibility. The key word in his last sentence above is *may*. I think teleology may be correct. It is certainly a question worth considering. But it is also one that needs to be open to being wrong.

The word *teleology* itself is interesting. Some words, perhaps because they are used frequently, transmit their meaning to the reader immediately. Teleology is not one such word. At first glance, it looks like it would mean "the study of distance." But that would be the root word, "tele," not "teleo." The root word, "teleo" means, "entire, perfect, complete."

Coined in 1740 by German philosopher, Baron Christian von Wolff, from the Modern Latin form, "teleologia," teleology is the study of final causes, or evidence of "design" or "purpose" in nature. This hypothesis suggests that the universe and nature (and life, especially human life) are too beautiful and meaningful to have sprung "by chance or accident," and that all we observe in the universe is evidence *itself* of a "Creator," just as we are products of our parents and just as any life form creates its progeny. It is very understandable that this thought occurs. However, simply because something appears incongruous to us doesn't mean that the universe has to operate according to our perceptions or preconceptions. In fact, just the opposite has been true in many cases. Humans have been wrong many times in their assumptions of how the universe must operate. So the idea of teleology as the foundation for the creation of the universe, and all life in it, could also be mistaken.

One of Schroeder's boldest proposals (that I touched on in Part I) is his attempt at a reconciliation between the six days of creation in Genesis and 6,000 years of human history, with the scientifically estimated 13.799 billion-year-old universe, 4.6 billion-year-old Earth (measured from the time since the Big Bang), and 2.5 million years since the appearance of the genus, *Homo*, or the earliest known ancestors of modern humans.

Two things seem clear at first: 1) that the scientific dating has the advantage of time with regard to much greater accuracy of mathematical measurement, and 2) that the biblical dating and the scientific dating—differing by an immense margin—cannot both be right. However, in his book, *Genesis and the Big Bang*, Schroeder attempts to demonstrate that they can indeed both be right.

Sympathetically, he admits that the wording of the first chapter of the Bible clearly creates a conflict—between the six days of Creation in Genesis and the scientific 15 * billion-year-old universe—for those desiring both a belief in God and an accurate understanding of modern science. There is no avoiding the issue.

So he asks, "Which understanding is correct?" Then he answers, "Both are. Literally. With no allegorical modifications of these two simultaneous, yet different, time periods." [72] He asserts that with no allegory or mathematical adjustment, six 24-hour days and 15 billion years can be

---

* He writes the former calculation of 15 billion years consistently. The current, though still approximate, calculations of the age of the universe are 13.799 billion years, and more recently, 12.5 billion years.

perceived as exactly the same by the former theory he emphasizes is now fact: Einstein's discovery of Relativity. The two time durations can begin and end simultaneously. In other words, God's perception of time is different from ours. We only perceive the time intervals as vastly different when in reality, by Relativity, they are identical.

He then clarifies what he refers to as "stretching time." He says that modern archaeology is consistent with the Bible from the time after Adam, and that the biblical record can also be consistent with archaeology and paleontology, but only, "...if we practice an exercise in logic that we refer to as 'stretching time.' This is the very heart of the matter. How do we stretch six days to encompass 15 billion years? Or the reverse, how do we squeeze 15 billion years into six days?" [73] He bolsters the proposition by citing the Psalm of David 90:4: *A thousand years in your eyes are as a day that passes.* He explains that the Psalm, "...has the feel of time seeming to pass at different rates for different participants in an event, but not necessarily being different in reality. Einstein demonstrated that when a single event is viewed from two frames of reference, a thousand or even a billion years in one can indeed pass for days in the other...Einstein's *law* of relativity tells us that the dimensions in space and the passage of time are not absolute. Their measurement is an intimate function of the relationship between the observer and the observed." [74]

This proposal is not without merit or credence. It is a creative and curious hypothesis. It uses, as he points out, the fact of General and Special Relativity as evidence for the following: that varying perceptions of time could explain and validate both the six days of Creation *and* the scientifically estimated 13.799 billion-year-age of the universe.

But unlike Einstein's law (as Schroeder respectfully acknowledges as fact), the proven age of the universe and the fact of the evolution of life, this hypothesis of Schroeder's seems at best a leap of logic. It is imaginative and does draw from scientific theory and fact. But it is also tinged with reluctance to abandon ancient lore—an exaggerated effort to retain the speedy account of Creation when stronger scientific evidence reveals its discrepancy with a vastly older universe. Like each of Cinderella's sisters trying desperately to squeeze their foot into her single slipper, to use a word in Schroeder's own phrase, it's a "stretch." While Schroeder may certainly be correct, there are probably many atheists who would argue that his proposition is just another anxious attempt at clinging to fantasy.

Chapter 6

PATRICK GLYNN

It has been a tendency and popular in many periods of human history to think of the universe in geocentric terms. Genesis, from the Bible, is a prime example in the religious view. Claudius Ptolemy is one of the most notable examples in ancient astronomy. These examples, no matter their notoriety or naiveté, were understandable perspectives for their time. After all, the Earth is the planet on which all of us live for most of the duration of our lives. A few humans have had the incredible fortune to orbit the Earth and the Moon. Fewer still have actually *walked* on the Moon! But most of us are, in a manner of speaking, prisoners of our planet. So, since most of us are *physically* Earth-bound, it makes sense that we would also tend to *think* Earth-bound.

Such an Earth-bound, and therefore relatively limited, perspective is likely an influence on the contemporary scientific idea of the "anthropic principle." The adjective, anthropic, derives from the Greek word, *ánthrōpos*, meaning simply, "human being." (Sagan offered, and I concur, that the term should really be "anthropo*centric*." Like any geocentric model, the focus is still on human centrality in the universe.) The anthropic principle holds that the very existence of human beings on Earth, in all our varied and beautiful complexity, points almost by default to universal human inevitability. Not only is the planet Earth special for life in the Solar System (akin to Ptolemy's geocentric model), but human beings are special for life in the universe (akin to Genesis in the Bible). Since the moment of the Big Bang, the matter and energy in the universe not only contained the requisite raw materials for human life, but human life was its inevitable destination. Humanity won the universal lottery.

Like the argument against the "chance" or "accidental" origin of the universe, there is also a religious view of the anthropic principle. It holds that God created the universe *for* humanity, with central importance and purpose. This perspective stems, I think, from a similar perception to the original anthropic principle—that the chemistry and mathematics needed for something as intricately beautiful as human life could not have emerged and flourished on this one planet without some degree of divine cause or at least divine intervention. It bears some similarity to the concept of "Intelligent Design."

Richard Dawkins is quick to remind, though, that the anthropic principle originated as a scientific idea—posed in 1973, by Australian theoretical physicist, Brandon Carter—not a religious one. Similar to my outline above, Carter's anthropic principle suggests that the chemical and mathematical probabilities in the universe themselves predetermined human life. But contrary to the concept of Creation, Carter's proposition does not require a deity for any initial creation. Theologians, Dawkins says, misconstrue or augment this original anthropic principle by requiring a deity for its inception; this in an attempt to offer proof for God.

The theological interpretation of the anthropic principle is this: since human exist on Earth, no life has yet been discovered elsewhere, and God is the Earth's Creator in Genesis, then the universe is pre-programmed by God for human life on Earth. Therefore, human existence alone is proof of the existence of God. In a succinct statement: If humans exist, then God exists (implying that humans are God's creation). Or definitively, but hastily put: Since humans exist, God exists.

However, Dawkins rebuts this misinterpretation in, *The God Delusion*. He remarks, "It is a strange fact...that religious apologists love the anthropic principle. For some reason that makes no sense at all, they think it supports their case. Precisely the opposite is true. The anthropic principle, like natural selection, is an *alternative* to the design hypothesis. It provides a rational, design-free explanation for the fact that we find ourselves is a situation propitious to our existence." [75] What Dawkins is saying is that since the anthropic principle points to universal human inevitability, the religiously inclined swap physics for their "Originator." God replaces math and chemistry. But again, as Dawkins corrects, "...two candidate solutions are offered to the problem (of Earth as the sole life-friendly planet). God is one. The anthropic principle is the other. They are *alternatives*." [76] In other words, some theologians borrow the anthropic principle and simply give God credit for it, hence its slight similarity to "Intelligent Design." In my view, however, the original anthropic principle is also a bit unnecessary. It seems to me just a sophisticated term for natural law.

In, *A Brief History of Time*, Stephen Hawking explains the anthropic principle in detail and in two versions. The two versions are called the weak and the strong. The weak version, he says, states that in a universe that is presumed infinite in both space and time, conditions that allow for both the possibility and evolution of intelligent life will only be found in isolated regions which are governed by space and time. Beings in those areas should then not find it unusual that they exist. Hawking humorously adds, "It is a bit like a rich person living in a wealthy neighborhood not seeing any poverty." [77] The strong version, he says, is one that allows for multiple universes or many regions in the same universe. Either in each universe or in each region there could be completely different sets of natural laws. It is more likely that in only a few of these universes or regions complex life might arise and evolve into highly intelligent beings. If those beings asked (as we do) why they exist, he says the answer is simple, "If it had been different, we would not be here!" [78]

Hawking then raises two arguments against the strong anthropic principle. The first involves the inconsistency of the multiple universes or regions in one universe. In multiple universes, since each would likely have its own natural laws, each would be unobservable to the rest. And if each, in fact, has the same natural laws, so could be observed by all the others there would be no distinguishing one universe from the other and they would all reduce to one universe, or back to the weak anthropic principle. The second involves the contradiction between the fact of our extreme lack of centrality in the universe compared to the proposition that humanity was the universe's inevitability. The comparison is incongruent. Hawking notes, "...the strong anthropic principle would claim that this whole vast construction [universe] exists simply for our sake. This is very hard to believe. Our solar system is certainly a prerequisite for our existence, and one might extend this to the whole of our galaxy to allow for an earlier generation of stars that created the heavier elements. But there does not seem to be any need for all those other galaxies..." [79] Put another way, evidence points much more to Earth and life being a chance and random phenomenon at the fringes or outskirts of only one of many trillions of galaxies.* That fact renders the anthropic principle all but obsolete.

Regardless of the validity of either the weak or the strong anthropic principles (whether naturally destined or divinely intended) and their presumption of our primary importance in the universe or universes, many people simply have great difficulty with the idea that the universe and life

---

* This is one of the points at the heart of what Carl Sagan referred to as The Great Demotions. Demoting any notion humans harbor of our centrality or primary importance in the cosmos.

could generate itself, in any fashion, regardless of the clarity and accuracy of any anthropic principle explanation. Some people cannot fathom a universe and life without a "Creator." It's too large a mental and psychological hurdle.

This might also have roots in human sexual reproduction. It is clearly impossible for a woman to become pregnant without the union/conception of a sperm and an egg. The male-female sexual union is the "creator" of a new life, which develops into a human being—even in-vitro fertilization joins the sperm with the egg to form a human zygote. The creation of life, as we know it, seems to require some form of a creator. The idea that the "creator" of the universe could be the universe *itself* (as Hawking offered in Chapter 4 that the universe would just *be*) is totally foreign and completely contrary to most religious doctrine. That all the essential molecular and cellular elements necessary for life would assemble *themselves* to form life sounds equally contrary and preposterous.* In other words, the likelihood that the universe would have successfully "rolled the dice" to create *any* life (much less human life) randomly, by chance, by accident, by its own inertial energy, seems inconceivable to many people. And they may be exactly right. Life may indeed require divine direction, or at least divine assistance (though atheists certainly find *those* proposals inconceivable and preposterous).

That said, it is equally possible that because we are predominantly Earth-bound, that particular and perpetual perspective prevents some of us from imagining alternative origins, or from even moderately conceiving of causes

---

* Dawkins also relates in, *The God Delusion*, "The Ultimate 747 Gambit," or "The Tornado in the Junkyard" counterargument against random chance. These are different names for the same analogy: In a junkyard, all the old parts of a Boeing 747 are randomly lying around. If the natural phenomenon of a tornado hit the junkyard, the odds that the tornado, as it hurled everything into the air —including all those Boeing 747 parts—would successfully reassemble and reconstruct the original Boeing 747, are realistically nil. The theory is used to refute the proposition that the universe and life could create themselves. But the argument uses misleading logic. It doesn't factor the obvious: that evolution works over billions of years. Random tornado damage takes only minutes. Therefore, the nearly impossible odds of a tornado perfectly reassembling the scattered parts of a Boeing 747 is inapplicable.

or sources unconstrained by our own provinciality. It's hard to be non-subjective and cosmically aware of ourselves.

~~~

Patrick Glynn, Senior Technical Policy Advisor in the Office of the Deputy Director for Science Programs at the U.S. Department of Energy, is the author of *God: The Evidence: The Reconciliation of Faith and Reason in a Postsecular World* (Forum, 1997). In this book, he discusses his interpretation of Carter's anthropic principle. But he begins, in the Introduction, by stating that his early mindset and practice of skepticism was shaken and supplanted by the "...all-but-incontestable..." [80] realization that there was in fact a God, and a soul, and an afterlife. He senses a time soon when skepticism and unbelief will diminish even among intellectuals. He thinks new evidence is surfacing which will supplant secular society, evidence in support of, "...'faith,': the soul, the afterlife, and God." [81] Though only from his Introduction, these senses he shares seem somewhat vague in their advocacy for God. Strong on generalities but weak on specifics.

He continues to relate that it did not make him happy to acknowledge atheism. Though he hoped to be proven wrong, he observed that the whole of western philosophy seemed to be a refutation of religion, a contradiction of the concept of God. "Reason," he thought, "was the only path to truth...The yearnings for God, for a life after death, for justice in the universe, were just that: yearnings, wishes, with no basis in fact... humans...had widely varying notions of God or 'the gods.' All these were fictions, human 'conventions,' that human beings, in their ignorance, had mistaken for nature, reality...We were on our own." [82]

However, he says that while he was, "plumbing the depths of nihilism," [83] he learned of a transformation in science. In a lecture to the International Astronomical Union in Poland in 1973, physicist and cosmologist, Brandon Carter, discussed the idea of the anthropic principle which seemed to be a counter-refutation of science, or at least one hypothesis of science. The anthropic principle challenged the random universe.

Then he elaborates, but employing what Dawkins considers the religiously misinterpreted view of the anthropic principle. He sees Carter's idea as clearer evidence that the universe did not form autonomously with humans one of many accidents. But unlike Carter, he interprets the anthropic principle theologically by putting God at the wheel. He states, "For hundreds of years science had been whittling away at the proposition that the universe was created or designed. Suddenly, scientists came upon a series of facts that seem to point toward precisely such a conclusion—that the universe is the product of intelligence and aim, that in the absence of intelligent organization of a thousand details vast and small, we would not exist." [84]

However, to use an inverse argument, just because humans exist doesn't mean that the anthropic principle (the original or the religious misinterpretation) is the answer by default. And when he mentions a "...series of facts..." the author doesn't cite or itemize the specific facts to bolster his proposal. Similar to C.S. Lewis, in my estimation Glynn's error is assuming that in order for human beings and everything in the cosmos as we know it to exist, it would have to be produced (or created) by an "Intelligence." We could neither be autonomous nor the product of random chance.

Many of us (including, it seems, Glynn) place primary value on human life, so it would be easy to suppose that we are the predominantly valuable life form in the universe. I think we are certainly *one* very valuable form of life and highly intelligent, but I don't think that we are the *only* valuable or intelligent form of life on our planet or, hopefully, in the universe (just ask anyone who studies or has studied chimpanzees, dolphins, or whales). We have no way of knowing that yet. To decide that we are the primarily important intelligent life in the universe seems to me a premature assumption. It actually sounds arrogant, conceited, and ego-centric.

Glynn spoke directly to that presumption. Carter, he said, had emphasized that the Copernican discovery of the heliocentric universe demoted human privilege and centrality. But, said Glynn, "...the explanation was not so simple. Too many values had seemingly been arranged around the central task of producing us... even if our position in the universe was not 'central,' it was 'inevitably privileged to some extent.'" [85] Privileged because the molecular elements that would form life and humans were present in the universe at the Big Bang. So the anthropic principle holds that the universe and life were not random chance. Glynn again, "The vast, fifteen-billion-year evolution of the universe had apparently been directed toward one goal: the creation of human life." [86] Clearly an anthropocentric argument. The existence of the universe was intended for homo sapiens.

Glynn then ties Carter's explanation of the anthropic principle to Intelligent Design. He argues that since life was "...pre-planned..." [87] from the origin of the universe, all the laws of nature and molecular structures had to be "...just right..." [88] at the outset. In other words, if even the slightest difference in formation and chemistry had occurred, the universe would be extremely different from the one in which we have found ourselves. Says Glynn, "Far from being accidental, life appeared to be the goal toward which the entire universe from the first moment of its existence had been orchestrated, fine-tuned... Indeed, today the case for design looks very strong." [89]

These arguments from Glynn (and Carter) are, in my view, once again making erroneous and illogical assumptions. It is erroneous and illogical to *assume* that any of the order we observe in the universe proves a "Designer," and to suggest or imply any designer without defining the designer.

~~~

One simple formula for testing whether logic leans more correct or erroneous are "If...then..." statements. They are another principle of deductive thinking that I learned in my senior high school geometry class. They are a very helpful way to compare conflicting ideas, illuminate and adjust faulty logic, or confirm correct logic. They help make sense of confusion. Before applying "If...then..." statements to Glynn's comments above, let me share two other examples. They are amusing and almost identical examples of faulty logic.

First, a picture in the textbook, *Geometry*, by Harold Jacobs (Second Edition; the one used for my geometry class), shows a suburban neighborhood of identical-looking houses and yard landscapes. Parked in front of each house is an identical Volkswagen (VW) van. The caption reads: "If the world looked like this and you wanted to buy a car that sticks out a little you probably wouldn't buy a Volkswagen Station Wagon. But in case you haven't noticed, the world doesn't look like this. So if you want a car that sticks out a little, [then] you know just what to do."

And second, a 2013 television commercial for the Audi Q5[*] shows the same kind of scene as in the Jacobs geometry book. It is a neighborhood

---

[*] http://www.youtube.com/watch?v=soJs3ZUYtLI

where every house and family is nearly identical, including everyone's cars (though not a VW van). An Audi Q5 drives up to drop a young boy off at school. It is clearly different from the other cars in the neighborhood, and a classier one at that! The point of the commercial is nevertheless the same as the picture above in Jacob's geometry book: the Audi Q5 is the car to buy because it is the *only* different car. Humorous text at the end of the commercial quotes Oscar Wilde: "Be yourself. Everyone else is already taken."

Just as with Glynn's arguments on the anthropic principle, both the picture of the VW vans in the Jacobs textbook and the Audi Q5 television commercial use faulty "If...then..." statements to promote their points/sell their products. *If* the world looked like the picture/commercial, *then* the premises would be accurate. However, since the world doesn't look like the picture/commercial, neither car will be as unique because the initial premises/conditions are erroneous. The scenarios in which the VW van "sticks out" and the Audi Q5 is unique are being compared don't exist. I think that the situation is similar for Glynn's arguments supporting the anthropic principle. The scenarios set for them are wholly speculative and logically erroneous.

Applying an "If...then..." statement to Glynn's interpretation of the anthropic principle might be, "*If* we exist, *then* God created the universe for us." We certainly seem to exist. The universe certainly seems to exist. But does it immediately follow that humans were the *intended result* of the universe, and that a "God" is the *obvious instigator* for the intention. I think the answer is it's possible, but not obvious.

The universe does have extraordinary mathematical laws by which it appears to operate. The fact of life in the cosmos appears to be governed by those same mathematical laws. But I don't think it automatically follows that the beauty and phenomena of the universe, including the mathematical laws and human existence, means that a Creator, God, is necessary or required (it is, of course, still possible). It is an erroneous assumption, a faulty premise. A serious argument would have to eliminate random chance with more detailed and thorough examples.

Or, another, inverse "If...then..." example for Glynn's view of the same interpretation might be: "*If* the anthropic principle is incorrect, *then* humans (and maybe the rest of the observable universe) would not be here, or would be very different." Again, this is possible but not necessarily true. The statement begins by assuming the validity of either interpretation of the anthropic principle. It is beginning with an assumption, which is never wise. It is true that the universe could have generated very different conditions than it did, and we would know no better because either we might not be here to observe the difference, or our perceptions might be different and we might be asking different questions. But the universe could also have randomly generated life—including humans and everything in the universe—with neither an Intelligence nor ideal mathematical odds, but by simple natural law. In which case, the anthropic principle would be an entirely pointless concept.

In an austere scene of official conference in the novel, *Aztec*, by Gary Jennings, the protagonist Mixtli and the Lord Speaker Motecuzóma (Montezuma) are discussing what to make of recent repeated reports: Reports of strange and large white men who recently landed by even more strange vessels on the nearby coast. Motecuzóma makes the assumption, or supposition, that because of their size, lighter skin color, and enormous vessels, they must be gods. To which Mixtli offers this tentative and humble thought, "Lord Speaker, I have erred before. I may err now in supposing the white men to be no gods or forerunners of any god. But might you not err more gravely in supposing that they are?" [90]

Like Mixtli's remark, I think the safest and most honest answer/rebuttal to either Brandon Carter's original anthropic principle, or the theological interpretation of the anthropic principle is, as with any hypothesis, perhaps but perhaps not. Glynn needs to prove how the mathematical formulas/numbers that exist in nature come from an Intelligent Designer, a Creator, and not as a result of the natural phenomena of the universe. The feeling that generates his (I think insufficient) logic is still rooted too much, it seems to me, in the provinciality of our narrow, Earth-bound perceptions.

Like the perception of some of our ancestors, both interpretations of the anthropic principle err on the side of imagining "the world revolving around us," a perception most of us now consider juvenile. Plus, the theological interpretation of the anthropic principle is, I think, influenced by another old and elementary notion: that because God created the universe and Earth for humans, God must *look* human ("God created man in His own image"), and like a human *male*. It is a very terrestrial and patriarchal perspective. Again, it also seems arrogant. Those who purport the anthropic principal—particularly theologically—seem not only to promote primary human significance in the cosmos, but to also to lean toward the idea of a patriarchal deity.

Chapter 7

JOHN POLKINGHORNE

The Reverend John Polkinghorne is a notable and interesting example of a man who, in a manner of speaking, "has his feet in both camps." He is a theoretical physicist who, after teaching mathematical physics for years at the University of Cambridge, resigned to become an Anglican priest. He is the author of many books on both the subjects of science and religion, with a stress on the similarities, symbiosis, and synthesis between the two.

Polkinghorne's perspective on the blending of science and religion is not dissimilar to Patrick Glynn, though he is likely more steeped in scientific knowledge. Along with the ideas of teleology and the anthropic principle, Polkinghorne discusses the origin of *value,* a quality that most of us would refer to—about our own most meaningful treasures and grandest accomplishments—as "valuable." He feels strongly that the universe is not the result of chance or random occurrences, but is the product of careful and intentional intelligence.

However, like the words, God, believe (belief), and faith, value is also a somewhat vague word because it refers generally to what is valu*able* to each person. And, of course, what is valuable to each person is different because feelings about what is valuable to each of us are, once again, subjective, the same reason for my sense and encouragement that religious belief remain a personal and private practice.

It is interesting that in contemporary politics, the general word, value (or in its plural form, values) is used to indicate a specific issue. "Family values" is an example. And the word, values, by itself, is often used when someone, or a political candidate, is citing a category of their political agenda. Again, a vague word used when a specific one would be more helpful and clear. (I suspect that the lack of more specific choices of words in politics may be entirely intentional, designed to manipulate and lure rather than adequately inform voters. Could the same be said of organized religion with its believers?)

So just as I'm arguing that the words, God, believe, and faith are used with too unspecific or unclear an understanding, so, too, a word like value has been used and accepted with too general and unclear an understanding.

In his book, *Belief in God in an Age of Science,* Polkinghorne asserts that value is the underlying energy of the universe, the "mind of God" [91] (somewhat similar to the view of C.S. Lewis). He says, "Theism presents an adequately rich basis for understanding the world in that it readily accommodates the many-layered character of a reality shot through with value." [92] He allows that science is, "...a partial reading of the 'mind of God...,'" but qualifies, "Yet there is much more to the mind of God than science will ever discover." [93] He stresses that human moral intuition, aesthetic senses, and religious inclinations are, "...intimations of the perfect divine will...," "...sharing in the Creator's joy...," and, "...whispers of God's presence...," [94] respectively. Thus, he summarizes, "The natural understanding of the value-laden character of our world is that there is a supreme Source of Value whose nature is reflected in all that is held in being. Otherwise the pervasive presence of value is hard to understand." [95]

Polkinghorne is certainly unambiguous in his focus on a religious perspective, both by beginning this particular passage with the word *theism,* and by the other religious references, most of which are capitalized: "mind of God," "God," "Creator," and, "Source of Value.*"* Regardless of one's philosophical leaning, he is not being unclear with his vocabulary in pairing value with theology.

There is no question that theism is a form of the word, theology, and both words denote belief in God, so he is due credit for some specificity. What is interesting to me here is the same thing that I find curiously presuming about many other religious perspectives, namely the assumed attribution of value and morality to a god rather than to the autonomy of nature. When he says, "Otherwise the pervasive presence of value is hard to understand," he is essentially saying that he doesn't understand how value (or morality) can exist without a god. This strikes me as an emotional/subjective opinion/position rather than an opinion formed from having considered enough other reasonable possibilities and perhaps even tested some of them.

But Polkinghorne's opinion is not unique, nor is it necessarily wrong. I have heard many religious people argue that value and morality are not something that can be scientifically quantified, and they may be right. But it certainly does not directly follow that if value and morality did not originate scientifically or within the laws of nature, that they then obviously originated from a god. That would also be an erroneous "If...then..." statement. It would be as erroneous as presuming that value and morality are born from nature alone. Both would be jumping to a premature conclusion. Possible, yes. Evident, no.

Similar to the search Stephen Hawking related for a unified theory of the universe by a proposed "Unified Theory of Gravity," in an August 1996 essay entitled, *So Finely Tuned A Universe* (adapted from his lecture at Connecticut College) [96], Polkinghorne discusses in detail *his* search for a unified theory of the universe, but through science to theology. It is another, and quite admirable example of a genuine attempt at blending science and religion while simultaneously respecting the individuality of both.

He begins by stating that, in his view, theology is the best basis for a unified theory. "Theology is the drive to find the most profound and comprehensive understanding of our encounter with reality." With that as his foundation, he outlines two "...alternative strategies..." in searching for a unified theory, and reminds that with any explanation, *Ex nihilo nihil fit*, or "Nothing comes from nothing." It is a slight assumption that everything must have some kind of creator, some instigator. Or, that nothing can spontaneously create itself.

The first alternative strategy, or starting point he describes as, "...the brute fact of the physical world...the brute fact of matter as your unexplained basis." He highlights the Enlightenment philosopher, David Hume, as an example of that view. The second alternative strategy. or starting point he describes as, "...the brute fact (if that's the word to use) of God. In other words, one can appeal to the will of an agent, the purpose of a Creator, as the basic unexplained starting point for understanding the world." He says, obviously enough, that the first strategy is that of atheism and the second strategy is that of theism. It is his desire to defend why he feels that theism, a belief in God, gives the most comprehensive and unified understanding of the universe.

He acknowledges that the scientific laws of nature are indisputably evident throughout the universe. What he insists is that the laws of nature are not sufficiently satisfying as a unifying basis to explain the universe. For him, the laws of nature do not account for morality, purpose, and love in the universe. He thinks the laws of nature actually "...point beyond themselves...to a deeper level of intelligibility." He sees the fact of a rational order of the universe as speaking clearly of a "Creator" for that rational order. He says, "The two fit together like a pair of gloves. That is a rather significant fact about the world." Then asks, "Why, we should ask, are our minds so perfectly shaped to understand the deep patterns of the world around us?"

Polkinghorne then delves into quantum physics to further his theological argument. He says that physics is not confined to, "...the everyday world, but the counter-intuitive, unpictureable quantum world." He correctly notes that the quantum world is one that we cannot visualize—see directly—but one that we can measure by intricate mathematics. It's another way of saying, seeing is *not necessarily* believing. Or, something doesn't have to be visible to exist. To support that point he states, "The theoretical physicist Paul Dirac discovered something called quantum field theory which is fundamental to our understanding of the physical world. I can't believe Dirac's ability to discover that theory, or Einstein's ability to discover the General Theory of Relativity, is a sort of spin-off from our ancestors having to dodge saber-toothed tigers. Something much more profound, much more mysterious, is going on." He even offers a reason why many scientific agnostics contest extreme atheism. He says, "...many agnostic scientists feel that the rational beauty and the finely tuned fruitfulness of the world suggest that there is some intelligence or purpose behind the universe."

Clearly, the inability for anything at the quantum level to be visualized, seen with the unaided eye, could be compared with the apparent inability to see God. The intricately beautiful can also be invisible. Polkinghorne certainly seems to be drawing that comparison—that, like quantum physics, God is invisible. But unlike what is known about quantum physics, God is also taught as incorporeal, omniscient, and omnipresent, qualities that quantum physics may or may not possess. The foundation of Polkinghorne's proposition of a unified theory is, unequivocally, God.

Regardless of whether one thinks more religiously or scientifically, and concurs with a Creator as the source of both, I must say that his ideas in the lecture/essay strike me as particularly thoughtful and thorough. I credit him for describing and explaining, with specific examples and concepts, exactly what he means and why. He clearly feels convinced that the mere presence of humans in the universe is too incredible a phenomenon to be explained by scientific fact alone, or even predominantly by science. For him, the "art"—the profundity of the existence of the universe, life, and humans—requires an "Artist."

That said, it is still most curious to me that no matter how well the various sciences have done (and will likely continue to do) in presenting extremely clear and concrete physical evidence and explanations about nature and the universe—of which we were previously ignorant, thereby rendering most ancient gods to mythology—that *any* modern gods still seem necessary. Plus, the transformation of multiple gods into a single god, entity, or being, personified as "God,"—as the necessary explanation for the *entire* universe—still persists. As I've said before, that persistence may be because it's entirely right. But it may also be correct that regardless of the veracity or fallacy of God, or the success and sufficiency of scientific explanation, the innate human psychological and emotional need to believe in at least *one* god, a "Supreme Being," may simply be too strong.

Later though, again in *Belief in God in an Age of Science,* Polkinghorne writes with subtle sensitivity and awareness about the pitfalls of premature religious conclusions, and the importance of a multi-faceted, or unified and experiential understanding of nature: "I am a passionate believer in the unity of knowledge and I believe that those who are seeking...understanding...and who will not settle for a facile and premature conclusion to that search, are seeking God, whether they acknowledge that divine quest or not. Theism is concerned with making total sense of the world. The force of its claims depends on the degree to which belief in God affords the best explanation of the varieties, not just of religious experience, but of all human experience." [97]

This support of a focus on the gamut of human experience in religious thought and practice is most impressive. Though from a theological perspective, it is exactly the point I feel strongly about of the necessity for the combination of intuitive and intellectual thinking in the pursuit of any study, particularly the study of the origin of the universe and on the question of the meaning and existence of God. Polkinghorne's refreshing comments encourage non-segregation and an openness to discovery, whether one interprets the discoveries theologically or scientifically, or a combination of both.

Chapter 8

STEPHEN JAY GOULD

Maybe the most pragmatic and diplomatic approach to the debate between science and religion came from science historian, evolutionary biologist, and former Harvard University and New York University professor, Stephen Jay Gould. Gould proposes a somewhat mollifying and almost segregated approach to the two disciplines. Instead of attempting to find common ground, Gould notes that science and religion have evolved separately by their own nature and should remain separate. He thinks this apparent because, in his view, they each offer such fundamentally different human needs that it is unnatural to try to find common ground.

Gould coined the acronym, NOMA, or Non-Overlapping MAgisteria (*magisteria* being the plural of the Latin word *magesterium* meaning "the office of a teacher"). According to Gould, science and religion are so different and unrelated that they should not be overlapped. It is an interesting proposition. It certainly takes the pressure off either discipline to have to conform to the other. But it also risks avoidance of what should be a healthy dialogue and debate. On one hand, there is a point to "letting well enough alone." On the other hand, growth is rarely accomplished when deeply entrenched ideas and notions are never challenged. Finally, NOMA seems to me too much of a posture of resignation. It's choosing the "safe route." If Galileo Galilei and Nicolaus Copernicus had lived by the equivalent of NOMA, how much longer would much of the world have been ignorant of our heliocentric Solar System?

In Gould's, *Rocks of Ages*, he cites the 1950 encyclical of Pope Pius XII entitled, *Humani Generis* (*Humankind*, or *Humanity*). Though not an admirer of Pius XII, Gould nevertheless found himself in agreement with one of the encyclical's declarations regarding science. Catholics, cautioned Pius XII, could accept scientific facts about the evolution of the human body, but they also had to accept that God had given the human body a soul. Gould found himself accepting this papal decree because it matched his own view of science and religion, that both had their separate magisterium, or domain of teaching authority.

Instead of trying to reconcile or merge religion and science, Gould somewhat echoes Pius XII's emphasis that the two are intrinsically incompatible, inert. Gould describes the difference, which simultaneously explains his book's title, "...the net, or magisterium, of science covers the empirical universe: what is it made of (fact) and why does it work this way (theory). The net of religion extends over questions of moral meaning and value. These two magisteria do not overlap, nor do they encompass all inquiry (consider, for starters, the magisterium of art and the meaning of beauty). To cite the old clichés, science gets the age of rocks, and religion the rock of ages; science studies how the heavens go, religion how to go to heaven...Many of our deepest questions call upon aspects of both for different parts of a full answer." [98]

A very interesting and well-formulated approach. It's hard to argue with clear, creative thinking. Nevertheless, I would still argue that not overlapping science and religion, each by avoiding challenging the other with critical questions, does a service to neither. As I pointed out previously, I'm not at all sure that science can never answer questions of morality. Nor would I say that religion cannot answer questions of theory or fact. I do think that in the typical teaching of both science and religion that morality has been more the domain of religion and fact more that of science.[*] But I feel somewhat opposite to Gould. As well-intentioned and pragmatic as Gould seems to be with his offering of NOMA, I think that what is needed is *precisely an overlap*, a sharing of ideas between science and religion, not their separation. It's similar to my feeling (and this is certainly not my original idea) that what could continue to help diminish much prejudice in the world is more interracial relationships/marriages. Different races dating, marrying, and having children together not only brings races closer and to a deeper, healthier understanding of each other, but the offspring of interracial couples are consistently and incomparably beautiful and intelligent. I have not met one biracial or multiracial person who was not strikingly attractive: physically, mentally, and personally. Biracial procreation seems to be a nearly perfect genetic blueprint. Likewise (though perhaps not as quickly), I

---

[*] A humorous note: In Season 5, Episode 19 of *The Simpsons*, Superintendent Chalmers hears Ned Flanders (who is acting as interim school principal since Principal Skinner was fired for havoc occurring at the school on his watch) recite a devotional over the school intercom system. Ned Flanders ends the devotional with "Thank the Lord." Superintendent Chalmers exclaims, "Thank the Lord? That sounded like a prayer. A prayer. A prayer in a public school! God has no place within these walls, just like facts have no place within organized religion!" Clearly, a very funny reference to the separation of church and state in the Bill of Rights. But my idea of the cooperation between science and religion would not infringe on the First Amendment!

think that the union and cooperation of science and religion could only serve to strengthen, embolden, and nourish both disciplines.

Chapter 9

JAMES PORTER (J. P.) MOORELAND
AND
KAI NIELSEN

Though perhaps not quite as famous as the debate between Clarence Darrow and William Jennings Bryan on the teaching of evolution in the "Scopes Monkey Trial," the debate between philosopher, theologian, and Christian, James Porter (J.P.) Moreland, and atheist, Kai Nielsen, is nevertheless an excellent example of a healthy head-to-head debate on the comparison of religion and science.

In the book, *Does God Exist?: The Debate Between Theists and Atheists*, J.P. Moreland defends one's innate epistemic right to believe in God and the unlikelihood of morality having been created spontaneously from the Big Bang. Kai Nielsen argues that since gods originated as anthropomorphic deities, and that there is as yet no evidence of anthropomorphic deities, that one cannot really know what one means when they say they believe in God. He implies that the concept of God seems to be relegated to the realm of the imagination.

Mooreland starts by asking if it's reasonable in modern scientific society to still have a belief in God. His answer is yes. He hastens to add that he does not mean that the existence of God can be proven mathematically, but that he thinks that there are rational reasons for believing in God and that one is, "well within her epistemic rights in believing that God exists." [99] He quotes an anonymous scientist, which actually sounds a little bit like the anthropic principle, "The universe seems to have evolved with life in mind." [100] He also quotes Paul Davies, theoretical physicist at Cambridge who said, "It is hard to resist the impression that...the universe, apparently so sensitive to minor alterations in the numbers, has been rather carefully thought out...the seemingly miraculous concurrence of these numerical values must remain the most compelling evidence for cosmic design." [101]

Mooreland then outlines several specific arguments. One, that the Artist's (God's) signature is in the molecular makeup of life: our DNA. He references Carl Sagan's example of a potential and unambiguous extraterrestrial message. Sagan, Mooreland relates, said that all such a message would need to contain would be not just order, but information. Information clearly distinguished from the laws of nature. It doesn't even need to be translated. Just the simple presence of information would indicate intelligence. Mooreland adds, "Well, what is sauce for the artificial goose ought to be sauce for the DNA gander, and I argue that the information in DNA molecules is evidence of intelligence behind it." [102] Two, he also expresses the doubt or unlikelihood that morality would have been generated by the Big Bang. He finds it hard to imagine that our sense of right and wrong is a product of the universe, like matter and energy. He says, "It just doesn't seem that the Big Bang could spit out moral values, at least not at the rate it spit out hydrogen atoms." [103] Third, he mentions and disagrees with the atheistic argument that there are no irreducible truths in the universe, even moral ones. The atheistic view is that life creates morality itself through evolution. Mooreland concurs with the idea that morality is too intangible and transcendent from physics for our morals to autonomously generate with evolution. Morality, he feels strongly, is a divine gift from a "Creator." Finally, he points to archeological confirmations of the Bible and other religious texts, the questions of how not only morality but consciousness could spontaneously spring from matter, and the fact of the billions of people who do believe in God.

All of these arguments from Mooreland are worth considering and examining. For starters, what does Moreland mean by "epistemic rights?" Since the word *epistemic* means, "knowledge or the conditions for acquiring knowledge," "epistemic rights" could mean "the right to acquire knowledge." If so, this is a right that should go without saying. Clearly, one has a right to know, understand, to believe, and believe in anything. But does that mean that because one has that right, that *any* knowledge or belief is correct, concrete, well-defended, and infallible? If the knowledge or belief is simply a personal sense but with too many remaining questions for someone else, then I stress that while the belief is definitely within one's rights, it is not a concrete enough belief or knowledge for adequate sharing or corroboration.

Next, when he cites the example of Sagan's criteria for distinguishing extraterrestrial intelligence, in my opinion he is not specific enough. To be unambiguously intelligent, the message would have to be not just any information, but information that non-intelligent or uninhabited worlds would less likely produce. Sagan's later suggestion of a possible extraterrestrial message was presented in his only novel, *Contact* (it was made into a motion picture, posthumously, starring Jodie Foster). The "message" in this story was received by the SETI (Search for

ExtraTerrestrial Intelligence; the capital T is mine for clarity of the acronym) scientists in the form of a radio wave palimpsest. It began with a cyclical repetition of the consecutive prime numbers—which ordinary matter and energy would probably not emit—thus highly suggesting intelligent origin. (Disappointingly, the real-life SETI has never received such a signal from space; much radio "noise" but no mathematical numbers, much less *prime numbers*.) Two other layers of the palimpsest were a television video (of terrestrial origin, received by the extraterrestrials, and subsequently retransmitted by them to us), and the blueprints for building a space-faring machine (for traveling to the extraterrestrials). Those three layers were explosive and unambiguous physical evidence in the story (and would also be if they were actually received!). Therefore, it was not just general information that Sagan was eluding to, but *specific* information. That particular point from Moreland is another example of the relative absence of specificity within religious arguments. To be fair, Sagan's novel was published well after Moreland's commentary, but Moreland certainly could have offered a little bit more in the way of other strong specifics when he raised Sagan's earlier proposition as an example.

When he quotes the anonymous scientist who refers to the universe having evolved with "...life in mind." he sounds similar to C.S. Lewis's and John Polkinghorne's description of the Deity as a kind of "mind." And Paul Davies's comment that, "...the seemingly miraculous concurrence of these numerical values must remain the most compelling evidence for cosmic design." is a curious statement. The key phrase in Davies's remark is "seemingly miraculous." I would argue that often something only *seems* miraculous until one studies and understands it more thoroughly. Then it moves, perhaps, from the miraculous to the majestic, or maybe just the matter-of-fact. Something appearing or seeming to be miraculous is not compelling evidence.

It is so often the error of humans (with either science or religion) to easily jump to conclusions, to make assumptions. In Ruiz's, *The Four Agreements*, that I referenced in Part I, Chapter 4, when outlining my Four Fundamentals, the Third Agreement is "Don't Make Assumptions." This is of course borrowed from the cliché, "To assume makes an ass of you and me," (which, surprisingly, Ruiz does not mention). Ruiz includes it (and rightly so) because humans make incorrect assumptions all the time even though we know the cliché and its obvious wisdom. It is also wise for Ruiz to include it as a *reminder*, which is really the purpose of all his "Agreements." It would probably be unfair to say that religion tends to jump to conclusions and assumptions more often—though by the very pre-acceptance of the existence of and belief in God before study, religions tend not to set a better immediate example of withholding assumptions—and that the scientific method better insures that assumptions aren't made (which, I realize, is perhaps an assumption in itself). But Moreland's supporting arguments for believing in God seem to err on the side of assuming: presuming that choices of morality have to be of divine origin. I feel that it is an assumption, from anyone, that our perception of morality and spiritual purpose and peace cannot be a product of physics alone, independent of divine origin, or perhaps even proof of nature as its own creator.

In a word, Kai Nielsen thinks that belief in God is incoherent. To him it is, therefore, also irrational to believe in God. He starts by referencing the Greek god, Zeus. Zeus, he says, is a prime example because most mythical gods originated as anthropomorphic entities. Zeus is probably the most well-known anthropomorphic god in mythology.

Many, if not all, Greeks of antiquity believed in Zeus, just as many people today believe in God. But if most adults now have no trouble understanding that Zeus and all the Greek gods were myth and superstition, why then is the modern and contemporary God not also suspected as myth? Nielsen says that Zeus and the other Greek gods are now known to be myth because of the simple reason than there was no physical evidence for their existence, other than the believer's imaginations. Is there really much better evidence for our contemporary God?

Furthermore, notes Nielsen, if a modern, anthropomorphic God could be detected directly, it would not be the God of Judeo-Christianity. The reason is because, unlike Zeus, the Christian God (as well as the God of any monotheistic religion) is considered incorporeal. Zeus was not only corporeal and anthropomorphic, Zeus was depicted as a human male, exactly as most modern monotheistic gods have been imagined. Nielsen stresses, therefore, that believing in an incorporeal monotheistic God, or any incorporeal entity for which there is no clear evidence or image, is simply incoherent.

He also makes the point of a problematic premise—a definition or description that is as vague as its premise. Phrase descriptions of God tend to be no more clear than the word, God. For example, some standard phrase descriptions of God that Nielsen gives are, "God is the maker of the heavens and the earth," "The being transcendent to the world on whom all things depend and who depends on nothing himself," "...the being of infinite love to whom all things are owed," "...the infinite sustainer of the universe...," "...the heavenly father of us all...," and "God is the Ultimate Mystery." [104] But, says Nielsen, we need to have at least some concrete idea about what we are talking about if we are going to use phrases like that to describe in what (or in whom) we have faith and believe. None of the preceding phrases are for Nielsen anything approaching clear descriptions of God. These phrases are as, or more, problematic than the premise.

Then Nielsen makes a most interesting analogy. He essentially asks the religious believer to put themselves in an atheist's shoes when the word, God, is mentioned. Since the word, God, is nearly impossible to define, to an atheist God is empty of meaning. To make his analogy, Nielsen randomly makes up a word: *poy*. He asks how the religious believer would feel and react if he encouraged them to believe in poy? It is almost a guarantee that a religious person would scoff at the idea. He says that for the non-believer or atheist, the feeling is much the same regarding belief in God. Any historical reference aside, and going only by clarity of definition, to Nielsen choosing to believe in God is much the same as choosing to believe in poy. It makes almost no clear, rational sense.

In the same vein, it also makes no sense to allocate the concept of God to its own category or reality—*sui generis*, "of its own kind," or "unique." This proposed solution essentially remedies the lack of a clear definition of God by making God immune to and separated from the laws of physics. And not only immune to and separated from physics, but the *creator* of physics. It is a very convenient solution. As Nielsen rebuts, "God just has a distinct reality which is different from any other reality. It is not like mathematical reality; it is not like physical reality and so forth. But such talk of being *sui generis* is, I believe, evasive." [105] It essentially means that God is separated from, the cause of, and transcendent beyond physics, which immediately (and dismissively) solves the problem of defining God. However, to the rational and atheist mind, it only kicks the can down the road.

Clearly, Nielsen's remarks are from an atheistic point-of-view. But they do raise legitimate questions. For example, in many modern religious stories for children, God is indeed illustrated as anthropomorphic: a larger-than-life, slightly stout and senior male figure with white hair, a white beard, and a white robe. Redress the same figure in a red-and-white coat-and-hat and black boots and the figure is instantly Santa Claus, " 'Father' Christmas," a fictional character. Shouldn't the striking similarity in these iconic patriarchs, and thus the implication of God as also possible fiction, be obvious to all adults?

The depiction of something non-human as a human figure—particularly that of a deity, and a male deity—is the *meaning* of the word, anthropomorphic. Since many children are taught both an anthropomorphic God and Santa Claus, it should not be surprising that, as with Santa Claus, unless the imagery of an anthropomorphic God was later clarified as metaphor by their parents, as those children grow into adults they would more likely retain some if not all of the anthropomorphic association for God.

As I've mentioned already, God is certainly most often referred to by adults as the "Father," a male human being. (God is referenced in some passages of the Bible as ministering in a mother manner, and some people use the word, mother, as a substitute for the word, father, when referencing God out of personal preference. But the standard, default gender reference for God is Father, with the proper noun upper case "F".) So if God is *not* anthropomorphic, then what image is meant by the proper noun, Father? Why the human patriarchal depiction? It is confusing imagery. Therefore, it is perfectly reasonable for Nielsen to ask and challenge what any religious person means when they imagine God. Obviously, I am asking the same question.

One response I have heard is that the anthropomorphic depiction is a *practical* way to represent God. Since God is deemed *super*natural, it is difficult to accurately represent the deity in natural visual terms. I understand the dilemma. But, of course, this generates further questions. First, if God is indeed supernatural, and no physical image is immediately apparent to represent the Deity, then why is a *male human being* the default choice? Why a human being at all? Or, if a human figure is used, why not a female God? Or if physical form for God is discarded altogether—including the anthropomorphic model—how is one certain that the deity in fact exists?

It is like Sagan's analogy in the chapter, "The Dragon in My Garage," in his book, *The Demon-Haunted World: Science As a Candle in the Dark.* If God cannot be clearly drawn, seen, touched, heard, audio-recorded, videotaped, or verified by any other means of physics, what does it really mean to say that God—or "Allah," or "Yaweh," or "poy," for that matter, or any other name given to a modern, monotheistic deity—exists? Is it really sufficient to play the card of sui generis? This is exactly Nielsen's point. I would add though that Nielsen might also be violating Ruiz's Third Agreement by assuming as well. Nielsen might be hard-pressed to offer physical evidence and proof that God *does not* exist.

But I would still argue, as I have before, that the onus of proof lies with the ones making the proposition. Atheists did not propose the existence of God, religions did. Proof is less (or perhaps not at all) required of those who *question* a proposal already made, particularly if evidence for the proposal is scant or nonexistent. From Nielsen's perspective, like the requirements of verification by proof for most other disciplines, physical proof is also needed for God.

Chapter 10

KEN HAM AND BILL NYE

A more recent and significant debate between religion and science took place on February 4, 2014.[106] It was entitled, "Is Creation a Viable Model of Origins?," and was held at the Creation Museum in Petersburg, Kentucky. It featured Ken Ham and Bill Nye. Bill Nye is a science educator, professor at Cornell, and the CEO of The Planetary Society. He is best known, though, for his 1990s PBS children's series, "Bill Nye the Science Guy." Ken Ham is the founder of Answers in Genesis, a Christian fundamentalist organization which includes the Young Earth Creationist Ministry, the Creation Museum, and most recently, the Ark Encounter: A Life-Size Noah's Ark Experience.

The debate was substantive, and well prepared and presented by both men. As with any debate, the most convincing arguments depended to a large extent on the subjective prior convictions, opinions, and reactions of the audience, both live at the Creation Museum and streamed live online.

Ken Ham began the debate and made many specific points. His strongest point—upon which all of his other points were based—centered on his suggestion to separate science into two subcategories: *observational* science and *historical* science. Ham said these two categories or branches of science should be delineated because they serve different functions and yield confusing results and misinterpretation of evidence if combined. To Ham, only one of those categories of science is reliable as evidence: observational. He asserts that this is because all anyone can do is observe something in present time. Eye-witness testimony. Anything in the past—history—cannot be accurately observed as evidence because the event is no longer happening. In other words, any evidence from the past to prove evolution cannot be reliable or viable because, in Ham's words, "We weren't there." Past evidence is invalid.

Bill Nye's rebuttal comprised essentially two points as well. First, that Ken Ham is mistaken to suggest that science has two *separate* categories. To Nye, there is no separation of observational science and historical science—they are one in the same. As he puts it, "Science is science." The process of science is to *observe* evidence in *history*—all present observed time instantly becomes history—which is clearly combining the two into one. And second, that there is an abundance of physical evidence of evolution—fossils, collected specimens, rock strata, plate tectonics, multitudes of varying species proving that no present life is exactly the same since single-cell organisms first emerged millions of years ago instead of thousands of years ago, Einstein's General Theory of Relativity, etc.— which clearly shows that life and the universe are billions of years old, not 6,000 years old. All one has to do is be interested enough to seek and study the available evidence. One can "be there" in history intellectually if one observes the physical evidence already discovered, and the physical evidence *yet to be discovered.*

I would like to make two points of my own about this debate. First, that denying the validity of clear evidence—such as the fact of the fossil record— is very nearly as unreasonable and obliviously unobservant as denying, for example, the existence of gravity. Gravity is ever-present and plainly evident. It's easy to prove. It is also why gravity is the strongest candidate for a *"unified* theory" of the universe. The fossil record is not as immediately obvious, but it is accessible and apparent with a willingness not to deny that it can be found, and *has been* found. Second, I would differ with Ken Ham's point that past, or what he calls historical, evidence is invalid. Genesis in the Bible is also about the past. So according to Ham's invention of, and argument against, historical science, Genesis should also be untenable evidence because, to borrow his phrase, "we weren't there" either. Why should Genesis be accepted as valid past evidence if any past evidence that challenges Genesis cannot? It seems an inconsistent and irrational prohibition. It also seems ridiculous and ignorant. Like the phrase "argument from ignorance," if you begin with an irrational or ridiculous premise, you will only get irrational and ridiculous arguments and conclusions, which further perpetuates ignorance. This should apply to everything, including science and religion.

Though I admire both men for agreeing to participate and being well prepared in the debate, I found Bill Nye the more reasonably and rationally compelling. Though I certainly have more of a scientific leaning, any fundamentalist viewpoint, it seems to me, is beginning in irrationality and denial which is rarely an effective way to winnow wisdom. Logic is logic. Evidence is evidence. And, as Nye says, "Science is science." Illogic can't be logical just because someone says it came from God. That particular promotion of illogic speaks poorly of the concept of God. It promotes a God that (or who) is irrational, untrustworthy, and should certainly not be accepted solely on faith.

Chapter 11

KEITH WARD

Another term that is used by religion to describe the scientific view of the universe and explanations of its origin is the adjective *materialistic*, or its noun, *materialism*. Obviously both a form of the word *material*, this view stems directly from the desire and insistence by science for physical evidence. Materialism can sound like a focus on the importance of all things physical at the expense of anything emotional, spiritual, intuitive, etc. Both C.S. Lewis and Gerald Schroeder seemed to indict science as "materialist." This, in my opinion, is untrue about science, but the misunderstanding is not surprising.

Plainly put, we refer to many items of physical matter as material: fabric, the earth elements (soil, wood, metal, body tissue), and wealth and currency (i.e. Madonna's, "Material Girl"), to name only a few. Concisely put, physics is material matter. That said, though I and many scientists stress the insistence on physical evidence, it is also inaccurate to say that science is *only* concerned with physics. Science certainly focuses on what physical/material evidence suggests, implies, and reveals about nature and the universe, but science is just as much about being awed and humbled by the beauty and grandeur of the universe as is religion. Awe and humility are emotional responses, not intellectual. However, as I expressed in the Introduction, the emotions may be tied to physics as well, and therefore, material.

So the use of the term *materialistic* to describe science is at best a misconstruing, and at worst a derogatory reference by religion to its perceived lack of sensitivity to emotional intuition by science. Religion perceives science as oblivious to and even chastising of intuition. This is also untrue. Science certainly cautions to be skeptical when using intuition, particularly as the primary, or only source for evidence. But scientific quest, experiment, and exhilaration—dreaming, discovering, defining, and delighting—would be stagnant without the stirring sense of intuition. Intuition could be said to be the initial inspiration of science, and perhaps the first step of the scientific method.

This reference by religion to science as materialistic is accompanied by its criticism that science is devoid in its explanations of purpose to the universe, as I've already shown with other theological authors such as John

Polkinghorne. Both of these are addressed by Keith Ward in his book, *God, Chance, and Necessity*. Unfortunately, his commentary often takes a negative and even defensive tone. He writes that a form of materialism he has observed, "...has become fashionable in recent years..." is, "...entirely hostile to religion...," and "...mocks any idea of objective purpose and value in the universe..." [107] He cites several brilliant scientists—Francis Crick, Carl Sagan, Stephen Hawking, Richard Dawkins, Jacques Monod, and Peter Atkins—stating that many of their books, .."openly deride religious beliefs, and claim the authority of their own scientific work for their attacks." [108] He asserts that their work as scientists is irrelevant to religious faith, their espoused materialism a minority rather than a majority societal viewpoint, and that they regard theologians as not to be taken seriously or worthy of respect. He remarks "...theologian, of course, is for them, only a term of abuse." [109]

He states further that materialism can be strongly criticized for ignoring the facts of consciousness, truth, and virtue, and that it is misguided to think that scientific search and discovery can reveal or corroborate anything about religious values. Nor does he think that scientists consider seriously enough the work of major and esteemed theologians. Instead he feels that scientists are, "...content to lampoon the crudest versions of the most naive doctrines they can find. Their treatment of religion shows no dispassionate analysis, but a virulent contempt which can only be termed prejudice." [110] Ironically, while Ward accuses scientists of being prejudiced in their criticisms of religion, he seems to do just that in return, by using derogatory language to deride a viewpoint that challenges his own. He chooses words and phrases of condescension—"entirely hostile," "content to lampoon," "crudest versions," "naive doctrines," "virulent contempt"—rather than ones of valid criticism.

To my understanding, materialism is not a term used by scientists to describe their own philosophy. Rather than being an indication of denial, it more likely implies that any form of the word material would be insufficiently evocative for describing the beauty of science. If by materialism Ward means the physical evidence that these scientists insist on obtaining in order to verify pronouncements of knowledge, then probably most good scientists (and really many of us) are to some degree "materialists." (As in the example of Madonna's song that I mentioned, the terms *materialist* or *materialism* also carry with them the derogatory connotation of a fixation on physical acquisitions or material wealth. That is a very different focus than requiring physical evidence for a claimed phenomenon.) When Ward says that materialism "...has become fashionable in recent years...," it is interesting to note the opposite: the centuries in which credulous belief has been readily accepted/believed ("in fashion") by comparison. Therefore, insistence on "material" or "physical" evidence might be viewed more as a recent improvement rather than an impediment to knowledge.

When he suggests that this form of materialism "...is entirely hostile to religion....," does he mean that any specific criticism about religion should be taken as hostile? Does criticism imply hostility? Deriding criticism as hostility sounds too much like the stereotypical reaction of many religions that tend to feel threatened by intellectual inquiry. And when he says that this materialism, "...mocks any idea of objective purpose and value in the universe..." or "...theologian, of course, is for them, only a term of abuse...." his use of the word, mocks, and the word, abuse, sound derisive and disdainful. Few skilled scientific authors mock ideas with which they disagree, nor do they in any way abuse theology. They can be soberly critical of theology and religion, but not mocking or abusive. Mr. Ward's choices of these words are most unfortunate. They make him sound angry and pugnacious rather than forming a well-constructed rebuttal.

He also mentions that the scientists, "...claim the authority of their own scientific work for their attacks."[111] While the authors he specifies certainly point to their own work as part of their evidence (in addition to the evidence of other scientists and writers), it is actually a fundamental principle of science to shun the weight of authority. Aldous Huxley, in a sermon at St. Martin's Hall on January 7, 1866, stated, "Every great advance in natural knowledge has involved the absolute rejection of authority." And Sagan, in *Cosmos*, "It [science] is not perfect...It is only a tool. But it is by far the best tool we have, self-correcting, ongoing, applicable to everything. It has two rules. First: there are no sacred truths; all assumptions must be critically examined; arguments from authority are worthless. Second: whatever is inconsistent with the facts must be discarded or revised. The obvious is sometimes false; the unexpected is sometimes true." And in *Law and Order: Special Victims Unit (S.V.U.)*, "Fashionable Crimes," the character, John Munch (Richard Belzer), says this to Olivia Benson (Mariska Hargitay), after baby-sitting Olivia's on-screen-son, Noah. "I taught him a very important life lesson: 'Always question authority.'" Then he says playfully to Noah, "Repeat after me...*why*?" Noah repeats, "Why?" Olivia bursts out laughing! Then John adds, "You can thank me when he's a fully-functioning antidogmatic atheist!" [112]

The funny but pertinent lines from *S.V.U.* aside, Ward would have done well to revisit at least Huxley's and Sagan's works before making such an assertion.

The writers with which he is irritated are some of the finest writers in history. They became superb writers by steeping themselves in the works of their esteemed literary predecessors. They did not reject or ridicule the strictures of science. They submitted to the discipline of science and reaped its rewards. It is not the mocking, as he says, of "...any idea of objective purpose and value in the universe..." that scientists have in mind. There is a legitimate question posed: just like the words, God, believe, and faith, what exactly is *meant* by "purpose," "value," and "materialism" to the universe?

Science observes that the universe is governed by natural law. But the laws of the universe/nature have not been observed by science as necessarily having a purpose or value. The exact genesis of natural law is still a mystery, until more is discovered about the laws of nature before, during, and after the Big Bang. There may be *no* purpose to the universe. Nature may have no other cause or design than an infinity of random, chance reactions. We need to be willing to recognize this as a possibility. The concept of "purpose" or "value" to the universe may only be applicable to living organisms which, since they appear to have a much shorter life span than much of the rest of the matter in the universe, they would have more need for a concept of purpose. If you have *less time* you have to *purposely use the time*.

We humans are obviously living organisms. We sense a need for a purpose to our lives: the need to survive, love, and create accomplishments in the extremely short time of our lives. But the universe may have no such need. We may be projecting *our need* for a purpose to life on the universe because it is the only perspective we know. While this is normal, it is also important to recognize once again how we might be projecting our human perspective on the universe when the universe may not operate that way at all. The question of purpose and value may be ours alone. It may be that life is the beautiful and phenomenal result of random, molecular physics. In a secular sense, that in itself could be called *miraculous*.

On the other hand, if the universe *does* have a purpose for its existence, it is important that we not only feel and sense it intuitively, but that we understand it intellectually as well. If those two aspects of our thought process don't work together, our minds inform us by making us think of questions. That mental process is there for a reason. One can, of course, choose to ignore the need for an answer to a question. Or worse, it can simply not occur to one to ask. Using a term such as *materialism* to describe science, particularly in a negative way, does not help to further our understanding of the universe, intuitively or intellectually, whether it has a purpose or not.

Ward later gives a clearer, less accusatory assessment. He states that, "The root of materialism is probably a firm commitment to empirical scientific method as the only reliable way to discover truth. Commitment to experimental method is in itself entirely commendable." [113] He cautions, though, that excluding any and all non-scientific searches for truth could result in as limited an understanding of reality as an exclusively religious search for truth. This is a more thoughtful, balanced, and insightful point. Extremes of any kind are probably unhealthy and limiting in the long-term, and like science, religion carries its unique rewards. He summarizes, "The root of theism is probably a commitment to worship and prayer, which carries with it the belief that aesthetic, ethical, personal, and relational aspects of experience provide distinctive paths to truth, and that the highest truth of all lies in apprehension of an objective reality of supreme beauty and goodness." [114]

This is also a much more cogent, objective, and respectful observation. However, at the end he seems to suggest that the highest truth is a "supreme" one, which science does not offer but religion does (and by the word, "highest," ironically excluding every other truth just as this author is warning science not to do). An objective point of view would really be to acknowledge that a Supreme Being *may or may not* exist, but that religion is right to want the emotions, intuitions, and spirituality included in scientific inquiry.

But later, Ward again reverts to the negative. He laments those who see a universe devoid of God. Such a universe to him is, "...without point or hope..." [115] He also sees a scientific and rationally understood universe as Godless and, "...the result of deep ignorance, itself the product of immersion in self-centered desires." [116] It is, he says, "...a picture that creatures have largely drawn for themselves, a world estranged from God, pitiless and indifferent. From the viewpoint of such an estranged world, nature itself comes to seem cruel and uncaring, a breeding ground for millions of suffering, unhappy creatures, living and dying without point or purpose." [117] And he feels that when the concept of God is abandoned, the principles of Darwin turn divine beauty into meaningless molecules and lifeless laws of nature. In his view, this is "...the projection of a despairing mind in a universe estranged from the source of its existence...It is a universe in which egoism can corrupt the good and bring suffering to the innocent..." [118] In such a universe, he affirms that God's purposes, "...are destined to be realized, so that every suffering creature can be brought to experience an infinite personal good, and the positive potentialities of the universe can be brought to fruition." [119]

For better or worse, nature can seem to be cruel and uncaring. This is undoubtedly the origin of the phrase, "Life isn't fair." That phrase comes from the feeling that nature doesn't seem to make our health, general welfare, or the sparing of our lives (or any life) priority; particularly those lives which promote and deliver the most good. But it is likely that nature has no volition, positive or negative, so any question of its self-motivation may, itself, be meaningless.

Still, it is a fact that nature selects extinction more strongly than survival. That fact is certainly devoid of care on the part of nature. Nature seems not to have the slightest "intention," positively or negatively, about whatever lives are in its path. Nature just *operates* and life has to learn how to survive within. The "egoism" and "projection of a despairing mind" that Ward refers to seems to see Darwinian evolution and natural selection as bleak, meaningless, and without value compared with the concept of God. It is curious and a pity that in Ward's very attempt to show science as unfeeling, devoid of purpose, or self-centered, that his own derisive attitude toward intellectual scrutiny and skepticism in the absence of physical evidence casts a shadow of negativity on his otherwise potentially good points.

Later in the same book, he is not negative but still appeals to, "...a being of transcendent power and value...," which he refers to as, "...value-transforming..." [120] Ward seems to prefer the premise of value generated from an entity to the idea of an autonomous universe (the latter expounded by Daniel Dennett). He also encourages trust in the testimony of at least some who describe sincere religious experiences. He identifies and characterizes those experiences as, "...beyond human comprehension...," and offers that this, "...transcendent power...," [121] sets limits on human understanding which is why the concept of God does not conform to logic. But logic might be analogous with light. Light is the cosmic speed limit. Logic may be the human thought limit. To the religious mind, God has *no* speed or thought limit.

On the other hand, unlike Stephen Jay Gould, Ward encourages the union of reason and faith. Reason he describes as, "...the deepest understanding of the cosmos." [122] Faith he describes as, "...the trusting response to the mystery of divine love." [123] He summarizes, "Only reason and faith together can bring humans and all sentient creatures that maturity that is their proper form of life. Only then can the universe achieve that fully conscious relationship to its creator in which its created potentialities for good can find their proper fulfillment. That is the ultimate purpose of God and the goal of evolution." [124]

While this is more positive and respectful to both science and religion, it is still interesting that he uses many words/phrases to describe God that are more vague: "transcendent power," "value-transforming," "beyond human comprehension," and "divine love." It's hard to be clear and specific about a topic if one uses words or phrases to support the topic that are themselves unspecific. However, he *is* more specific about what the word, purpose, might mean in the next-to-last sentence above: "...the created potentialities for good." This is clearer and more optimistic. But it is also possible with or without a god. In short, like the presumption of God in Genesis, the premise of God's existence is still being assumed by Ward.

Chapter 12

NEIL deGRASSE TYSON

Without a doubt, the most impressive, engaging, and popular scientist of the current generation is astrophysicist, cosmologist, and science communicator, Neil deGrasse Tyson. In addition to his distinguished credentials and enormous influence in the scientific community, his enthusiasm and encouragement for the wonder and joy of scientific discovery is extraordinary. As well as the author of many best-selling books, he is the Director of the Hayden Planetarium at the American Museum of Natural History. And he is the host of the PBS television series, *Cosmos: A Spacetime Odyssey* which has brought science, physics, and astronomy back into the public awareness and experience. Unsurprisingly and fittingly, Tyson was a deep admirer of the late Carl Sagan, whose original 1970s television series, *Cosmos*, Tyson has revived and expanded. Articulate, jovial, humorous, brilliant, and profoundly well-educated, like Sagan, Tyson makes the exploration of science and the universe beautifully accessible.

As would be expected, he has also tackled the relationship between science and religion. Of his many interviews and speaking engagements (some available online), three that bridge these two subjects struck me as particularly insightful and historically thorough.

The first was on the PBS program, Moyers and Company. Bill Moyers interviewed Tyson in a three-part series on January 10, 17, and 24, 2014.[125] They discussed a wide variety of issues pertaining to science and religion. Perhaps the most intriguing question Moyers asked was more rhetorical. He speculates that many people leaving Tyson's planetarium presentation—on the invisible and elusive forces of dark matter and dark energy—would likely conclude that the inability to directly see either is finally the missing scientific evidence and proof for God. After replying wryly, "Is that a question?!," Tyson continued to say that throughout history, wherever people have reached the limit of their intellectual understanding, that limit is what they then relegate to a deity. He states that wherever there is mystery, God gets invoked. Over time, philosophers have referred to this as, "God of the Gaps." (In my words, instead of "God is in the details," it becomes, "God is where details are temporarily missing.") He says that if this is where one puts God, then God is, "...in every receding pocket of scientific ignorance."

240　A Supreme *Question*

God is often viewed, generally, as the mystery of the universe. But Tyson reminds that science is solving mysteries of the universe continually, and more and more rapidly. In his words, "one-by-one." He challenges that God needs to be more to the religious person that just, "...where science has yet to tread." Therefore, in response to the hypothetical question posed by Moyers—of any religious person asking if the mystery of dark matter and energy is God—Tyson replies that if the reason for the question is because it's still a mystery, then those religious people should not be surprised if that mystery is also solved soon by physics. In Tyson's words, "...get ready to have that [dark matter and energy as God] undone."

The second and third examples were eight years earlier. Tyson spoke on two occasions during Session 2 of the symposia, Beyond Belief: Science, Religion, Reason, and Survival, held November 5-7, 2006 at the Salk Institute for Biological Studies in La Jolla, California. On November 5, his discussion was titled, "Intelligent Design." On November 7, he explored the psychology and physiology of religious thinking in a presentation called, "A Final 'Sermon' on Cosmic Perspective." [126]

In his discussion on Intelligent Design, he points out first that, as with many religious ideas, the thinking behind the concept of Intelligent Design is not new but an historical pattern. He highlights scientists, Claudius Ptolemy, and, Isaac Newton, as examples. Both men, he says, evoked God only when they confronted the limits of their ability to explain aspects of natural and celestial phenomena scientifically. Anything they could not explain by physics they deemed the domain of the Deity.

For example, though he was obviously incorrect, Ptolemy, in his *Almagest* (*The Greatest*), formulated the geocentric universe using his best efforts at scientific thinking. It was an honest and admirable attempt to understand the Solar System and the universe. But Tyson relates that where Ptolemy could not calculate, he deferred to a deity. He quoted Ptolemy, "...when I trace at my pleasure the windings to and fro of the heavenly bodies, I no longer touch the earth with my feet: I stand in the presence of Zeus himself and take my fill of ambrosia."

Isaac Newton, discoverer of the law of gravitation (between any two objects) and laws of motion (between the Earth and the Moon)—both clearly and without question scientific fact—did exactly the same. In his, *Philosophiæ Naturalis Principia Mathematica* (*Mathematical Principles of Natural Philosophy*), Newton states, "The six primary Planets are revolv'd about the Sun, in circles concentric with the Sun, and with motions directed towards the same parts, and almost in the same plane...But it is not to be conceived that mere mechanical causes could give birth to so many regular motions...This most beautiful System of the Sun, Planets, and Comets, could only proceed from the counsel and dominion of an intelligent and powerful Being." Tyson exclaims emphatically, "This was Isaac Newton invoking Intelligent Design!" Tyson made note that Newton did not credit "...an intelligent and powerful Being..." with his discoveries of either the existence of gravity or the laws of motion because he figured them out scientifically. (In the famous story, he observed an apple fall from a tree and discovered gravity. He then extrapolated the same force engaged between the Earth and the Moon and correctly deduced the laws of motion.) He only attributed to God those observations which his mind could not grasp by physics: the origin and operation of the entire Solar System. Because he was a religious man, he surmised that the more complex and mysterious machinery of the Solar System (now known to simply be varying degrees of gravity and motion) must have a "Creator." Tyson firmly states another point, "I wanna' put on the table the fact that you have school systems wanting to put Intelligent Design into the classrooms, but you also have the most brilliant people who ever walked this Earth *doing the same thing*!! So it's a deeper challenge than simply educating the public."

He segues to another point about the religious belief of scientists by comparing the ratio of the percentage of the American *public* who believe in God with the percentage of American *scientists* who believe in God. The percentage of the American public who believe in God is about 90% (an obviously large and striking percentage). American scientists in general who believe in God, he says, are about 40% (a significantly smaller percentage).

But among elite scientists—members of the National Academy of Sciences—he cites an article in the July 23, 1998 publication of Nature, International Weekly Journal of Science.[*] The article found that in 1933, for example, a significant 85% of the most distinguished scientists rejected a personal God. In 1998 it was larger, at 93%. Or, the opposite. In 1933, only 15% of the most esteemed scientists believed in a personal God; in 1998, it was only 7%. However, Tyson notes that the 15% group (and the 1998 7% group) raises a key point and question. To Tyson, the writers/researchers of

---

[*]http://palgrave.nature.com/nature/journal/v394/n6691/full/394313a0.html

the 1998 article in Nature ("they" in the quote below) overlooked the obvious. Tyson again exclaims, "Wait a minute, they *missed the story*! Why isn't that number *zero*?!" *That's* the story!!" To Tyson, the 1933 15% and the 1998 7% groups reveal a larger point that I am exploring in this book. When science demands compelling physical evidence over faith, why do *any* scientists, particularly those most well educated, accept a personal God on faith at all?

In addition to the mystery of elusive evidence for God, there is another, perhaps deeper mystery (which I have alluded to already). The seeming innate need in many human beings, including some brilliant scientists, to believe by faith in some kind of universal beneficent Being. In my view, of all the mysteries of the universe and life, that need in a large segment of humanity is one of the *most* intriguing but confounding. In fact, Tyson concludes this talk by asking that very question. He reflects, "And the answer to that question [humanity's need to believe in a deity] would be very interesting indeed." Humanity (and all life) has evolved by natural selection because of *intelligence*, our brains. The intellect and logic. But it is interesting that natural selection has also *selected* faith. Though contrary to the intellect, skepticism, and logic, faith must also carry a substantial degree of survival value.

Regardless of the success of evolution by natural selection, humanity is of course not infallible. Though both were brilliant scientists in their day, Ptolemy and Newton were also human and fallible and influenced by some of the uneducated thinking of their time. Their two quotes above reveal the tendency in even some of the most brilliant of human thinkers to default to deities when the going gets most intellectually rough, when answers are the most elusive. Part of Tyson's point (and, humbly, mine) is that the invocation of any deity at any time and for any situation should perhaps be an alarm bell of warning not to prematurely end the search, not to presume that we cannot discover explanations solely by physics.

Tyson also highlights a different and wiser scientific reaction to universal mystery. He cited Pierre-Simon Laplace's discovery, more than one hundred years after Newton and that had eluded the discoverer of gravity and motion because of his religious beliefs. It is the phenomenon of perturbation theory. Perturbation theory demonstrated different degrees of gravitation between two or more objects, thus explaining by physics all the planetary motions in the Solar System. He relates Laplace's response to

Napoleon that I have mentioned, when the latter inquired why God was not depicted in Laplace's model of the Solar System. Laplace confidently but respectfully replied, "Sire, I have no need of that hypothesis."

Tyson adds that what concerns him is that even if one is as brilliant as someone like Newton, if your focus is primarily on God your thirst for discovery could stop. Focus on God can delay discovery. He remarked that Laplace's deduction of perturbation theory should have been "...crumbs for Newton." Too easy. For example, Newton invented the differential and integral calculus, almost on a dare. Newton was asked why planets orbit the Sun in ellipses and not some other shape. He didn't know the immediate answer, so he figured it out by inventing the calculus. However, his religious background then prevented him from applying his brilliant scientific thinking to decipher what Laplace later found. Tyson's point is that Newton terminated his intellectual investigation that would have tied gravity and motion to the perturbation theory in the Solar System because of his focus on God. Newton could have deduced the connection, but he didn't. Tyson remarked, "His religiosity *stopped him.*"

Then Tyson continues with an encapsulation and summation, what we can conclude based on these examples. He concludes, "Intelligent Design, while real in the history of science, while real in the presence of philosophical 'drivers,' is nonetheless a philosophy of ignorance. So regardless of what our political agenda is, all you have to say is, 'Science is a philosophy of discovery, Intelligent Design is a philosophy of ignorance.' That's all!" He quickly added that even though Intelligent Design is not science so should not be taught as science, it is nonetheless part of historical thinking and should be taught thusly. If it is not discussed at all, he said, "...you're neglecting something fundamental that's going on in people's minds when they confront things they don't understand. And it happens to the greatest of the minds [just] as it happens to everyone else...if not most, many people in the public."

In his talk, A Final "Sermon" on Cosmic Perspective [127], on the psychology and physiology of religious thinking (my third example), he goes farther than comparing science and Intelligent Design. He describes his own reverential feeling of awe and connection to the cosmos, and wonders if a religious person's feeling of connection to God and Jesus is the same. But rather than just speculate, he wants to scientifically test his hypothesis and invites the audience to perform an experiment on him.

Like Ann Druyan did for the Voyager Interstellar Record, he wants someone to put electrodes on his head and measure his brain waves. What he specifically wants to know is what part of his brain lights up when he thinks about marvels of scientific discovery. He notes the nifty common origin of the iron in the 15-ton meteorite at the Rose Center for Earth and Space and the iron in human blood: in the core of a star! He says, "Tell me what part of my brain is lighting up, because that excites me! That makes me wanna' grab people in the street and say, 'Have you *heard* this?!'" It's not simply, as Carl Sagan said, 'We are starstuff.' But there's a more poetic, and I think more accurate wayta' say it. It's quite literally true that we are...star*DUST*...[in a softer and more delicate voice]...in the highest exalted way one can use that phrase." *

He continues about measuring the commonality of scientific and religious feeling. He relates that he feels and expresses himself about the universe similarly to how religious people express themselves about God. He says, "I bask in the majesty of the cosmos." That is similar he thinks to people who say that they have revelations from Jesus or who go on pilgrimages to Mecca. He senses that there is a commonality of feeling between the religious and scientific experiences. He doesn't know exactly what the commonality is, but regarding the brain wave experiment that he wants performed on him, he says, "...if the same centers in my brain [that] are excited by these cosmic thoughts are the same as what are going on in the mind of a religious person, *that's something to know*! That's going to be a really interesting finding."

He then draws a parallel regarding one proof of the evident public joy of scientific discovery and its ties to spirituality. He says that when the news reported that the Hubble Telescope was going to be canceled, the largest outcry came not from astrophysicists or NASA but from the general public. The public had, in his phrase, "taken ownership" of the Hubble Telescope. This because images from it had been shown on television and made available for download online, so the universe was now transmitted to

---

* Like Joni Mitchell sang in her 1969 hit song, "Woodstock":
We are stardust, Billion-year-old carbon
We are golden, Caught in the devil's bargain
And we've got to get ourselves
Back to the garden

people's homes, and stored on their computers. They were, as Tyson put it, "...participant[s] on the frontier of discovery." He then states what I already feel very strongly, "...it's not just that we are in the universe, but in fact, given the chemistry of it all and the nuclear physics of it all, the universe *is-in-us*. And I don't know any deeper spiritual feeling than what that brings upon me."

I'm curious as to whether anyone volunteered and conducted the neural electrodes experiment he requested?! Regardless, Tyson's final statement above encapsulates the reality of the joy of science. For himself and the general public, he connects the intellectual and the emotional, the scientific with the spiritual. The visceral. The infinite.

PART III

PERSONAL PERSPECTIVES

Chapter 1

THE HARD LINE

*We believe with certainty that an ethical life can be lived
without religion.
And we know for a fact that the corollary holds true—
that religion has caused innumerable people
not just to conduct themselves no better than others,
but to award themselves permission to behave in ways
that would make a brothel-keeper or an ethnic cleanser
raise an eyebrow.*

Christopher Hitchens
God Is Not Great

Throughout history, Europeans of different faiths have fought and killed each other for this reason or that. But never until the coming of Christianity did men of our western world fight and kill each other because *of their faiths—one seeking to impose his on the other.*

Galindo paused to take another draft of his awful smoke.

However, the Arian Christians are at least tolerant of every other religion, and of paganism, and of those persons who profess no religious beliefs at all. Therefore, if the Goths should *prevail, they would not demand or even expect everyone else in the world to believe as they do.*

Saggws was galiuthjon! [Song was sung!]"

Gary Jennings
Raptor

(The Goths, a generally peaceful, tolerant, and kind people—
exemplified by their leader, King Theodoric the Great—
did not prevail.
They were obliterated by the early Catholic Church.
What followed was one of the longest periods
of intolerance and horror in human history—
the "Dark Ages.)

This chapter is my opportunity to do a little "venting" and "instructing." I ask the reader's patience and forgiveness in advance for my perhaps less than careful approach and in taking the risk of appearing offensive. I certainly never intend to be offensive. But I also feel the need to be direct for a moment in addition to being as clear as possible.

First, I always feel angry when I learn about people treating other people with unkindness, disrespect, and prejudice under the pretext of religious doctrine and dogma. In fact, there is much religious text and scripture that prohibits prejudice. For example, in Matthew 7:3-5 Jesus speaks clearly and unambiguously against judgment and prejudice:

> [3]Why do you look at the speck of sawdust in your brother's eye and pay no attention to the plank in your own eye? [4]How can you say to your brother, 'Let me take the speck out of your eye,' when all the time there is a plank in your own eye? [5]You hypocrite, first take the plank out of your own eye, and then you will see clearly to remove the speck from your brother's eye.

There are many current issues that become both distorted and problematic because this passage from biblical scripture is violated. From my point of view, though, it does not take referring to the Bible or any other religious text to know that judging others more severely than oneself, or even judging others at all, is highly unethical. The issues of gay marriage, or the ban on allowing gay and transgender people to serve openly in the military are examples of judgment and prejudice; the latter impressively and rightly reversed by the Obama administration on September 20, 2011 and June 30, 2016, respectively (though despicably and callously reversed for transgender people by the Trump administration on April 12, 2019), and the former gradually legalized later by some states and subsequently legalized nationwide by the Supreme Court on June 26, 2015. (I was among the millions who were jubilant about that Supreme Court Decision. In a country still so rife with prejudice, literally one vote helped to reunite the country with love.)

The prejudice against Lesbian/Gay/Bi-Sexual/Transgender/Queer (LGBTQ) rights is no different from racial prejudice except that the prejudice is aimed at homosexuality and transgender instead of race. Prejudice against sexuality (whether homosexual or heterosexual) is motivated by people who are insecure with their own sexuality and intimidated by those who are more comfortable with their sexuality. The former feel the need to control and dictate the sexuality of the latter, very likely to allay their own sexual insecurity; this in the hope that the issue, the feelings that accompany the issue, and any influence on society by the differing sexuality of others will disappear. The prejudice is most often aimed at homosexuality, but prejudice against heterosexuality undoubtedly exists, too. In other words, prejudice of any kind is unacceptable and abhorrent. The feelings that motivate prejudice need to be understood and worked with, but the practice of prejudice is simply inhumane.

In Harper Lee's novel, *Go Set A Watchman* (the author's prequel novel, *To Kill A Mockingbird*), the character, Uncle Jack Finch, reflects to Jean Louise "Scout" Finch on an ironic commonality between prejudice and faith—comparing both to reason. He remarks, "...the white supremacists fear reason, because they know cold reason beats them. Prejudice, a dirty word, and faith, a clean one, have something in common: they both begin where reason ends. That's odd, isn't it? It's one of the oddities of this world." [128] It seems to me, though, that reason and love—and trust (faith) in both—are antidotes to prejudice.

It seems to me extremely narrow to use as the primary source for any opinion any document that is extremely outdated and contains grave inconsistencies, such as the Bible, Qur'an, and other ancient religious texts. We have hopefully learned more deeply and genuinely how to treat our fellow human being (and all living things) since the time standard religious texts were written. Like the Fourteenth Dalai Lama, and Buddhism in general, encourages, we therefore need to utilize our natural senses of love and compassion in addition to the wisdom of writers, both ancient and contemporary. If we seriously hurt another person's feelings or infringe on their human rights by our behavior (my suggestion of the only definition of "sin"), and our behavior is motivated primarily by the purported wisdom of an ancient dictate, we need to seriously reexamine the dictate. Too often, religious teaching encourages people not to trust their own feelings, instincts, intellect, and natural sense of morality to one another, and instead to defer to ancient dogma that may no longer be healthy or applicable, or to have ever had any merit at all.

Of course, not all dictates are harmful. One example of a healthy dictate is effective and ethical civil law. Much of civil law is very effective. Documents such as England's *Magna Carta*, Switzerland's, *Golden Charter of Bern*, Russia's, *Treaty of St. Petersburg*, the *Morrocan-American Treaty of Friendship*, the *Treaty of Ghent*, the *London Protocols*, the *Geneva Conventions*, the *Treaty of Versailles*, the *Treaty of Tripoli*, the *Oslo Accords*, the *Kyoto Protocol*, the United States *Constitution*, Lincoln's, *Emancipation Proclamation*, and the abolishment of Apartheid, are all excellent examples of enacted (and, in many cases, successful) civil law.

Civil law is not derived primarily from religious belief or dogma and should, therefore, be separate from religious law. Civil law is derived from a mixture and compromise of general and civil ethical principles. Civil law is definitely dogmatic to the extent that laws, once established, are meant to be taken very seriously and upheld in principle and practice for the protection and regulation of peaceful society.

By contrast, religious law derives from deeply personal and private belief, one definition of subjectivity. Civil law is neither personal nor private. It is the citizens and the community, the designation of public or people. It is one form of objectivity, and therefore works more healthily and effectively for the benefit of society as a whole. The reason that religious law should not become civil law is because it is unfair and unethical to make laws based on any one private or individually subjective viewpoint, or any collectively subjective viewpoint. Civil law is based upon a *citizen* or *secular* majority rather than a *religious* majority, which is a *more objective* viewpoint upon which a majority can agree. In history, and currently, I think it is apparent that not everyone can agree on one single religious point of view. Therefore, because religious belief, teaching, and practice should remain private, one should never make the mistake of using religion as the basis for any kind of societal judgment. Prejudice is bad enough when it is felt privately. But when it moves into the establishment of civic or public policy, it is inexcusable. Too often, some people who expound the most about love coming from God are the quickest to pass judgment on others who don't share their subjective viewpoint (perhaps because the God in the Old Testament portion of the Bible can be quite judgmental as well).

The First Amendment of the Constitution of the United States clearly protects the freedom of private religious practice, and prohibits the foisting of any religious belief on society in any form of governance or legislation. On February 7, 2017, columnist, Jay Parini, of CNN offered this insightful perspective in his article, *Trump Needs To Learn Some American History*. "One thinks back to Roger Williams, who founded the Colony of Rhode Island and Providence Plantations. In his correspondence with John Cotton, a Puritan preacher, Williams famously wrote in praise of a 'hedge or wall of Separation between the Garden of the Church and the Wilderness of the World.' He worried that allowing this hedge to fade would imperil religion itself, and the practice of faith, which is always an individual thing and should never be imposed or curtailed."[*] Organized religion tends to forget that the First Amendment contains a permanent and free "individual insurance policy" of private religious freedom. An indelible gesture of respect to religion from the Enlightenment.

I have heard it argued from some Christians that the First Amendment is really intended to prevent the foisting onto society of any particular *denomination* within Christianity, not religion *in general*. This interpretation is used as an attempt to offer proof that the Founding Fathers intended for the United States to be a "Christian nation." Besides, for example, the Treaty of Tripoli (mentioned above—drafted in 1796 under George Washington and signed in 1797 by John Adams) directly and specifically refuting that notion in Article 11, it is also a very convenient and erroneous assertion.

First, neither the words *denomination* nor *Christian* appear anywhere in the First Amendment.

Second, a careful reading of the First Amendment makes it very clear that the intention is inclusion of all religious belief as well as no religious belief. The Amendment's protective shields are to neither prevent the private practice of any religion, nor to allow the adoption of any religion as a barometer for policy or legislation by the federal government; no religious persecution, and no theocracy.

Third, it is clear from the history of the writers of the Constitution that their intention for the United States be a Christian nation is completely and entirely untrue. Many of the early representatives of the Colonial States were

---

[*] http://www.cnn.com/2017/02/02/opinions/trump-needs-learn-american-history-opinion/

Deists or Secularists, not Christians. A *Deist* believed in a supernatural God as the initial "Creator," but also as the "absentee Father" since Creation. The belief was formulated and focused on reason and nature, not associated with any specific or divine religious leader for eternal redemption (such as Jesus Christ). It was a belief in God born by and in the education of the time, the "Enlightenment" (the time of the Classical period in music, for example, from which the general term *classical music* derives). A *Secularist* simply upheld the principle of secularism, or the separation of government and religion. The Framers wrote the First Amendment with the express purpose of ensuring that the same religious repression that had been experienced in England and elsewhere in the European countries did not occur in the "New World." The First Amendment was also written with the keen awareness of avoiding governmental tyrannies, and religious governmental tyrannies have been some of the worst. Any Inquisition in history is proof of that fact.

General religious freedom and its separation from government policy, therefore, is apparent and guaranteed in the First Amendment. However, religious freedom does not include *active* intolerance and prejudice. Freedom never means the ability to deny the human or civil rights of another. Using the issue of (now nationally legalized) gay marriage once again as an example of religious discrimination, my feeling is that any attempt for any reason to prevent *two adult people* from legally expressing their permanent love for each other through marriage, either in the behavior of society or by law, is unethical, amoral, and contrary to life and happiness. Any minister or officiator who refuses to perform a gay marriage now is not only uncompassionate, unkind, and unethical, but is breaking the law.

This includes the ridiculous, juvenile, unethical, and *illegal* behavior of Kim Davis who chose jail time rather than obeying the law when, as a Kentucky county clerk, she refused to issue a marriage license to a same-sex couple. Although professing her decision based on her Christian beliefs, besides breaking the law, her decision was unkind and un-Christian—though undocumented, Jesus probably sanctioned *all* marriages without hesitation or discrimination, and with pleasure and love!* Her decision was also veiled

---

* There is also no documentation that Jesus condemned same-sex relationships or marriage. His offering and teaching of unconditional love indicate exactly the opposite. Only the extremity of Levitical Law included that prohibition, which Christ, among other unloving human behavior, repudiated.

prejudiced. It was the equivalent of, post-Emancipation Proclamation, a white waitress or waiter refusing to serve an African-American person in a restaurant.

To me, her situation and decision should have been obvious: if her *private* religious belief prevented her from executing the responsibilities of her job as a *public* servant—issuing marriage licenses to all adult couples—she could have resigned and looked for a non-public-service job. Davis's reason for not resigning was as ridiculous and unwarranted as her decision not to issue the license. In an interview with Fox News anchor, Megyn Kelly, on September 23rd, 2015, Davis said, "If I resign, I lose my voice." [129] Besides American Constitutional law never causing anyone to lose their voice in freedom of expression by the First Amendment, she could just as easily have performed one of two possible alternative scenarios, without resigning: 1) She could have recognized her job responsibility in public not private service, and issued the marriage license herself. 2) She could have submitted a written request to her supervisor/boss/employer to have a colleague employee issue the marriage license, citing her private religious conviction as the reason for not issuing the license personally. In either scenario, she could subsequently have written President Obama a letter of protest, thereby complying with her professional public position, the law, and formally voicing her objection on religious grounds, all at the same time. My suspicion is that Davis was not only concerned with her religious belief. Just as she accused her detractors and the gay couple, whose complaint about her refusal was recorded on video, I think that she was also selfishly tempted by the lure of media attention. Both above scenarios would have meant less likelihood of world-wide notoriety. Frustratingly, and typically, the media not only complied, it was solicitous.

By direct contrast, in a country in which many of its citizens tend to deeply distrust the federal government, it was their Vice President, Joe Biden, who set the finest example on this issue. Using his platform as deputy to the Commander in Chief, he took the ethical and loving reins when he stated his support of marriage equality directly and succinctly to David Gregory on March 6, 2012 on *Meet the Press*: "The good news is that as more and more Americans come to understand what this is about, it's a simple proposition. Who do you love? Who do you love? And will you be loyal to the person you love? And that's what people are finding out. It's what all marriages, at their root, are about. Whether they're marriages of lesbians, or gay men, or heterosexuals...I'm Vice President of the United States of America...the president sets the policy. I am absolutely comfortable with the fact that men marrying men, women marrying women and heterosexual—men and women marrying—are entitled to the same exact rights, all the civil rights, all the civil liberties. And quite frankly, I don't see much of a distinction beyond that." [130]

I was particularly proud that the Vice-President of the United States of America would have the courage to say that, and on national television. It was also a moment (among many) in which Joe Biden did not make a verbal gaffe. Very much the contrary. It was of his best documented moments. Significantly, not only was he in a safer position politically than the president to verbalize his opinion on the issue, but instead of being politely reprimanded or contradicted by the president, he "opened the door" for President Obama, who, on May 9, 2012 to Robin Roberts of ABC News, followed suit by also verbally supporting gay marriage on national television. [131] Clearly, the president had wanted to support gay marriage all along, but felt more cautious and reticent in making his support public; the Vice-President's courage created the opportunity. In verbally and publicly supporting same-sex marriage, Vice-President Joe Biden—and then President Barack Obama—declared and clarified that marriage is about the civil human right to the legal, ceremonial, and formal expression of deep love between any two adult human beings.

Personally, I want nothing to do with any religion (or religious official) that seeks to discriminate against anyone, for any reason, including marriage. The Supreme Court's decision affirmed that gay marriage should be as allowed and honored by society as heterosexual marriage, without judgment or bias. It is simply inhumane to encourage otherwise.

My late uncle, Frank Ayre Lee, had this to say in another one of our recorded conversations in April, 2010. The conversation covered a variety of topics, but included homosexuality (in the arts, specifically), gay marriage, and child-rearing by gay couples. He said, "If we *didn't* have the homosexual community, we would be *far poorer* [in the arts, but also in general] than we are. And a loving union of two people of the same sex is wonderful, I think it's *magnificent*! And why *shouldn't* they raise children? You know...surround a child with love...*what's wrong with that*? Which puts me at *complete odds* with the Republican establishment...but it [anti-gay marriage] doesn't make any *sense*! And I'm absolutely convinced that this is…this is *in the genes*. You can't…you know, this is not a matter of choice. This is in the genes. I just…I can't see why there should be *any prejudice at all*. Any more than I can see why there should be prejudice because of *the shade of one's skin*." And regarding the Republican/Tea Party argument against gay marriage because it threatens the "sanctity of marriage," he exclaimed, "It's *nonsense!*…that this *threatens marriage*…I'll tell you what threatens marriage…*DIVORCE*!! [He laughs! Frank Lee was married to my Aunt Bettye for 65 years, until his death in 2011] That's one of the most absurd arguments I ever heard in my life." Then with slight sarcasm, as if quoting someone characteristically conservative, " 'This threatens the sanctity of marriage'…*Sheesh*!!!"

It was reassuring and elevating to hear my uncle so strongly express that point. It was particularly significant because he was 86 years old when we had that discussion. Many people in that generation, particularly *men*, are unable to acknowledge or embrace homosexuality at all, much less gay marriage.

Prior to June 26, 2015, I was extremely pleased that more and more states were choosing to legalize gay marriage. I thought and hoped that it would just be a matter of a relatively short time until gay marriage would be legal in the entire United States of America. Thankfully and magnificently, like the eventual ratification of the *Emancipation Proclamation*, June 26, 2015 saw gay marriage legalized nationally in a single Supreme Court decision, and by a single vote. A non-divisive victory for a still deeply divided country. All Americans instantly became more equal. What an accomplishment and a happy day that was!

I think marriage could even be performed for two animals if their owners wanted to. (It's been done on YouTube!) It might be a bit silly, but clearly animals have deep feelings and a marriage ceremony for two animals, if nothing else, would be adorable. (The animals' owners would really be performing the wedding for themselves. Though animals have deep feelings, they would likely be oblivious to the meaning of a wedding.) Obviously, all living creatures have some degree of intelligence and feelings. Any form of life does or it wouldn't be "alive." This is one of my interpretations of Genesis 7. In this section of biblical scripture, animals were considered important and worthy enough of dignity and respect that they (or at least some species) were included on board the Ark—along with the human being, Noah—to be spared from the Great Flood. I consider this and many religious stories allegory and not to be taken literally, but at least animals were given some respect and dignity in this story.

But humans are probably the most intelligent of all the animals (with respect to chimpanzees, dolphins, and whales), so it is us whom we deem deserving of the most serious laws. Unlike two animals, marriage between two humans of the same sex is between two people who are not at all oblivious to the meaning of marriage. Gay marriage is to be taken just as seriously as marriage between humans of the opposite sex. Religion should not be a factor. Just like health care, marriage is a *civil right*.

~~~

Though science is fundamentally self-correcting, it cannot claim immunity to dogma. A significant challenge to the long-accepted scientific fact of natural selection—as the underlying force propelling evolution—has been submitted for many years by molecular evolutionary biologist, Masatoshi Nei (whom I cited in Part I). He has been questioning natural selection for decades through research and the publication of his books. His most recent book, *Mutation-Driven Evolution*, proposes that it is subtle mutations in the characteristics of life, not primarily natural selection, that most prominently produce the extraordinarily gradual changes in evolution. He is not suggesting that natural selection doesn't occur at all, only that natural selection is not the underlying engine of evolution as first proposed by Darwin, and since then considered fact by science. In the March, 2014 issue of *Discover* magazine [132], Nei states the following in an interview with Gemma Tarlach, "My position is mutation creates variation, then natural selection may or may not operate, it may or may not choose the good variation and eliminate the bad one, but natural selection is not the driving force...In mutation-driven evolutionary theory, evolution is a process of increasing or decreasing an organism's complexity. We tend to believe natural selection selects one type. But there are many types, and they're still OK. They can survive, no problem." According to Nei, Darwin was correct about evolution but incorrect about natural selection being the primary operating force. Darwin was of course limited by the degree to which his observations were accurate and conclusive at the time (and how brilliantly accurate they largely were!). Time has proven Darwin largely correct, but certainly not infallible. On this issue, Nei makes a striking comparative observation of science with religion: that much of the scientific community has erred in being as dogmatic about natural selection as many religions have been dogmatic about religious scripture. He elaborates on this in the same interview, "But anytime a scientific idea is treated like dogma, you have to question it. The dogma of natural selection has existed for a long time. Most people have not questioned it. Most textbooks still state that it is so. Most students are educated with these books...You have to question dogma. Use common sense. You have to think for yourself, without preconceptions. That is what's important in science." Clearly, this is an example of where science can err in the same way as religion. Whether Nei is correct or not in his theory of mutation being the actual heartbeat of evolution, he is very right in challenging natural selection if he has evidence to support his differing theory, particularly if the scientific community is sluggish and resistant to his evidence. Dogma of any kind is a deterrent to knowledge.

I know a man (whose identity I will protect) who converted to Mormonism as a twenty-year-old because he was searching for life meaning and wanted to feel that he belonged to some kind of stable spiritual group. However, this man told me that because he was in his twenties (he is now in his mid-60s) he was required by the Mormon Church to report his progress with avoiding transgressions to the proper church authority. One of the transgressions was (and perhaps still is) masturbation. He told me that he tried very hard to refrain from masturbating, but in fact lied when asked in one interview when he said that he was successfully refraining. Most healthy people now know that, other than occasional circumstances of sexual addictions, masturbation is a normal, healthy, and exciting human desire and private activity.

Sadly, it is typical of many organized religions to attempt to repress anything sexual. This man's experience with the Mormon Church's prohibition on masturbation was bad enough. But though he protected himself by lying in order to pass that particular interview, this same man was later excommunicated by the Mormon Church when the church discovered that he was gay. I have many Mormon friends (as I will share in the next chapter) and have great respect and love for them. But both of those forms of behavior and treatment of my friend by the Mormon Church are abhorrent to me, particularly their decision to excommunicate him based on his homosexuality.

He told me that in New York, where he lived for years in his 20s and 30s, many members of the Mormon Church—even some *officials* of the Mormon Church whom he either knew personally or indirectly, and knew were gay, lesbian, or bi-sexual—successfully kept the sexual part of their personal lives hidden from the church. I told him that, like the negative reaction of the U.S. Episcopal Church to the ordination of Bishop V. Gene Robinson in 2003, I don't see the value of an organization that promotes any kind of prejudicial discrimination. One is better off without the organization. To the U.S. Episcopal Church's eventual credit, the ban on openly gay members or gay officials in the church was ended in July of 2009. But it is a ban that should never have been imposed. At least the U.S. Episcopal Church learned from its mistake and abolished the discriminating policy. My friend was not so lucky. In fact, indicated in the letter that he received from the Mormon Church as the reason for his excommunication was written, "Homosexual." This is despicable treatment of another human being by anyone, individual or organization, and should be cause for embarrassment and shame for the organization—and a reversal of its decision, like the U.S. Episcopal Church's 2009 ruling—whatever the organization might be.

In short, we humans can be extremely judgmental of each other and not enough of ourselves. (This is the purpose for the principle of Al-Anon, the support group for families of alcoholics: "Keep the focus on oneself.") If we all truly kept the focus on ourselves (not to be confused with being self*ish*) and worked to love each other more, what a better world community we would create.

However, according to both views of the anthropic principle—which in my view is really a selfish, ego-centric principle in disguise—we like to think that we are a special species on a special planet. But we are only special to the degree of our behavior and the potential of our learning capacity. We are stupid and cruel in other ways. The word, stupid, may sound like too harsh a word, but it is applicable whenever humans are inhumane. When it comes to any kind of prejudice and inhumane behavior, stupid is really a mild assessment. Prejudice is utterly hateful and repugnant. It is also a severe form of shunning. Shunning (which is "ex-communication") on the basis of homosexuality or heterosexuality or any other natural and normal human biology or commitment celebration (such as not allowing two gay people to marry each other) is stupid at best. But it is also prejudiced, inhumane, ridiculous, ignorant, unfair, judgmental, presumptuous, unkind, and amoral. I have said that I would rather meet and get to know a nice, kind, loving, unprejudiced person—gay, straight, transgendered, religious, respectfully religious, or non-religious—than meet and try to get to know a prejudiced religious or science fundamentalist. I feel very uncomfortable with, and sometimes even repulsed by the views and behavior of the latter. The former, for me, is a joy and pleasure to know and be around.

In an interview on May 2, 2004, comic icon of Monty Python, Eric Idle, had this to say about God, "…I'm an Alzheimer's agnostic: I can't remember whether I don't believe in anything or not. However, I do believe religions are the cause of most of the problems in the world today and there should be a moratorium on the use of the G-word. I think it should be replaced by something less controversial that we can all agree on. Like Chocolate." [*]

American author and minister, Rob Bell, has much the same sentiment. Founder and pastor of the Mars Hill Bible Church in Grandville, Michigan, until 2012, Bell's emphasis has evolved to more of a focus on love rather than God. He has come to realize that, in addition to benevolence, the word, God, can conjure intangible and supernatural authority, wrath, and judgment—all negative, fearful, inaccessible, and less nurturing qualities. He also understands better what I have stressed, the need for greater clarity with interpretation and terminology in religious teaching. As a result, he uses the "G-word" now much less, expressing himself in more secular or, if you will, spiritual terms. He says about the word, God, "When a word becomes too toxic and too abused and too associated with ideas and understandings that aren't true to the mystery behind the mystery, it's important to set it aside and search for new and better ways to talk about it." [†]

---

[*] http://www.justabovesunset.com/id108.html
[†] http://www.buzzfeed.com/jonathanmerritt/god-a-trigger-word#.gl7geYe5g5

"Organized religion is a sham and a crutch for weak-minded people who need strength in numbers. It tells people to go out and stick their noses in other people's business. I live by the golden rule: Treat others as you'd want them to treat you. The religious right wants to tell people how to live." [133] It was no surprise that this comment from Jesse Ventura, former governor of Minnesota, sparked much consternation and resentment from the religious community.

It also elicited this clarification from Ventura in his 1999 memoir, *I Ain't Got Time To Bleed.* [134] "I'd like to clarify [my comments published in *Playboy*] about religious people being weak-minded. I didn't mean all religious people. I don't have any problem with the vast majority of religious folks. I count myself among them, more or less. But I believe because it makes sense to me, not because I think it can be proven. There are lots of people out there who think they know the truth about God and religion, but does anybody really know for sure? That's why the Founding Fathers built freedom of religious belief into the structure of this nation, so that everybody could make up their minds for themselves. But I do have a problem with the people who think they have some right to try to impose their beliefs on others. I hate what the fundamentalist fanatics are doing to our country. It seems as though, if everybody doesn't accept their version of reality, that somehow invalidates it for them. Everybody must believe the same things they do. That's what I find weak and destructive."

Curious how, even in a country such as the United States where the First Amendment to the Constitution also allows for the freedom of speech, that people who openly express themselves critically often feel pressure to then abandon their Constitutional right and recant their honest comments because of negative popular reaction (though perhaps in this case, it was probably helpful that Ventura elaborated to further clarify his point). It is another form of prejudice and hypocrisy on the part of the public. It's as if that hypocrisy were saying that everyone has the Constitutional right to express themselves verbally, artistically, or in writing *except when someone else disagrees*. It is an obvious paradox and contradiction.

I think Jesse Ventura's comments (before and after he recanted), are well worth considering. I also think that this is an example of where the negative public reaction is an indication of the age-old phrase, "The truth hurts." There is probably some degree of truth in Ventura's opinion that organized religion is "...a sham for weak-minded people who need strength in numbers." (It's difficult *not* to think of the uninquisitive or uncircumspect as a bit weak-minded.) Where I would differ with Ventura is that I think that it can be a positive characteristic to need strength in numbers. Where I agree with Ventura is that I think organized religion tends not to encourage people to think critically or question for themselves, which certainly means less, or weaker mental exercise. Organized religion may not directly *discourage* people from thinking or questioning, but it tends to err by not making thinking and questioning as virtuous and as much of a *priority* as believing.

I think the reason for that is two-fold: First, there are many writings of scripture in religious texts that do not make rational, logical sense or simply appear absurd based upon what we now know to be plausible. Organized religion often encourages people to *ignore the absurdities* or at least errs by not pointing out the absurdities for discussion and debate. Or the absurdities are suppressed. Or worse, not even noticed. And second (the focus of this book), by not encouraging the questioning of the most basic premise of most religions: the meaning and existence of the Deity (God, Allah, Yaweh, Adonai, Elohim, Jehovah, Para Brahman, Krishna, Shangdi, Shen, Bahá, etc.). Not to at least *question* the legitimacy of these and other religious premises is simply, in my view, abdicating thought and initiating in ignorance. I don't understand how any intelligent, thinking, non-weak-minded person would *not* question them.

I have explained and given my own examples of both logical and illogical "If...then..." statements. But here is one that I offer as a possible consequence of early religious teaching:

> *If* God, Creation, and religious morality are the primary part of one's earliest education and life association,
> *then* it will be more difficult to understand that morality and an understanding of the universe can come from any other source. (Other sources would be genetics, excellent parenting, a liberal arts education, exposure to and possibly immersion in the performing arts, and general positive life experience.)

Of course, the opposite "If...then..." statement could also be applied:

> *If* one has little-to-no early religious education,

then it will be harder to understand how a deeply religious person feels and views the universe.

At the very least, I think Jesse Ventura's comment is productive because it forces us to look at what we think and/or believe in and why, a mental exercise that I feel should be applied to any and all ideas.

~~~

I would like to share, with another specific example, my opinion on what I consider to be a lack of clarity in a famous religious story. My example is an additional angle or interpretation of the story of Cain and Abel. The standard interpretation is as the story and prohibition of the first murder. I suggest that there could be an additional, unapparent interpretation: one of abuse.

Both Cain and Abel give gifts (make offerings) to God of their respective professions: Abel, a shepherd, one of the fat of his flock; Cain, a farmer, some of his produce. Here is the verse from Genesis 4: 1-12 (King James Bible; the LORD is understood as God):

> 1 And Adam knew Eve his wife; and she conceived, and bare Cain, and said, I have gotten a man from the LORD.
> 2 And she again bare his brother Abel. And Abel was a keeper of sheep, but Cain was a tiller of the ground.
> 3 And in process of time it came to pass, that Cain brought of the fruit of the ground an offering unto the LORD.
> 4 And Abel, he also brought of the firstlings of his flock and of the fat thereof. And the LORD had respect unto Abel and to his offering:
> 5 but unto Cain and to his offering he had not respect. And Cain was very wroth, and his countenance fell.
> 6 And the LORD said unto Cain, Why art thou wroth? and why is thy countenance fallen?
> 7 If thou doest well, shalt thou not be accepted? and if thou doest not well, sin lieth at the door: and unto thee shall be his desire, and thou shalt rule over him.
> 8 And Cain talked with Abel his brother: and it came to pass, when they were in the field, that Cain rose up against Abel his brother, and slew him.

> 9 And the LORD said unto Cain, Where is Abel thy brother? And he said, I know not: Am I my brother's keeper?
> 10 And he said, What hast thou done? the voice of thy brother's blood crieth unto me from the ground.
> 11 And now art thou cursed from the earth, which hath opened her mouth to receive thy brother's blood from thy hand.
> 12 When thou tillest the ground, it shall not henceforth yield unto thee her strength; a fugitive and a vagabond shalt thou be in the earth.

Though this story is clearly one of denouncing the act of murder (and very necessarily so), I think another transgression exists in it as well. No transgression—even murder—is without motive or provocation, and I feel strongly that there is unacknowledged provocation and motive for Cain in the verse. (Not justification. As I explored and emphasized in Part I, murder is one transgression that should *absolutely never* be justified.)

God accepts Abel's offering of meat from his flock but refuses Cain's offering of the vegetables he has grown. Why? Other than the distinction of "the fat thereof" as an additional description of Abel's offering and the potential implication of the superiority of his offering, there is no clear explanation of why God favors meat over crops/produce (perhaps that is agreeable to carnivores, but not to vegetarians or vegans). It is a very vague differentiation, especially for preferential treatment. Even if this, some, or all other religious stories are viewed metaphorically, the preferential treatment is still unclear.

Like the assumption of the existence of God in the opening sentence of Genesis, this example of the story of Cain and Abel is also very early in Genesis, where clarity should be strongest. It is another example, in my view, of why clarity needs to be sought in instances where it is lacking. God's reason for favoring Abel's offering is not at all clear. In fact, it not only seems to me unclear, it also strikes me as unreasonable and unkind—almost intentional, baiting. It's as if God intentionally rejects Cain as a lure, to test his response to random rejection—a cruel, unfair, unethical, and inhumane test.

It is also not clear how old Cain and Abel are. Paintings of this story suggest that the brothers are adults, but the verse indicates nothing about their ages. Regardless, demonstrating acceptance or favoritism for someone without adequate or ample reason is hurtful to the person(s) being rejected no matter how old they are. It is mean and manipulative. Understandably, Cain felt dismissed and rejected, and as a result, hurt and resentful. Cain's retaliation by murdering Abel was deplorable and morally repugnant, but it was not, I think, without provocation.

The provocation, I submit, comes from God. God is initially culpable for rejecting Cain's offering without sufficient explanation. Though Cain's response was hideous and amoral, God's behavior was equally so, if not worse. It was especially reprehensible coming from a character who is supposed to be without equal in setting a superb moral example. To so blatantly favor one person over another without adequate reason and explanation is a form of abuse. In this case, emotional child abuse, since God is considered the Creator (the "Father") of all humanity. The contradiction is increased exponentially since God is purported as perfect[*] and the verses are considered by many as literal and unerring.

Though it is obviously important to teach the rule of law against murder, this story is, in my opinion, an example of the lack of sufficient detail and clarity in the Bible. There should never be an excuse for murder, but causes are always important to consider and should be given significant stress as part of a story or lesson. God's inadequately explained favoritism of Abel over Cain, in my estimation, contributed strongly to Cain's murdering Abel. (It was not the direct cause, of course. Cain was responsible for his own direct—and inexcusable—action.). If this was a contemporary story, God would not only have demonstrated exceedingly poor skill as a father (or grandfather), he would undoubtedly be guilty of child abuse. For me, that makes the lesson prohibiting murder in these verses of scripture less compelling, the opposite of their desired effect.

At the very least, this story (and any other religious text) should be read and understood from a modern, current, and liberal arts educated perspective. In that spirit, if most (or all) religious stories—and the concept of a Supreme Being—were simply related by religion as allegory and myth,

---

[*] I have heard the perfection of God questioned before. The Great Flood, for example, was enacted by God because of God's dissatisfaction with humans. But how could God be dissatisfied with any part of ("His") Creation if God is perfect? As I have questioned before, how could a perfect entity create anything *imperfect*?

the severity of my question about a deity's behavior, in this and any religious story, would be tempered considering its mythology.

~~~

From my senior year of high school through my graduation with my doctorate degree, I was a music major in cello performance (with a doctoral minor in instrumental conducting). Any area of the performing arts requires the strictest of education, discipline, and practice. The performing arts are unique in this way, I think, because they are a combination of physical and mental study, discipline, and skill that requires intricacies of the mind and the body not found in many other subjects or professions. The arts also require that one intensely explore their emotions for self-expression and to respect the self-expression of others. It is not possible to delve deeply into oneself emotionally or intellectually and not find many questions while searching for answers. In fact, even though the hope is to find answers and solutions (to performing and thinking about one's craft and artistic history) one will find many more questions than there are answers. The posing of questions and search for answers is one of the pleasures and joys of life, and it certainly is in the arts.

I am certainly not without error as a cellist. But I'm also relatively successful, and it is due in large part to very tough and rigorous teaching that I was fortunate to receive. That toughness included direct, but constructive criticism from my teachers: the necessity for me to think about what I was doing, how I was doing it, and why and to support and celebrate the work and success of others. Since that has been my education as an artist, and it requires emotional and intellectual expression—and because I am an emotional and intellectual person—I can't help but apply that tough rigorous training to many other areas of my life, including the question of, and my curiosity about, the origin of the universe and of life in general. So part of the equation of any thought, it seems to me, is a willingness to accept the "toughness" of inquiry and criticism. Too often, not being tough and directly honest leaves too many questions *not asked* much less answered.

I read a very interesting example of tough teaching in a story that had nothing to do with music or the arts, but reminded me of the effectiveness of strict (and, at times, personally and emotionally painful) teaching. Although teaching is not the focus of this book per se, thinking, learning, and teaching are all components of considering and respecting other points of view, which is certainly at the heart of exploring both the origin of the universe and of the meaning of the concept of a "God."

The example of tough general teaching I want to share is from, *The Horse Whisperer*, by Nicholas Evans. It is from the scene toward the end of the book in which the horse whisperer himself, Tom Booker, is attempting to reenable Grace to ride her seriously injured horse, Pilgrim. Though methodical and calculated, Booker's rehabilitation method appears severe. After gently forcing— "hobbling"—Grace's horse, Pilgrim, to a lying position on the corral ground with ropes tied to his legs, he is about to coach Grace on how to get back on Pilgrim. Up to this point in the story, Pilgrim has not allowed anyone to ride him after suffering a nearly fatal accident when he, with Grace on his back, collided head-on with a tractor-trailer moving full-speed down a mountain road early in the story. Tom Booker is now attempting to restore faith and trust between Pilgrim and Grace. But Grace has been watching Tom "hobble" Pilgrim, and the relentless force of Tom's arms, indeed the entire process of pulling the horse down, has been extremely difficult and upsetting for her to watch. Pilgrim has been fighting to stay standing and it has looked as if Tom has been purposely making Pilgrim suffer. Grace is crying because, to her, it looks like brutality.

Once Tom and his friend and assistant, Smoky, have Pilgrim successfully supine, Tom calls to Grace to come to where he and Smoky are standing. When Grace refuses, Tom walks over to Annie and Grace. He gently asks Grace again to come with him to where Pilgrim is lying. After expressing more reluctance, she finally allows Tom to lead her over to Pilgrim. Tom asks Grace to stroke Pilgrim from flank to forehead which, though hesitant at first, she does. Then Tom makes a startling request. He asks her to stand on Pilgrim. She is stunned. Tom gently repeats the request. Alarmed again, she tries to adamantly refuse, but Tom persists insistently. Annie, now also alarmed, calls Tom's name reproachfully, but Tom firmly asks her to be quiet. Then, again to Grace, he speaks more forcefully, "Do as I say Grace. Stand on him. Now!" Grace begins to cry but realizes that she needs to cease protesting Tom and trust him. Sobbing, she steps up onto Pilgrim's midsection and stands on him with both feet, tears running down her face in anguish at the brutality she feels she is inflicting on her horse.

After a few moments, Tom allows Grace to step down from Pilgrim. As Grace is stepping down, Annie, who has walked up to stand beside Grace and Tom, challenges Tom on what seems to her and Grace as his severe and brutal therapy. She tells him it seems cruel and humiliating. Keeping his eyes on assisting Grace down, Tom firmly counters her, "No, you're wrong...It's not cruel...He had the choice to go on fighting life or to accept it...and he chose to accept it." Then he turns to Grace and says, "What just happened to him, laying down like that, was the worst thing he could imagine. And you know what? He found out it was okay. Even you standing on him was okay. He saw you meant him no harm. The darkest hour comes before the dawn. That was Pilgrim's darkest hour and he survived it...Sometimes what seems like surrender isn't surrender at all. It's about...seeing clearly the way life is and accepting it and being true to it, whatever the pain, because the pain of not being true to it is far, far greater." [135]

The point that the character, Tom Booker, makes is very similar to the one made by Sagan, "Better by far to embrace the hard truth than a reassuring fable." [136] Face your fears, especially when given wise and perspicacious guidance.

My point in including and describing this scene in *The Horse Whisperer* is that tough teaching, and the willingness to be strictly taught, are both great gifts. The most progress is made when one is willing to have their most entrenched notions challenged, to have their deepest fears explored, and to consider the wisdom of opposing perspectives. Religion and science need to do the same: A willingness to be mutually and rigorously taught.

Although fiction, this is an excellent example of the need for persistence and discipline in any endeavor or issue, but motivated by love. It is sometimes necessary to appear firm and forceful, temporarily, if the desired end is known to be worthwhile and will likely be successful. The horse whisperer, Tom Booker, knew that both Grace and her horse, after suffering such a terrible accident, needed to be put in another extremely vulnerable position, but one that was safe, loving, and non-life-threatening.

Grace's initial refusal to follow Tom's instruction is also a lesson about life in general: that resistance to tough issues and lessons guided by caring and dedicated instructors and leaders is a serious mistake. As Matthew 7:3-5 reminds, one of life's lessons is to admit that we human beings have the capacity to be extremely judgmental toward others, lenient and flattering with ourselves, and to treat each other (and other living things) with too much cruelty and hatred, particularly toward differences in religious belief or thought; differences in ethnicity as well, obviously, but that is not a specific focus of this book. If the Inquisitions, or unsafe or dishonest scientific pursuit (the explosion of the Challenger Space Shuttle, for example) have taught us nothing else, they taught that killing each other either in the name of religion or through scientific deception—both motivated by selfishness, impatience, mediocrity, fear, and paranoia—are in the category of insanity, the complete opposite of healthy human peace and existence. I think most us could agree that insanity is surely something to avoid, and that health, peace, and love are goals for which to strive.

Chapter 2

A LENIENT TACK

In the early days of the Christianity, my daughter, all the catechumens were thrice immersed at their baptism. It was only with the emergence of Arianism that the Catholics changed their liturgy to specify a single immersion. It was done simply to set their creed apart from ours, you see, much as the Church had long ago made Sunday its Sabbath day, to dissociate itself from the Jews' Saturday Sabbath, and also had made Easter a movable feast, simply to set it as far as possible from the fixed Passover of the Jews. But we Arians do not dwell on the differences between the Catholics and ourselves. We believe that Jesus desired his followers to practice generosity and tolerance, not exclusivity. If you were to decide this minute, Caia Veleda, that you want to convert to, say, Judaism—or even revert to the paganism of our ancestors—

why, I should simply wish you happiness in your choice.

I [Veleda] was astounded.

But St.Paul said, 'Preach the word; reprove, entreat, rebuke; do the work of an evangelist.'

Tata Avilf, you would not even council against my making such a drastic departure from the Christian Church?

Ne, ni allis. So long as you live a virtuous life, daughter, doing harm to no other, we Arians would aver that you are obeying what St. Paul called 'the word.'

Gary Jennings

Raptor

In this chapter, I'd like to do the opposite of the preceding chapter. I'd like to stress the importance of tolerance, leniency, and cooperation. First, by leaving either discipline, science or religion, "well enough alone," "to each their own," and "in peace." This is similar to Stephen Jay Gould's idea of Non-Overlapping MAgisteria (NOMA)—the respectful separation of science and religion—discussed briefly in Part II. Second, by encouraging healthy dialogue and discussion. As I mentioned before, where I differ with Gould is that I think it's healthy for these two disciplines to share and debate; sharing and debating are different than attacking or deriding. But in addition to sharing and debating, the diminishing of insistent and constant criticism is also necessary.

I mentioned in previous chapters my opinion and feeling that religion remain a private practice, individually and within church sanctuaries. That, again, is the intent of the First Amendment of the Constitution and what is meant by "the separation of church and state." Unlike the scientific method—which is a principle (and a set of principles) that helps calculate, clarify, and conclude to improve our ability to understand the universe emotionally, intellectually, and aesthetically—religion is a personal philosophy of faith for inner peace which should be privately and subjectively cherished, but cannot and should not be utilized or dictated by any civic governing body. Actually, neither science nor religion should be "dictated" by a governing body; "dictating" is the definition and genesis of a dictatorship. Sadly, religion has a pattern in human civilization of doing exactly that. Science has had that tendency less. But science has also had its share of occasional dogmatic posturing and been responsible for human fatality. That said, this chapter is about being less critical of either science or religion, of encouraging their integration, of being more tolerant of both.

To recap, the First Amendment to the Constitution of the United States provides for the freedom to believe and practice any religion *and* to ensure that no single religion be adopted by either federal or state governments. As I attempted to clarify in the preceding chapter, the idea that this country was established as a "Christian nation," is in direct contradiction to the wording of the First Amendment. Civil morality is handled by governments.

Religious morality is not. The Framers of the Constitution determined that religion was best left to free, private practice rather than be controlled or adopted by any governmental entity. It is, in my view, one of the wisest aspects and decisions in the Constitution, and in global human organizational history. Our Colonial ancestors drew from the political lessons of all human history (albeit largely from their most recent political history with Great Britain), and applied it protectively to the future of the United States of America exceedingly well.

Religious practice has also been responsible for many beautiful accomplishments in humanity. There are countless religious charities that have helped the poor, destitute, hungry, homeless, exiled, mentally ill, handicapped, and the unlawful (convicted felons).[*]

And there are many non-judgmental and non-fundamentalist religious people in society who are loving and compassionate and are deeply loved and emulated. It would be prejudice as well for the non-religious to harshly and generally criticize and judge the philosophy, intention, and ethical motivation of these religious people and organizations; unless of course those charities, individuals within a charity, or other religious people clearly violate civil law (like the chronic and heinous sex-abuse within the Catholic Church). In other words, just as it is improper for religion to attempt to dictate civil law, so must civil society respect the privacy of religious practice. This should be one of the symbiotic relationships between science and religion. Where they can work together they should do so with respect and cooperation. Where they differ, the differences should be allowed. As Gould offers, science and religion are in many ways unique and differing approaches to human thought and that uniqueness should be honored. I add that their similarities should also be acknowledged and nurtured, and where possible, mutually instructive.

In avoiding either science or religion dictating civil policy, like the main horror premise in George Orwell's, *1984*, no society should ever allow a "thought police." No one has any right to tell someone else how to *think*. As Sagan noted, "The cure for a fallacious argument is a better argument, not

---

[*] A comprehensive, though by no means exhaustive list can be found at *GuideStar*, Directory of Charities and Nonprofit Organizations: http://www.guidestar.org/nonprofit-directory/religion.aspx).

the suppression of ideas." [137] Society is bettered by the existence of both scientific and religious inquiry and pursuit.

Unfortunately, as in Jerry Falwell's "Moral Majority" and in the misinterpretation of a "Christian nation," there are many religious people and leaders who feel strongly that what is missing from civil governments and the federal government is the "morality" of religious influence on the public, or the non-private practice of religion. While we should understand, sympathize, and respect some of the genuinely benevolent feelings that accompany this motivation, it is nevertheless in grave error.

First, it overlooks the fundamental principle of the need for privacy with regard to religious practice.

Second—and this is particularly striking—that very principle of privacy of religious belief, and its separation from government in the First Amendment, works both to protect society from the imposition and prejudice of religion *on society*, but also to protect religion from prejudice and discrimination *from society*. The separation is startlingly symbiotic.

It is obvious and tragic that many religions have experienced persecution and genocide in history: the early Protestant Church, the Jews, the Palestinians, the Arabians, the Quakers, the Mennonites, the Mormons, and the Amish, to name but a few examples. Just like with prejudice, persecution of any kind is intolerable and should be condemned and abolished whenever and wherever it happens.

But many of the world's religions have also been guilty of persecution, making erroneous moral pronouncements on individuals and society, as well as the hideous treatment of individuals throughout human history: every Inquisition; the completely spurious and fallacious accusations and house arrest of Galileo Galilei; the 10-year *fatua* by the Ayatollah Khomeini in 1989 against Salmon Rushdie (since 2000 he has returned to a normal life); and the 27-year imprisonment by the Apartheid government of South Africa of the late Nelson Mandela (who, after his release in 1990, was elected President of South Africa from 1994-99), to name only a few. These atrocities notwithstanding, religious thought and practice must be honored and respected like any other private or privately organized pursuit. Just as anyone or any group is free to pursue scientific inquiry and experiment, so must anyone or any group be allowed to pursue their religious beliefs free from judgment or harassment.

I would like to make special mention and commendation of one religious organization in the United States that I find especially exemplary. It is the Cooperative Baptist Fellowship (CBF). This moderate and inclusive group of Baptist churches is the result of their courageous departure from the highly conservative Southern Baptist Convention (SBC). Born initially from a splinter group in 1986 called The Southern Baptist Alliance—which became the still current umbrella group, the Alliance of Baptists—the Cooperative Baptist Fellowship is among the more liberal and non-prejudicial of the world religious denominations. They demonstrated their commitment to compassion and priority of love over belief and dogma when, in 1991, they broke ties with some of their brethren in the Southern Baptist Convention who had chosen a fundamentalist path for the SBC. Though I would like to hear not only inclusiveness of all religious faiths and no religious faith, but also *interest* in all faiths and philosophies including atheism and skepticism of their own faith, the advocates and adherents of the CBF were and continue to be an excellent example of churches that genuinely practice the love they preach. Even the words *cooperative* and *fellowship* in their organization's name indicates an unambiguous desire and focus for flexibility and unity. For non-fundamentalism.

It always takes courage to speak out and/or defy or denounce any authoritative body felt to be promoting and pursuing unethical principles and behavior, particularly, like Dorothy, when it's in one's own backyard. But the CBF did that and, in the process, rejuvenated the reputation of the Baptist Church globally. I admit, with chagrin, my previous ignorance of the CBF, which proves that it is often the loudest and most negative voices which dominate and overshadow those more kind and gentle. But it has been my pleasure learning that the unconditionally loving and welcoming members of the Cooperative Baptist Fellowship have been active and growing ever since the establishment of the initial Baptist Church in England in 1612.

As I mentioned in the Introduction, though I rarely attend church and seldom derive deep inspiration from church sermons or services, there are three ministers who I hold in particularly high regard. As it happens, they are all Presbyterian ministers.

Sharon Youngs is the pastor at First Presbyterian Church in Oak Ridge, Tennessee. Although (and sadly and shamefully) it is still somewhat rare that women are ordained ministers, much less head pastors at a church, Sharon is exemplary as a first-class minister, theologian, and human being. She is a dear friend of mine, and I have attended several of her church services and heard her sermons. She is warm and sensitive, with a welcoming smile and bright eyes. She is also an excellent speaker and her sermons are extremely progressive and inclusive. Though she and I probably differ about the source of her faith—the necessity of God—she is one of the few ministers whose sermons I consistently enjoy. I also have deep respect for her belief and faith in God. The references to God notwithstanding, I just greatly enjoy *her*, so I just internally substitute the word *universe* for God and I continue to thoroughly enjoy everything she has to say. She is loving, compassionate, thoughtful, witty, and very globally and culturally aware. She even threw in a fun analogy in one of her recent sermons, using the famous quote from Garrison Keillor about Powdermilk Biscuits, "Gives shy persons the strength to get up and do what needs to be done!" Curiously, I had just been talking about that quote the previous day, so Sharon's choice to include it in her sermon struck me as particularly clever, comical, and coincidental—and maybe even providential!

John Shuck is a Presbyterian minister affiliated with the First Baptist Church in Elizabethton, Virginia. Unlike my friend, Pastor Sharon Youngs, I have never met or seen Pastor Shuck in person. But he is also the creator and author of the blog, *Shuck and Jive*, which questions a wide range of religious dogma. Among progressive ministers, he is probably the most remarkably progressive. So much so that he freely offers that he does not believe in God. Not only is that highly unusual for any minister to say (including the already progressive Unitarians), but he takes issue with *all* the supernatural aspects of religion. As a guest in a blog called FriendlyAtheist.com[*] he writes, "In short, I regard the symbols of Christianity from a non-supernatural point of view. And yet, even though I hold those beliefs, I am still a proud minister. Why is [it] that so many people

---

[*] http://www.patheos.com/blogs/friendlyatheist/2015/03/17/im-a-presbyterian-minister-who-doesnt-believe-in-god-2/

think my affirmations are antithetical to Christianity? I think it is because Christianity has placed all of its eggs in the belief basket. We all have been trained to think that Christianity is about believing things. Its symbols and artifacts (God, Bible, Jesus, Heaven, etc) must be accepted in a certain way. And when times change and these beliefs are no longer credible, the choices we are left with are either rejection or fundamentalism. I think of Christianity as a culture. It has produced 2,000 years of artifacts: literature, music, art, ethics, architecture, and, yes, beliefs. But cultures evolve and Christianity will have to adapt in order to survive in the modern era."

He shares his own specific beliefs as well, in six points (incidentally, two groups of 111!):

- Religion is a human construct
- The symbols of faith are products of human cultural evolution
- Jesus may have been an historical figure, but most of what we know…is …legend
- God is a symbol of myth-making and not credible as a supernatural being or force
- The Bible is a human product as opposed to special revelation from a divine being
- Human consciousness is the result of natural selection, so there's no afterlife

Regardless of whether he is right or wrong in these opinions, for me his honesty is incredibly refreshing. I admire his personal candor and courage, and his willingness to highlight, discuss, and challenge some of the most sensitive doctrines of religious teaching.

Dr. Alexander Jeffrey ("Sandy") McKelway was Professor of Theology at Davidson College all the years of my youth. He and his wife Adelaide ("Babs") McKelway were two of my late parents' dearest friends, and their three sons were some of my brothers and my best friends.

In addition to having known, loved, and admired their family, Sandy McKelway spoke at both my father's funeral in 1977 and at a memorial concert that my brothers and I organized in our mother's honor in November, 1997. He is a very distinguished man, in posture, countenance, and credentials, and he is a comforting and commanding person and orator. Because my father's funeral was not recorded or videotaped, my memory of

Sandy's speaking at that time is a bit patchy. But I do remember that it was very tender and that it was obvious that Sandy loved my father and already missed him acutely. Sandy's speech at my mother's memorial concert *was* videotaped, so we have it to enjoy permanently.

I want to share portions of that particular speech of Sandy's because it was one of the most exquisite elocutions I've ever heard. It was a speech, a sermon, poetry, an essay, a mini-dissertation, and an intimately written meditation all-in-one. His words were, as Sandy introduced at the beginning, both as a theologian and as a long-time friend. He even joked that the theologian reference would have made my mother "...somewhat apprehensive...because she was in no ordinary sense religious." His speech was thus not only remarkable and eloquent in its wording and delivery, and contained religious references, but it was also deeply respectful of our mother and her own relative disinterest in and skepticism of religious belief. It was an endearing speech and sermon.

I also call it a "sermon" because, since he is a Presbyterian minister, there were definite references to God and divinity within his oration. But there were equal acknowledgments of the limitations of religious dogma and tradition, particularly regarding the abolishment of the arts by the early Reformed Church (founded by John Calvin) from some of their worship services. But as Sandy McKelway significantly pointed out, that stricture had forgotten what Calvin himself had emphasized called, "Common Grace." It held that *all* humans (a fact that we clearly have in *common* but tend to forget too easily) would receive God's grace, not just ones who adhere to a particular faith or purportedly chosen for grace by God. By extension, magnificent human endeavors and accomplishments, like the arts, enhance rather than detract from religious worship. McKelway also offered that art and artists augment religion—rising above the dogma of any particular faith to reach a wider circle of people. This is a feeling that I've always sensed. In addition to being awed by the universe and the beauty of life, I also feel the most religious (re-bound, re-tied, re-linked) and connected with the universe when I witness a great performance or a great presentation of any kind of art.

In the same speech, McKelway very graciously and gratefully related the first time he and his wife, Babs, heard my mother play. It was at a solo recital she performed at their church—the Presbyterian Church in Davidson,

North Carolina—in 1965. Prior to that recital, he and his wife had not yet met my parents. Here is a transcribed portion of his speech:

> Elaine's sons have asked me to speak briefly about their mother, and to do so not only as a long-time friend but also as a theologian. [*slight pause…*] Now, the prospect of that kind of commentary would make Elaine herself somewhat apprehensive [*the audience lightly laughs*]…for she was in no ordinary sense religious. Yet it was in a very religious setting that I first became really aware of Elaine and her art and the importance both would have for my life and, of course, for the lives of many others. [*long pause*] The year was 1965 and my wife Babs and I had just arrived in Davidson. We had lived in Vienna and Basel and worked for several years at Dartmouth in New Hampshire, and wondered what sort of cultural environment this small southern town might offer. Elaine was performing one evening at the Presbyterian Church, and we went not knowing exactly what to expect. Elaine entered, strode in her majestic way to the center of the chancel, raised her bow and began to play one of Bach's sonatas for solo violin. [*another long pause…*] As her music filled the church with such subtle technique and understanding, we both knew that things would be alright.

That last endearing accolade is one of the most loving and respectful things I've ever heard anyone say about another person. It is also an accolade of *faith*. Sandy and Babs felt (trusted, had faith in) a sharing of universal love and peace from my mother through her violin playing, without having met her, and thus unaware that she was not religious. That is faith through music…through sound…tangible, physical evidence.

Sandy's sweet comment was not only loving and admirable, it was also innocently free from religious prejudice. Since he was unaware of my mother's non-religiosity, his comment was human-to-human, particularly striking coming from a theologian to someone non-religious. (Some time later, after becoming dear friends with my parents, including learning of their non-religious lifestyle, he later made another significant and unprejudiced comment. He told them that were Jesus and they somehow able to meet, Jesus would probably prefer my parents' principles and ethics of love to some professed religious people whose ethics were less consistently compassionate; an even stronger and deeper compliment to bestow on a non-believer.)

Sandy and Babs are Presbyterian. As Sandy noted, their experience of my mother's recital that night was not wholly unreligious. Connecting the "Common Grace" with my mother's playing, in the same speech Sandy added:

> And so as I listened to Elaine play that evening, there seemed to me a marvelous symmetry between the sanctuary and the music she made in it. Above her and to one side stood the pulpit, where each Sunday morning—and with more or less success—the goodness of God and His Creation was expounded. And now standing alone, this young woman—using creative things...little bits of steel, and horsehair, and wood—very unconsciously, and *without the slightest intention to do so*, reminded us with great power of that same God and His goodness.

Once again, since he and his wife did not know that my parents were not religious, their feeling of comfort and contentment listening to my mother play that evening was completely unprejudiced and humanitarian. Love and music were the common languages.

I'm reminded of a similar musical moment—this time that my mother and I shared—years later in England, in 1971, which transcended cultural customs rather than religious rites. Our family was living in Sevenoaks, Kent, because my father was on sabbatical from Davidson College. I was attending the local Wildernesse (Secondary) School and my mother came one day to play a duet with me (I was still a violinist at the time) for the whole school's Assembly hour. It was not a religious school, but it was extremely conservative and properly British. I don't remember the name of the duet we played, but I remember well the response of the headmaster when we finished playing. His name was Mr. Pizer. He was a stern man, straight out of a Dickens novel, of some significant girth and height, with white hair on his large, imposing head, and an authoritative, yet dignified countenance. He projected and spoke with regal and solemn severity. However, this time, after a moment of silence, he smiled and formally but genially offered, "I don't usually say this to strangers, but...*do come back*!"

I participated, for the first time as a cello student, in the Snowbird Summer Arts Institute in Snowbird, Utah for four summers, from 1975 to 1979. Because Snowbird is just up Little Cottonwood Canyon from Salt Lake City, many of the other music students came from Mormon families. I had known Mormons before but not as many closer to my own age. It was both an education and a pleasure getting to know them. I must say that not only did I find them nice, friendly, hard-working, disciplined, very family-oriented, attractive, and interesting, I found their faith more interesting than some other religions to which I had already been exposed. I even took the "Seven Lessons" (the regiment of study taught by Mormon missionaries with the goal toward conversion), partly out of respect for the religion and partly motivated, I confess, by my romantic interest in a particularly lovely young Mormon woman! Though I did not find myself interested in converting when I completed those lessons with the missionaries, I did learn quite a lot about the Mormon faith, which added to my general appreciation for the Mormons and their commitment to a healthy and productive life.

The parents of one Mormon family that we got to know quite well were particularly exemplary. Three of their children were violinists and studied with my mother. In addition to their musical talent and ability, the whole family was kind, loving, friendly, supportive, disciplined, and welcoming of everyone. Next to my own father and both my uncles, I remember the father, John Grant Reed, as one of the kindest men and loving fathers I have ever known. He was a very sweet man, tall and lean, with an almost deferential smile and a light, tenor laugh. And next to my own mother and both aunts, the mother, Edith Carlquist Reed, was also one of the nicest women and most loving mothers I've ever known. (I also like both their full names. They are very dignified, sophisticated, and aristocratic names, like they were as people.) She was a little bit stronger a personality but no less kind, and she had a very sweet smile and a noble, almost regal presence. He and his wife clearly loved their children because all of their children exuded the same sweetness and immediate, infectious smile of their parents.

I was not present the fifth summer that my family returned to the Snowbird Institute, but that summer, in 1980, my father was terminally ill with brain cancer. My mother told me that John Reed walked slowly with my father holding onto his arm because my father could not walk easily by himself. Like all my Mormon friends, this family knew that my family was not L.D.S. (Latter Day Saints), but it didn't matter. Mr. Reed would probably have helped my father if he had been Charles Manson or Jeffrey Dahmer. He had not the slightest prejudice or judgment. He only cared and wanted to help another fellow human being in need.

Tragically, years later, while driving, John Reed was hit by a drunk driver and died not long after. I don't often say that the world is an unfair place because I sense that Darwin's discovery of the principle and force of evolution in nature indicates that life is fragile by nature, survival the exception not the rule, and that often there simply may be no apparent reason for life or death other than the pure chance, accident, and biological struggle for survival. But the death of Mr. Reed, and by a drunk driver, felt deeply and completely unfair to me. (The death of my own father from brain cancer at the age of 49 felt similarly unfair of nature. For me, if anything should be primarily rewarded in nature with survival it should be loving kindness, a trait that John Reed and David Richey shared). That kind and loving man paid the price of his life nearly instantly, through no fault of his own, and by a person irresponsible and uncaring enough to recklessly drink and drive.[*] It seems horribly cruel of nature. It is also wrenchingly ironic because one of the ways in which the Mormons are healthy is that they completely abstain from alcohol consumption. For this man to have been hurt at all, much less killed, by an inebriated driver is hideous and ironic injustice. If only that inebriated person who involuntarily killed my Mormon friend could have benefitted from Alcoholics Anonymous, the effects of the disease on him might have been abated, the two cars would have passed each other without incident, and Mr. Reed would probably have lived many more years sharing his love and kindness with his family and others.

~~~

My Life Coach, R. J. Solomon, is another example of a wonderful human being who is also religious (Jewish). Besides being my dear friend, confidante, and honorary "big sister," she helped me in many areas of my personal and professional life. In particular, she was influential in

---

[*] I know that what causes one to drink enough alcohol to adversely affect their safe operation of a motor vehicle is the same subject—physical/mental addictive disease—that motivated the formation of the original Twelve-Step organization that I discussed in the Introduction, Alcoholics Anonymous (AA).

encouraging me to set aside some of my religious preconceptions and prejudices in order to gain a better understanding of, and benefit from, a religiously-influenced but internationally-successful program and tradition: Twelve-Step work.

As I mentioned in the Introduction, it was (and sometimes still is) hard for me not to be distracted by the references to God or even a "Higher Power" in Twelve-Step meetings without wishing that the wording would be more non-religious, and/or that all capitalizations creating implied personal pronouns would be omitted. However, to be so distracted by the choice of words and capitalizations that one doesn't allow themselves to experience the benefit *behind* some of the wording, is as prejudiced as someone somewhat less educated who is put off by a marvelous story or orator because the vocabulary seems too erudite. Both are hindrances to learning and growing.

Ms. Solomon was of great help in bringing to my attention my own preconceived notions of, and reactions toward, religion. She helped me to temper (what I still consider in some cases justifiable) reactions that I know I have toward religious vocabulary; this so that I can appreciate and absorb the wisdom behind some of the wording unique to, or adopted by, Twelve-Step meetings. She also sometimes shared anecdotes of her faith with me that I found fascinating and illuminating. Mostly though, she is simply a dear person and an example of someone very committed to her faith who is a sweet, insightful, perspicacious, kind, and compassionate woman.

My point in the examples of this late Mormon man and my former Jewish Life Coach is that, while I don't necessarily think that it takes religion or science to make someone loving and kind, I do think it's important to simultaneously respect the benefit that one's religious faith or scientific pursuit provides. What causes someone to be loving and kind, or have any personal characteristics at all, is still largely a mystery, or at least not yet specifically substantiated (whether because of genetics, environment, religious faith, scientific study, or a combination of these four and other possibilities). In my perception, John Reed, like my own father, was kind, gracious, and loving *by nature*. But unlike my father, he also happened to be a Mormon. R. J. Solomon also has a kind and loving nature, and she happens to be Jewish. Though I don't think that his being L.D.S. or her being Jewish are the primary reasons for their loving kindness, their religiosity is clearly not to their detriment. It may, in fact, be much more of a significant influence in their lives than I'm aware, which would simultaneously illuminate my ignorance and further my own positive education. Therefore, I can only acknowledge and credit those specific religions with a substantial amount of excellent qualities, or this man and this woman would probably not have remained with their respective faiths.

Religion, like anything in human society, has been both beneficial and damaging. But I think it would be entirely fair and safe to say that the original and continuing intention of religion, private or organized, has been the yearning for understanding, benevolence, and love. After all, why is God so often equated with love? The phrase "God is love" is quoted both metaphorically and literally. Personally, I think that even if the concept of a single, divine entity as creator of the universe and all of life *is* mythological, the word or term "God" could easily be acknowledged as both a metaphor for the beauty, energy, and total force of love, *and* as a metaphor for our aesthetic, emotional, and reverential connection to the universe. The universe, as evident in countless photographs and video footage, is magnificent beyond measure. Though unseen, the sense and feeling of love in life is obvious, unmistakable, and ubiquitously and physically evident. In other words, though invisible—like Sandy and Babs McKelway felt through my mother's violin playing—there is abundant proof of love.

Therefore, I want to offer a personal proposal of my own possible belief in God (external to the universe or not). It is simultaneously an "If...then..." statement and the transitive property of equality (If a = b and b = c, then a = c). In my proposal, "a" stands for love, "b" for God, and "c" for believing:

If the force and energy of love is (called) God (If a = b)
then I believe in God (and b = c)
because I believe in love (then a = c).

But then that is what Sagan meant when he said, "Whether we believe in God depends very much on what we mean by God." [138]

My next question, however, is this: why does love need to be called anything else, including God or any other abstract term? What can't love exist for its own sake? Like Stephen Hawking said about the universe, why can't love just *be*. I feel that defining love as God (or reflexively, God as love), while sweetly poetic, also creates abstraction, distraction, and confusion. And at least for me, it is unnecessary to the natural beauty and experience of love. (I realize, though, that for anyone who is religious, God is not only necessary and a deep enhancement of love, but is the incorporeal presence, source, and origin of love.)

Though I think organized religion tends to fall into a trap of fearfully resisting intellectual inquiry, I don't think religions, by and large, have primarily negative motivations. Mostly, and regardless of my own opinion, I think it would be correct to credit religion, and churches in general, for being motivated more by love than by hate. That said, I think religions need to be as consistent in the *practice* of their faiths as in their *quoting of scripture*, by demonstrating that professed love in their *behavior to and interest in all people*, not just with their fellow-believers. I think that that is what most, if not all, of the most prominent historical religious figures have taught, and are what my Life Coach and my late Mormon friend exemplify.

Chapter 3

IN
TENTATIVE CONCLUSION

Truly the dear world is as fair here as in the woodland shades.
Who calls it a vale of tears?
Methinks it is but the darkness in our minds
that bringeth gloom to the world.

Robin Hood
The Merry Adventures of Robin Hood
Howard Pyle

Each of us is a God, Buddha had said.
Each of us knows all.
We need only open our minds to hear our own wisdom.

Angels and Demons
Dan Brown

The best explanation of a comparison between a scientific view and a religious view of the universe was related to me by a friend who is a Catholic woman and is as follows: That the feelings and senses of both views are identical. Only the terminology is different.

I will gladly share and express that I have deep feelings and senses. I am a very emotional and expressive person, in addition to being intellectually interested. My emotions and expressions are why I am a performing musician and love all the arts. And my intellectual interest motivated me to write this book. They are both why I stress the beautiful pairing of the emotions *and* the intellect. I have never thought or felt that in navigating life, it should be a question of one *or* the other.

I inherited my feelings, sensations, expressions, and intellect. They are in my DNA. I know that assessment is a more of a scientific view. Perhaps if I had been raised in a religious home environment, I would automatically, or at least more readily, attribute all my sensations, my desire for expression, and my intellectual pursuits as gifts from God. But I was not raised with religion so I don't sense that interpretation. And I have no way to turn back my life clock to test for that alternate scenario. The best I, or anyone, can do is try to understand, empathize with, love, and respect all other senses and perceptions, the same that we all wish from others. The "Golden Rule."

But if I *had* to stress one more than the other—the emotions or the intellect—I would choose the emotions. The right-brain. Feelings. Love. I would stress love more than thought; like my friend said, our feelings are our most important thing. I sense that love runs more deeply in humans (and maybe in the universe—God?) than thought. It would be my hypothesis and theory that love is the strongest force in living creatures and in the universe. That would match the religious phrase, "God is love," though I would substitute the word, God, with the word, universe. I sense that all life (known and unknown) in the universe is most deeply driven by love. I sense that because of my observation of life and because of how I feel when I feel love and feel loved by others. It is the closest I come to believing in or affirming faith in something relatively intangible. I cannot prove that love exists. But I experience its existence. (Those last two sentences sound, to me, very similar to a religious person's description of sensing God, albeit with a different possessive pronoun.) I have faith that love ultimately triumphs hate because of how powerfully wonderful love feels, both individually and shared. I don't feel or think that the intellect has quite the same energy, power, or force.* But perhaps thought has a different and hidden function: maybe thought leads us to the best situation in which to love!

I've quoted my late grandmother Richey a couple of times earlier, and two other poignant and quotable moments from her come to mind for me now regarding love. Though she was a Methodist and knew that my mother was not religious nor raised with religion, she treated my mother—and everyone else—with unconditional love. However, it did bother my grandmother somewhat that my mother and my two brothers and I were not religious, and that we voiced constructive criticism of religion. People of my grandmother's generation, particularly women, were much less openly skeptical or critical of anything, especially religious authority. My mother was raised in an openly skeptical family, just as she raised my brothers and me. So though my grandmother Richey was a very independent, courageous, outspoken, and admirably feisty woman, she was also a product of her generation, including a religious upbringing. Her Christian faith was strong and extremely emotional, like her personality. My immediate family's lack of religious belief saddened her and made her feel lonely anytime the subject of religious belief came up in our conversations (a fact and byproduct of religious teaching that I find sad in itself, and self-incriminating of religion in general).

But my mother related two lovely things that my grandmother said to her once after a slightly sensitive conversation they had about their differing views on religious faith. Because she loved my mother and our family unconditionally, and love really was more important to her than religious faith, she said simply, "We believe the same thing!" She also said once, "It's not hard for me to love people." In the spirit of those true and beautiful statements, I encourage all of us to have unconditional love and respect for each other and our beliefs, regardless of any differing terminology. Love should be easy to give and receive, and terminology easy to adjust and accommodate.

---

* I sense and think that C. S. Lewis did not give the question of autonomous love (no deity required) enough credit when he chastised the term, "Life Force." I sense the possibility that the universally autonomous life force may indeed be love.

A term is simply a name or title we give to something that we have discovered or sensed. But terminology is invented, reinvented, discarded, and swapped all the time. If our discoveries or senses are similar, then all we have to do is realize the similarity and try to be as specific as possible, but flexible, about the terms or words we use to describe our senses/discoveries. Terms are also a somewhat superficial part of discovery. The process by which we pursue discovery—whether by the scientific method or through religious reflection—and discovery itself are the important things, respectively. The term we apply to discoveries are less important. Unfortunately, terms are not unimportant altogether; they are probably necessary, even if only as temporary references. However, as I explored in detail in the Introduction and chapters of Part I, terms can be confusing if they are too general, not well enough defined, and/or not clearly enough understood. The words/terms, *religion, believe, faith, spiritual, materialistic, value, miracle,* and *free-will* are all examples. The same seems to be the case with the word/term, *God.*

The Unitarian Church was founded on the principle of 'cross' or 'multi' theologies to try to help remedy the confusion of varying terms and perceptions of God. "God *as we understood Him*" is the final phrase of the third step in The Twelve-Steps of Alcoholics Anonymous. The word or term, *God*, is obviously confusing to enough people or these adaptations and changes would not have taken place; and if it was not as confusing, there would be far fewer skeptics. As I have offered, I don't think it's the fault of skepticism. The error, as I see it, lies with an acceptance of unclear terminology and a lack of the disciplined critical thinking needed to clarify the terminology.

Even the specific words, religious, non-religious, fundamentalist, agnostic, and atheist are all terms that only approximate our subjective views and feelings. While I think it is extremely important to understand and use words well, and there seems to be an almost infinite number of deeply, specifically, and beautifully descriptive words, it is probably true that no words can completely evoke the feelings they define and represent. A phrase that comes to mind is one I've heard many times: "Words fall so short." This is expressed by some people who feel that, like the stricture and requisite of science for physical evidence to support a proposition or claim, the use of words to describe religious or spiritual phenomena are a limitation, an impediment to the experience of deep and visceral feelings. There is a point to this. Like the feeling and energy of love, feelings in general are difficult (and maybe impossible) to quantify or measure. Their effects can be clearly felt, and measured electronically, but the source and origin of feelings is often elusive to physical evidence and verbal and written description. Feelings may or may not be attributable to physics.

In, *Dying To Be Me: My Journey From Cancer, To Near Death, To True Healing*, by Anita Moorjani, she describes her feeling of being enveloped in unconditional love during her near-death experience (NDE) and the inadequacy of even the word, love, to describe the depth of that feeling. "I then had a sense of being encompassed by something that I can only describe as pure, unconditional love, but even the word *love* doesn't do it justice. It was the deepest kind of caring, and I'd never experienced it before. It was beyond any physical form of affection that we can imagine, and it was *unconditional*—this was *mine*, regardless of what I'd ever done. I didn't have to do anything or behave in a certain way to deserve it. This was love for me, no matter what!" [139] She then clarifies more specifically the meaning of her feeling. "My heightened awareness in that expanded realm was indescribable, despite my best efforts to explain it. The clarity was amazing. *The universe makes sense!* I realized. *I finally understand—I know why I have cancer!* I was too caught up in the wonder of that moment to dwell on the cause, although I'd soon examine it more closely. I also seemed to comprehend why I'd come into this life in the first place— I knew my true purpose. *Why do I suddenly understand all this?* I wanted to know. *Who's giving me this information? Is it God? Krishna? Buddha? Jesus?* And then I was overwhelmed by the realization that God isn't a *being*, but a *state of being...and I was now that state of being!* " [140]

While this sharing does not itself constitute proof of her definition of God, it is beautifully and clearly related. The last sentence, in particular, is refreshingly specific. Her expressions evoke the strong sense she felt of a love that exceeded all the love she had experienced in life and the elusiveness of words to describe the depth and grandeur of her feeling. Her last statement bolsters the significant point that Paul Tillich and Stephen Hawking made, respectively: of God as *the state of being* but not *a being*, and that the universe could just *be*.

However, just because something is elusive does not mean it is unattainable. Searching for deeply descriptive words for feelings and searching for physical evidence for the meaning and existence of God are, to me, very similar searches.

A new and creative religious term that I heard and enjoyed came from a woman who was raised Baptist, feels a close connection to Jesus Christ and God, but now feels most comfortable as a free-thinker. She described herself philosophically, religiously, and *humorously*, as an "Agnostic Christian." I liked the term immediately, and it gave me an instant realization: if we were being truly honest, I think we might *all* call ourselves agnostics. God or no God, how can any of us *really* know how everything got here? *I* sure don't!!

Like my Catholic friend, I sense that the scientific and religious views are not as different as they seem. In Part I, Chapter 1, I outlined and defined both the religious term, *God*, and the scientific terms, *cosmos/universe*, and pointed out how I think those terms, though applied differently in practice, are more similar than they are different. Where the similarity ends, in my view, is with the concept of the cosmos, or the creator of the cosmos, in the form of a person, a proper noun. But if the religious person and the scientist can acknowledge this and minor differences in other word and phrase definitions, maybe a better agreement can be reached. In religion, for example, allowing that God as a proper noun, a person, might be a metaphor and not a reality, and that the religious, "...ultimate reality..." may be the same as the scientific "...orderly harmonious systematic universe..." (or my phrase in the same chapter, "the totality of the observable universe"). In science, for example, that scientific thinking and the demand for physical evidence be open to *all* evidence (including potential non-physical evidence), as long as the evidence is superbly proposed and demonstrated.

I have stressed several times my feeling of the need for religious belief to be held and practiced privately—individually and in buildings of worship—rather than risk the permanent adoption of any single religious faith into public life and legislation.[*] Science is less problematic when applied publicly, and I outlined my feelings about why in Chapter 1 of this part of the book.

---

[*] This does not include seasonal public religious expressions, such as Christmas, Hanukkah, Easter, or any other *temporary* public religious/holiday decoration or celebration. Temporary expression does nothing to interfere with or intervene into long-term public policy.

In Tentative Conclusion   293

I was watching CBS This Morning on February 14 (Valentine's Day), 2014, when the program ran the story of the death of Ralph Waite. The report was significant for me in two ways. First, I loved *The Waltons* when I was a child and very much enjoyed Waite's portrayal of John Walton. Second, the news piece included a video segment from the series between John Walton and John Boy Walton that was directly germane to this particular point: of the necessity of private practice for religion. The discussion between the two characters in the scene is about the similarities and differences of religious/spiritual thought—while emphasizing the commonality—of the parents, John and Olivia Walton, about which the plot of the episode centers. It raises both the importance of religious privacy and the commonality between secular/scientific and spiritual/religious thinking. In Season 1, Episode 7, of *The Waltons*, "The Sinner," John Walton (Ralph Waite) expresses this to John Boy Walton (Richard Thomas):

> John Sr: I guess you're old enough to travel your own road son.
> John Boy: I love you and Momma both.
> John Sr: 'ell, there's no choice there. It's not a question of one bein' right and the other wrong.
> John Boy: Well, I know Mom's a Baptist, but I don't truly know what you believe, Daddy.
> John Sr.: Well...I believe life's a mystery...a sacred one...as for faith, that's a personal and private thing, it's not something like you pull on like you pull your pants on in the morning. [John Boy laughs] I don't think that's much different from whacha Mom thinks.

It is a thoughtful and tender scene. I was struck not only with the beauty of the scene and its application to the importance and necessity I feel for religious belief and practice to remain private, but I was also highly impressed by the taste, preference, and judgment of the party or parties at CBS This Morning who were responsible for choosing that scene as the example of Waite's acting to air on the broadcast.

The importance and boundary of privacy is too often forgotten, both as an individual right and as an ethical principle to respect and demonstrate toward others. Privacy is applicable to all issues, but should be particularly applied to religious belief, both for the protection of religion and for the protection of those non-religious.* However, beyond the issue of religious privacy, how extremely important the need is for *sharing love*, privately and publicly, regardless of religious or scientific background. The sharing of love is expressed and exemplified in the 1965 hit song, "What the World Needs Now Is Love," with lyrics by Hal David and music by Burt Bacharach. How lovely it would be if, not only as a wishful momentary thought, love was as physically abundant as oxygen and water. Perhaps it can be. That would be a constant satiation and fulfillment of love.

~~~

Similar to the "trinity" of my own personal spiritual/religious feelings that I described in the Introduction (love and respect for myself, all of life, and for the universe), I would like to close with a trinity of a slightly different kind—three scenarios of what I imagine to be *possibilities* of the meaning, existence, or non-existence of God:

1) There is **one God, or many Gods**. Religion, theism, and deism have been and are correct. God(s) are void of form or gender and elusive to physical evidence and proof. But the existence, energy, and presence of a supernatural God (or gods) is (are) real.

2) There is **no God**. Science, atheism, agnosticism, and spirituality have been and are correct. God(s) is(are) mythological, a human invention in the

---

* A relatively new term for a non-religious person has been coined by the religious community. It is the "nones," or no religious affiliation. I find the term rather unflattering. It sounds like it could mean "one who has nothing" as if having no religious belief rendered one less spiritually secure. I much prefer the word, *philosophical*. To their credit, some admirable religious leaders are not only including the non-religious in their respect for all beliefs, but others yet are offering concerned responsibility for helping to increase their numbers.

https://baptistnews.com/opinion/columns/item/30505-making-more-nones-asap
https://baptistnews.com/ministry/people/item/30602-bjc-exec-blasts-religious-bigotry

imagination. There is no supernatural. The universe(s) and life as observed, studied, and understood by modern science, physics, and astronomy is reality.

3) We are **our own God**. Humans, all life on Earth, and all possible life in the universe or universes are autonomous. *Both* religion and science are our unique inventions, but there are no external entities or deities except in our imaginations. Thus life on Earth has a profound and proud power: Like the universe, we evolved, exist, live, and love together as *a collective entity*. No conceit, arrogance, narcissism, or anthropic principle is implied. Dignity and autonomy of life (known and sought), awe, humility, love, comfort with cosmic phenomena and ambiguity, and relishing all these together, are reality. (Numbers 2 and 3 can coexist.)

Though all three of these possibilities are deeply intriguing to me, the latter, number 3, is the *tentative conclusion* that I am suggesting in this book:

<blockquote>
The meaning of God is ***us***...
our unified, united, and universal ***love***.*
</blockquote>

Like the Whos singing joyfully together, hand-in-hand, in *How the Grinch Stole Christmas*, and the sense of loving humanity in the song, "We Are The World," we don't need love from a deity because we have love for ourselves and for each other.† Our *internal* love shared *externally* with others. As Ayya Khema said, "Breathe-in peace, breathe-out love." That, to me, *is* spirituality. Or, as Neil deGrasse Tyson said, "...the universe *is in us*." We just forget that we never lost it, like Dorothy.

---

* I noticed two things after writing this tentatively conclusive phrase. One, that the first line comprises three word-pairs: 1) The concept 2) of God 3) is us. A trinity. And two, that the second line comprises a four word-phrase rhythm: 1) Our unified 2) united 3) and universal 4) love. It matches the number of my suggested fundamentals. Four. At least my subconscious was somewhat consistent!

† In Carl Sagan's 1985 novel, *Contact*, Ellie Arroway reflects: "For small creatures such as we, the vastness is only bearable through love." And in the 1997 motion picture, *Contact,* based on the same novel, the extraterrestrial (Ellie Arroway's "father") offers to Ellie, "...you feel so lost...so alone...only you're not. In all our searching, the only thing we've found that makes the emptiness bearable...is [loving] each other."

As if in support of this, the "Words of Offering" in the service program of the Unitarian Universalist Church in Winston-Salem, N.C. on December 29, 2013, which I attended, expressed this beautifully (although I question, once again, the need for the capitalization of "Fellowship"):

> We come to this place because we love what exists here. The Fellowship is a living entity, and like all living things, it must have nurture and sustenance. Its breath and its heartbeat...its life itself, can only be derived from its living components: us.

Christophe Galfard said the same in his book, *The Universe In Your Hand: A Journey Through Space, Time, and Beyond*:

> ...you suddenly sense that your home world [Earth], despite its ability to heal, is fragile, almost defenseless...almost. But not quite. It now has us. It has you. [141]

Reza Aslan said much the same in his book, *God: A Human History*:

> ...perhaps we should consider the possibility that the entire reason we have a cognitive impulse to think of God as a divine reflection of ourselves is because we are, *every one of us*, God. [142]

Cat Stevens expressed the teaching of love in the closing lyrics of his song, "The Boy with a Moon and Star on His Head." Any wonderful teacher of any gender in history is my interpretation of the "The Boy." And to me, "The Moon And Star" are our collective entity of love, respect, and sharing of the universe:

> Until the gift that someone left, a basket by my door.
> And in there lay the fairest little baby crying to be fed,
> I got down on my knees and kissed the Moon and star on his head.
> As years went by the boy grew high and the village looked on in awe
> They'd never seen anything like the boy with the Moon and star before.
> And people would ride from far and wide just to seek the word he spread
> I'll tell you everything I've learned, and Love is all, he said.

Although perhaps unintentionally, I think Canned Heat also intended this sense of love and unity in their 1970 single, "Let's Work Together." Originally written and sung by Wilbert Harrison in 1962 as the single, "Let's Stick together," the Canned Heat version single was sung by Meryl Streep and Rick Springfield in the final wedding scene of the 2015 film, *Ricki And The Flash*. Rousing lyrics of the 1970 song are:

> Come on come on let's work together
> Now now people
> Say now together we will stand
> Every boy girl woman and man

Keith Thompson's and Dr. Robert Landy's 2007 musical *God Lives In Glass: Reflections Of God Through The Eyes Of Children* expresses this unity of all religious and spiritual belief. In the song, "God Lives," the final choral cadence concludes, "…in the human heart, inside of you."

And maybe The Jackson 5 said the same thing in their 1970 hit song, "ABC":

> ABC…Easy as
> One, two, three…Or simple as
> Do re mi,
> ABC,
> one, two, three,
> baby, you and me…
> That's how easy love can be.

As it happens, ABC/One, two, three/Do, Re, Mi are all groups of three: small trinities and 111s! These three triad groups also match my four fundamental principles, respectively: 1 and 2, Reading and Writing (ABC) 3, Arithmetic (One, two, three) 4, Music and the performing arts (Do, Re, Mi)—all products of a possible cosmic trinity of beauty, intelligence, and love. And the three-word phrase, "…you and me…," in the above song could be a metaphor for life unity. How nice if love *could* be that easy!

Like my earlier example of the billion-piece evolutionary picture-puzzle, I met a very sweet and smart young woman recently who made a striking puzzle analogy. She was talking about her enjoyment of puzzles and remarked that completing them was like putting people together again to make a unified global community. She also shared a significant and surprisingly aware fact about herself. She said, unabashedly, "I'm autistic." Despite that, she is clearly functional, intelligent, and insightful. The date I met her was also somewhat significant and fun. It was the 4th of July, 2016.

So whether one feels religious, scientific, spiritual, philosophical, or a healthy mixture of philosophies and beliefs, not only are we all aware of and sense the same universe and arriving at slightly different ideas and terms as explanations, but our real strength is within ourselves and living proudly and peacefully together—the family of life on Earth. Coexisting. I encourage all of us not only to acknowledge this possibility but, like the jubilant 1970 song by Three Dog Night, "Celebrate!" *

To that end, here are my specific hopes:

- That we love ourselves and each other unconditionally
- That we revel in the unity of our global human community
- That we respect the welfare and balance of all life
- That we promote and nurture artistic beauty and excellence
- That we not assume anything (Ruiz's Third Agreement)
- And that we continue learning and our search for knowledge unbiased to any and all possibilities.†

Both the scientist and religious person alike can glean from the other's insight, which should only be a compliment to all points of view. It may be that there *is* an Intelligence, an Entity, a Deity external to, responsible for, and Creator of, the universe. God. But that could just as possibly be fiction or fantasy. It may be that the universe, nature, and life have always existed (somewhere in the cosmic vastness), and will continue to exist, infinitely, by their own inertial natural law, devoid of supernatural powers or deities. Both of these perspectives are possible until determined more conclusively—a determination or conclusion that, at present, still remains hidden. The

---

* Curiously, the last three of those four song examples—by Canned Heat, The Jackson 5, and Three Dog Night—were all released in 1970.

† I noticed after formulating these that I had emphasized six points. Six is two threes: two trinities, or two 111s. However, contrary to my emphasis on concrete evidence, now *I'm* probably reaching for insignificant significance!

acquired knowledge and art, trust in ourselves, love and admiration to and from each other, and the enjoyment of having figured out so much about ourselves and the universe, are our greatest assets and attributes. Not bad results and rewards for being tiny creatures on a tiny planet in an immense universe, regardless of its initial source.

Our job as human beings, in tribute to the gift of intelligence from the universe—whether "Created," or naturally evolved, or both—is to leave open all possible conclusions and continue rigorous, disciplined, and enthusiastic inquiry. Like Stephen Hawking and Paul Tillich posed, if we truly love and trust ourselves and each other, our collective intelligence, experience, perseverance, creatively critical thinking and artistic expression, and unreserved global love and compassion may be our supreme *being*.

Epilogue

As I shared in the Introduction, I have seen only a few rare cosmic phenomena. I have seen Comet Hale-Bopp with my naked eye, Jupiter and its four moons through a telescope at the Griffith Observatory in Los Angeles, the Moon through a telescope, a few falling stars, and a couple of lunar eclipses. They were all breathtakingly beautiful and gave me the same viscerally connected feeling that Neil deGrasse Tyson spoke of when he compared the iron in stars to the same stuff in our bodies. Star*dust* as he called us.

On August 21, 2017, I had the chance to increase my experience sighting cosmic phenomena. And not to behold just *any* cosmic phenomenon, but *the* cosmic sighting across the United States in nearly a century: a *totality* Solar Eclipse.

I was prevented from seeing the totality of the Solar Eclipse in the late summer of 1999 in Paris, France by a large cloud. It floated from the left, reached out its oblivious and unkind hand and completely covered the Sun just moments before "full corona," as totality is also called. As the cloud approached and began and covering the sun, a French woman standing beside me began shouting profanely but pointlessly at the cloud, and in an agitated and strettoed crescendo, "merde, merde, merdE, merDE, meRDE, mERDE, MERDE!!!!," She shouted this sequence of "shit" as if she could somehow keep the offending cloud from advancing, or at least divert it into a trajectory away from the nearly consumed Sun by the Moon. But it was not to be. The cloud completely covered both the Sun and the Moon for several minutes, long enough for totality to be blocked. When that cloud finally passed to the right and the Sun and Moon were again revealed, the Moon was making its way *off* the Sun, to the left, opposite from whence it had come.

I will relate my most recent experience of disappointment in a moment. I will share that disappointment partly out of need for personal peace and tranquility, and partly to offer perspective on proof. But first I must say that, germane to my advocacy for searching for concrete physical evidence, there is no greater evidence, and proof of that evidence, than to experience something not just for oneself, but along with many other people, and have the mass experience not just be overwhelmingly exhilarating, but match exactly—beginning, middle, and end—with frequent and consistent scientific calculation and prediction. Such was the case and experience for millions of people in the United States with the Solar Eclipse on August 21, 2017.[*] I had planned and prepared for over a year to be, "at the right place at the right time," to view that complete Solar Eclipse, including totality. I was determined not to miss it again. Sadly, my determination was to be deflected yet again. This time not by a cloud, but by me.

In the spring of 2015, I suffered a health issue with my left eye that is permanent but not life-threatening. I was one of only a small number of unlucky people who experienced a detached retina—not once, but twice—after cataract surgery. I learned that a detached retina is one possible, random, and unavoidable repercussion for a very few people following cataract surgery. I was one of those unlucky few.

The first time my left retina detached, I was advised by my cataract surgeon to choose laser and gas bubble surgery. He advised that method because he knew that I was a musician and would risk permanent near-sightedness if I elected the other surgical method, scleral buckle surgery. Gas bubble surgery is less invasive, but requires the nearly impossible regiment of remaining upright and altitude pressure-free for three weeks, including while sleeping. It is extraordinarily difficult to maintain, and I know I did not remain consistently upright when I slept. I was also due in Colorado two weeks following the surgery, which would be a large change in altitude one week before the end of my instruction to avoid altitude pressure. As I approached Denver and was aware of the gradual increase in altitude, I did as well as I could in following the doctor's direction—stopping

---

[*] I have heard an observation made (with irony and frustration) that many of the same people who trusted scientists to predict that specific total Solar Eclipse to the exact minute, don't extend anywhere near that same degree of trust to scientists who have repeatedly warned about the devastating damage humans are wreaking on the Earth by recklessly contributing to global warming. Unflatteringly, it proves that those who chronically deny the severity of global warming, place more trust in science for their personal entertainment (natural or human-made) than in protecting the global environment for all life. The double irony is that with little-or-no acknowledgment and adjustment in human awareness and behavior to reverse this exponential global warming, the likely fact is that there may soon be no habitable Earth on which to be entertained.

for a 30-minute break if I could feel pressure in my eye. But I was under a travel time constraint for arriving in Boulder, and I pressed on at moments when I probably should have taken another break to let the pressure subside. I had been in Boulder only about a week when a follow-up appointment with a local retina surgeon revealed that my left retina had redetached. That surgeon insisted on emergency scleral buckle surgery.

During the surgery, that surgeon discovered that the redetachment had torn a small hole in the macula. The macula is much too tiny a membrane to surgically repair, so I had to lie face-down for five days to close the hole. It was a semi-torturous five days, but I managed and successfully closed the hole. The upside is that I can still see—albeit fuzzily— in my left eye. The downside is that the hole closed with scar tissue and that is as impossible to surgically smooth as was the original hole. So, because of the minutely bumpy scar tissue on my left macula, I now have permanently squeezed vision in the center of my left eye. I can see somewhat clearly around the periphery of my left eye, but the center looks like objects disappearing into quicksand. Smudged and blurred if visible at all. My right eye still sees nearly perfectly, save for my continued need of reading glasses.

As a result of this damage to my left retina, I have also learned that the brain adjusts for the relative loss of vision in one eye by making the still healthy eye compensate, "take over" and see for both eyes. (The Department of Motor Vehicles (DMV) calls the condition a "one-eyed driver.") With only a slightly hazy or filmy look from my interfering left eye, I am able to see everything very well with my right eye as if my left eye was not at all damaged. This is, in my view, one proof of evolution in the very short term. The brain makes a nearly automatic adjustment to the injury so that the person is nearly unaware of the injury. That is a remarkable evolutionary survival function of the brain, and not in years, but almost immediately. In my opinion, that is one concrete proof that evolution is a fact. The body quickly adapts to insure its continued use and survival. As you might guess, since my second detached retina surgery, I have been and am still very cautious and protective of my eyes, particularly my right eye. In the case of the August 2017 total Solar Eclipse, *too* cautious and protective.

I went with friends to Lake Tellico, in Tennessee to experience the event. I also took the inspiration from my friends to view the eclipse while floating on my back in the lake. About twenty minutes before we knew the eclipse would begin in our geographical location, I paddled out on the lake on a kayak and picked my position. Since I had gotten into position early, I began watching the Sun through my eclipse glasses when the Sun was as yet unobstructed. That view remained unchanged for what felt like many minutes. Then suddenly, but almost imperceptibly, I thought I saw something make a light smudge on the Sun at the Sun's upper right curve (from my floating perspective on the lake, which changed as I floated and turned on my kayak). I was right. My right eye assisting my left had seen correctly. It was the Moon. Gradually the smudge became a nibble at the Sun and then a small bite. Then a larger bite. I continued to observe the Moon's entire, perfectly patient progression across the Sun in larger and larger bites, creating a greater and greater crescent Sun, all the while exercising great caution with my eclipse glasses to make sure that I was completely covering and protecting my eyes.

Caution is a very prudent response in moments or situations of uncertainty. The adage, "Better safe than sorry," was not first thought of to encourage being hasty. But in the case of diligently shielding my eyes from Sun with the eclipse glasses, caution would turn out to be to my eventual disadvantage. I'm not sure what I was expecting to see through the glasses at totality, but when the last sliver of the Sun was blocked by the Moon, I thought I might see a muted version of totality in my eclipse glasses (so I would know that I could safely remove the glasses to enjoy totality). When I still saw only black through the eclipse glasses, I thought the Moon just hadn't quite completely covered the Sun.

It had and was. In my extreme caution to protect my eyes, I waited too long. A moment later I saw a sudden splash of sunlight wash over the lake to my right, and a sliver of the Sun appear on the opposite, or right side, of the Moon. Unwittingly—and to my tremendous, frustrated chagrin and disappointment—I realized that I had blocked my own view of totality.

Fortunately, there will be another chance to view a Solar Eclipse in my lifetime. The next one will occur on April 8, 2024 and will cross a path from Texas to Maine. I am looking forward to that one and will know that I not only *may* remove my eclipse glasses when the last sliver of the Sun disappears behind the Moon, but that I *must* remove my eclipse glasses in order to see the totality. Curiously, not a single news article that I read prior to August 21, 2017—detailing preparation for watching the eclipse—ever emphasized that it was not only safe to remove the eclipse glasses during totality, but that it was *absolutely necessary*. It would have helped me, with my damaged left eye, to read that significant point. But then I think few people needed that advice. The more common error is to not use the glasses enough before totality, not during totality. In fact, I felt for a while after the eclipse was over like probably the only person observing in the path of totality, and during totality, to naively and ridiculously keep their eclipse glasses *on*!! It actually took me several days to comfort and forgive myself for what I felt was my colossal stupidity.

But now that some more time has passed, and I feel more peace and even some humor at my overly prudent, but sincerely safe error, I can realize that I was trying to be smart for my eyesight and my musical career reading music and text, and give myself that consolation. Also, what's done is done. Que sera, sera! The Serenity Prayer.* It's certainly not the end of the world. No Armageddon. A good and kind friend of mine (who saw the entire Solar Eclipse *including* the totality), with whom I shared all this, compassionately offered, "You saw most if it!" That was nice of him and it's true. I will remember all of this recent Solar Eclipse I saw with pleasure. I also have another opportunity to see it again, *with the totality*, and relatively soon. Actually, to borrow a religious phrase, one might say that I am particularly and eagerly awaiting the, "second coming!"

---

* By Reinhold Niebuhr.

Acknowledgments

I wish to thank the following people who helped make my writing of this book possible:

In addition to the dedication of the book to my parents, David Frank Richey and Elaine Lee Richey, I want to first and foremost thank my two brothers, Craig Johnson Richey, and Evan Frazer Richey, whose love and support during our lifetimes has helped me maintain the personal confidence I needed to persevere working over many years toward its completion and publication.

I want to thank my late Uncle Frank Ayre Lee, who I emulated and admired all the years of my life. Any visit with him, whether on my own or with a friend and/or family, were days spent immersed in a riveting smorgasbord of cultural fun: listening to him share personal stories; listening to a wide variety of music; watching fun segments of or full movies; getting annihilated by him on the tennis court (he was a superb tennis player until his death at age 86); and discussing a wide range of thought-provoking and emotionally-entrancing topics. He spoke beautifully, as if he was writing a well-written book—and no need for editing—with eloquence, a musically commanding bass voice, and a nearly-dictionary-perfect vocabulary. I will be forever grateful to him for inspiring me, and for his permission to audio record many of our marvelous conversations. I was also moved beyond measure by his tireless commitment in caring for his wife, my Aunt Bettye, who is the only person and relative I have ever directly experienced suffer from the hideousness of Alzheimer's Disease. My Aunt Bettye was also a dear and sweet soul, and she and my Uncle Frank were always examples to me of people who deeply and unconditionally loved each other and their family, and bestowed that unconditional love to anyone with whom they came into contact.

I want to thank their children, my cousins, Gary, Linda, Janet, and Clifford, for their permission to use quotes from my recorded conversations with their father, so that I could reinforce my points with his stronger points and profound wisdom.

My deepest gratitude as well to Dr. Walter Gray, my teacher of musical styles courses at the (University of) North Carolina School of the Arts from

1977 to 1981. Dr. Gray was the first spectacular teacher of music history I ever had. He always had his lectures memorized and delivered them eloquently and beautifully. I hung on his every historical word. He also encouraged me to read and write as much as I could which made me much better equipped to write my both doctoral dissertation and this book.

Also my deepest gratitude to my friend and Life Coach of eight years, R. J. Solomon. She helped me in ways I can never thank her enough, with my confidence, my organization, my creative writing (journaling), reminding me to keep the critical focus on myself, and to continue to see the glass full even if only one drop remains. She also encouraged me to stay aware and participating in Twelve-Step work, which kept my focus not only on myself, but on the love everyone has inside and deserves to feel and receive, and feeling that love as a global community, my definition of a higher power. I owe my continued awareness of those to her.

A very special thank you to Peg Robarchek and Carolyn Krause for their patient help with editing and proofreading of the manuscript at various stages of my writing. In addition to pointing out common errors, they both offered insights and perspectives, particularly on the development of women's views on religion.

A very special thank you to Dr. Bill Blevins for his willingness to read my manuscript and offer his valuable input and wisdom.

A very special thank you to Dr. Bill Leonard for his willingness to read a portion of my manuscript and offer his valuable input and wisdom on the details of the story of the Immaculate Conception.

A very special thank you to Dr. Alexander Jeffrey "Sandy" McKelway for his willingness to read my manuscript and offer his valuable input and wisdom, particularly on the history and specifics of John Calvin.

A very special thank you to Mary Culver for her willingness to read my manuscript several times and offer her very instructive and insightful comments in the early stages of my writing.

Another special thank you to my high school Geometry teacher, Ms. Judy Land for giving me the greatest educational experience of mathematics of my life.

A deeply expressed personal thank you to Meredith Reed Campbell for her permission to include my description of her father, the late John Reed, and her mother, the late Edith Carlquist Reed.

Thank you again, so much, to all of you!

Notes

Epigraphs:

Part I, Chapter 1
Pagels, p. 120
Ann Druyan, Introduction, ix

Part I, Chapter 2
McKelway, p.123
Sagan/Druyan p. 149

Part I, Chapter 3
Paul Tillich, p. 127

Part I, Chapter 4
King Hussein 1 of Jordan,
https://www.brainyquote.com/quotes/hussein_of_jordan_193927
The Reverend Jerry Falwell,
https://rockvillecogop.com/blog/2015/03/19/weekend-encounter-by-richard-dick-innes-229/

Part I, Chapter 5
Richard Preston, p. 58-59
Oh, God!, https://sundaykafunda.blogspot.com/

Part I, Chapter 6
Broca's Brain, pp.13-14

Part I, Chapter 7
St. Thomas Aquinas, online
Richard Dawkins, online
Dan Brown, The Da Vinci Code, pp. 341-342

Part III, Chapter 1

Christopher Hitchens, pp. 5-6
Gary Jennings, Raptor, p. 609

Part III, Chapter 2
Raptor, p. 337

Part III, Chapter 3
The Merry Adventures of Robin Hood,
of Great Renown in Nottinghamshire
Written and Illustrated by Howard Pyle
Dover Publications, N.Y. 1968
Originally published by Charles Schribner's Sons in 1883
p. 144
Angels and Demons, p. 484

Quotes:

---

[1] Part I, Chapter 1, p. 11: https://www.huffpost.com/entry/proof-of-the-soul_b_10112150

[2] Part I, Chapter 1, p. 18: *The Grapes of Wrath*, John Steinbeck. Penguin Books, 1939 p. 250

[3] Part I, Chapter 2, p. 26: *Broca's Brain*, Carl Sagan. Ballantine Books, 1980 p. 330

[4] Part I, Chapter 2, p. 27: *The God We Never Knew: Beyond Dogmatic Religion to a More Authentic Contemporary Faith*, Marcus J. Borg. Harper Collins. 1997 p. 11

[5] Part I, Chapter 2, p. 27: *God: A Human History*, Reza Aslan. Random House, 2017 p. 168

[6] Part I, Chapter 2, p. 29: *Dogmatic Theology* Anglican Province of Christ the King's (APCK) American Church Union, 1907 https://prydain.wordpress.com/francis-j-halls-dogmatic-theology/

[7] Part I, Chapter 2, p. 30: *The God Delusion*, Richard Dawkins. Houghton Mifflin Company, New York, 2006 p. 104

[8] Part I, Chapter 2, p. 34: https://www.goodreads.com/quotes/312349-interviewer-didn-t-author-sagan-10538-want-to-believe-druyan-author-he-10538-didn-t-want

[9] Part I, Chapter 2, p. 35: *The Demon-Haunted World*, Carl Sagan. Random House, New York, 1995 p. 207

[10] Part I, Chapter 2, p. 35: https://www.theguardian.com/science/2011/may/15/stephen-hawking-interview-there-is-no-heaven

[11] Part I, Chapter 4, p. 56: *Under the Banner of Heaven*, John Krakauer. Doubleday, a division of Random House, Inc. 2003. p. 30

[12] Part I, Chapter 4, p. 67: *The Demon-Haunted World*, Carl Sagan. Random House, New York 1995. (Trade Paperback) p. 278

[13] Part I, Chapter 4, p. 75: *Broca's Brain*, Carl Sagan. Ballantine Books, 1980 p. 365

[14] Part I, Chapter 4, p. 75-76: ibid. pp. 336-337

[15] Part I, Chapter 5, p. 81: *Chronology of the World: The History of the World from The Big Bang to Modern Times*, Isaac Azimov. HarperCollins 1991. p. 3

[16] Part I, Chapter 5, p. 82: *Don't Know Much About The Bible*, Kenneth C. Davis. Eagle Brook, William Morrow and Company, 1998 p. 49

[17] Part I, Chapter 5, p. 82: *Cosmos*, Carl Sagan. Ballantine Books, 2013 (Trade Paperback) p. 22

[18] Part I, Chapter 5, p. 82: *Dragons of Eden*, Carl Sagan. Random House p. 6

[19] Part I, Chapter 5, pp. 82-83: *An Interview With Isaac Azimov on Science and the Bible*, Paul Kurtz, interviewer. *Free Inquiry*, Volume 2, Number 2, Spring, 1982. p. 2 https://secularhumanism.org/1982/04/an-interview-with-isaac-asimov-on-science-and-the-bible/

[20] Part I, Chapter 5, p. 83: *The God Delusion*, Richard Dawkins. Houghton Mifflin Company, 2006 p. 300

[21] Part I, Chapter 6, p. 95: *irreligion: A Mathematician Explains Why The Arguments For God Just Don't Add Up*, John Allen Paulos. Hill and Wang, a division of Farrar, Strauss, and Giroux. p. xi

[22] Part I, Chapter 6, p. 101: *An Altar in the World,* Barbara Brown Taylor. HarperCollins. iBooks. p. 14

[23] Part I, Chapter 7, p. 106 *The Wisdom of Insecurity, A Message for an Age of Anxiety*, Alan W. Watts, Vintage Books, A Division of Random House, N.Y. 1951. pp. 137 and 198

[24] Part I, Chapter 7, p. 107: *Under the banner of Heaven*, John Krakauer. Doubleday, a division of Random House, Inc. 2003. p. 68

[25] Part I, Chapter 7, p. 109: *Aztec*, Gary Jennings. Forge, A Tom Doherty Associates Book, 1908. pp. 50-51

[26] Part I, Chapter 7, p. 112: *God, The Evidence: The Reconciliation of Faith and Reason in a Postsecular World* (Forum, 1997), Patrick Glynn. iBooks. p. 69

[27] Part I, Chapter 7, p. 114: *The Demon-Haunted World* Random House, New York 1996, p. 65

[28] Part I, Chapter 7, p. 114: *The Gods of Eden*, Avon Books, p. 453

[29] Part I, Chapter 8, p. 125: *A Raisin in the Sun*, Lorraine Hansberry, 1958. Thirteenth Anniversary Edition, Samuel French Acting Edition, 1988. p. 39

[30] Part I, Chapter 9, p. 146: *The God Delusion*, Richard Dawkins. Houghton Mifflin Company, 2006. pp. 348-49

[31] Part I, Chapter 9, p. 150: *Essentials of Christian Theology*, "Does It Make Sense To Talk About God?" William C. Placher. Westminster John Knox Press, 2003 p. 60

[32] Part II, Chapter 1, p. 161: http://www.newsweek.com/religion-and-brain-152895

[33] Part II, Chapter 1, p. 162: http://www.newsweek.com/religion-and-brain-152895

[34] Part II, Chapter 1, p. 162: *Mere Christianity* A revised and enlarged edition, with a new introduction, of the three books *The Case for Christianity*, *Christian Behavior* and *Beyond Personality*). Colliers Books, Macmillan Publishing Company. p. 21

[35] Part II, Chapter 1, p. 164: ibid. p. 19

[36] Part II, Chapter 1, p. 164: ibid. p. 19

[37] Part II, Chapter 1, p. 166: ibid. pp. 17-18

[38] Part II, Chapter 1, p. 166: ibid. p. 18

[39] Part II, Chapter 1, p. 167: ibid. p. 17

[40] Part II, Chapter 1, p. 167: ibid. p. 18

[41] Part II, Chapter 1, p. 168: ibid. p. 18

[42] Part II, Chapter 1, p. 169: ibid. p. 17

[43] Part II, Chapter 2, p. 174: *A Severe Mercy*, HarperSanFransisco, A Division of Harper Collins Publishers. pp. 98-99

⁴⁴ Part II, Chapter 2, p. 175: ibid. p. 210

⁴⁵ Part II, Chapter 2, p. 176: ibid. p. 99

⁴⁶ Part II, Chapter 2, p. 176: ibid. p. 98

⁴⁷ Part II, Chapter 2, p. 177: *The Da Vinci Code*, Doubleday, a division of Random House, Inc. New York 2003. pp. 266-67

⁴⁸ Part II, Chapter 2, p. 179: *Kidnapped*, Robert Louis Stevenson. Biographical Edition, iBooks p. 315

⁴⁹ Part II, Chapter 3, p.183: *The Universe in a Single Atom: A Convergence of Science and Spirituality*. Morgan Road Books. pp. 73-74

⁵⁰ Part II, Chapter 3, pp.183-184: ibid. p. 119

⁵¹ Part II, Chapter 3, p.184: ibid. p. 120

⁵² Part II, Chapter 3, p.185: ibid. p. 24

⁵³ Part II, Chapter 3, p.185: ibid. pp. 24-25

⁵⁴ Part II, Chapter 4, p. 188: *Astrophysics for People in a Hurry*, Neil deGrasse Tyson. W.W. Norton and Company, 2017. p. 18

⁵⁵ Part II, Chapter 4, p. 188: ibid.

⁵⁶ Part II, Chapter 4, p. 188: *A Brief History of Time*, Stephen Hawking. Bantam Books, 1988 (Trade Paperback) p. 13

⁵⁷ Part II, Chapter 4, p. 188: ibid. p. 13

⁵⁸ Part II, Chapter 4, p. 189: ibid. p. 13

⁵⁹ Part II, Chapter 4, p. 189: ibid. p. 15

⁶⁰ Part II, Chapter 4, p. 189: ibid. p. 135

⁶¹ Part II, Chapter 4, p. 189: ibid. p. 135

⁶² Part II, Chapter 4, p. 189: ibid. p. 135

⁶³ Part II, Chapter 4, p. 189: ibid. p. 136

⁶⁴ Part II, Chapter 4, pp. 189-190: ibid. p. 151

⁶⁵ Part II, Chapter 4, p. 190: *The Grand Design*, Stephen Hawking. Bantam Books, an imprint of the Random House, New York, 2010. iBooks, pp. 320-321. https://www.theguardian.com/science/2010/sep/12/the-grand-design-stephen-hawking

⁶⁶ Part II, Chapter 5, p. 194: *The Science of God*, Gerald Schroeder. Free Press, A Division of Simon and Schuster, 1997 iBooks. p. 412

⁶⁷ Part II, Chapter 5, p. 194: ibid. p. 412

⁶⁸ Part II, Chapter 5, p. 194: ibid. pp. 412-413

⁶⁹ Part II, Chapter 5, p. 194: ibid. p. 454

⁷⁰ Part II, Chapter 5, p. 194: ibid. p. 454

⁷¹ Part II, Chapter 5, p. 194: ibid. pp. 454-455

⁷² Part II, Chapter 5, p. 195: *Genesis and the Big Bang,* Gerald Schroeder. A Bantam Book, 1990. iBooks. p. 35

⁷³ Part II, Chapter 5, p. 196: ibid. p. 44

⁷⁴ Part II, Chapter 5, p. 196: ibid. pp. 44-45

⁷⁵ Part II, Chapter 6, p. 199: *The God Delusion,* Houghton Mifflin Company, 2006 p. 136

⁷⁶ Part II, Chapter 6, p. 199: ibid. p. 136

⁷⁷ Part II, Chapter 6, p. 200: *A Brief History of Time,* Stephen Hawking. Bantam Books, 1988 (Trade Paperback) p. 137

⁷⁸ Part II, Chapter 6, p. 200: ibid. p. 138

⁷⁹ Part II, Chapter 6, p. 200: ibid. p. 140

⁸⁰ Part II, Chapter 6, p. 202: *God: The Evidence: The Reconciliation of Faith and Reason in a Postsecular World* (Forum, 1997), Patrick Glynn. Three Rivers Press, iBooks p. 12

⁸¹ Part II, Chapter 6, p. 202: ibid. p. 12

⁸² Part II, Chapter 6, p. 202: ibid. pp. 16-18

⁸³ Part II, Chapter 6, p. 202: ibid. p. 18

⁸⁴ Part II, Chapter 6, p. 203: ibid. p. 21

⁸⁵ Part II, Chapter 6, p. 203: ibid. p. 44

⁸⁶ Part II, Chapter 6, p. 203: ibid. p. 44

⁸⁷ Part II, Chapter 6, p. 204: ibid. p. 19

⁸⁸ Part II, Chapter 6, p. 204: ibid. p. 19

⁸⁹ Part II, Chapter 6, p. 204: ibid. p. 20

⁹⁰ Part I, Chapter 6, p. 206: *Aztec*, Forge, A Tom Doherty Associates Book, 1908 (Trade Paperback) p. 598

⁹¹ Part II, Chapter 7, p. 210: *Belief in God in an Age of Science*, John Polkinghorne. Yale University Press, 1993. iBooks. p. 23

⁹² Part II, Chapter 7, p. 210: ibid. pp. 46-47

⁹³ Part II, Chapter 7, p. 210: ibid. p. 47

⁹⁴ Part II, Chapter 7, p. 210: ibid. p. 47

⁹⁵ Part II, Chapter 7, p. 210: ibid. p. 47

⁹⁶ https://paulgavrilyuk.files.wordpress.com/2017/11/polkinghorne.pdf

⁹⁷ Part II, Chapter 7, p. 213: *Belief in God in an Age of Science*, John Polkinghorne. Yale University Press, 1993. iBooks. p. 54

[98] Part II, Chapter 8, p. 216: *Rock of Ages*, Stephen Jay Gould. Ballantine Publishing Group, New York, 1999. iBooks. p.16

[99] Part II, Chapter 9, p. 219: *Does God Exist? The Debate Between Theists and Atheists*, J.P. Mooreland and Kai Nielsen. Prometheus Books, 1993. p. 35

[100] Part II, Chapter 9, p. 219: ibid. p.35

[101] Part II, Chapter 9, p. 219: ibid. p.35

[102] Part II, Chapter 9, p. 220: ibid. p. 36

[103] Part II, Chapter 9, p. 220: ibid. p.36

[104] Part II, Chapter 9, p. 223: ibid. p. 51

[105] Part II, Chapter 9, p. 223: ibid. p. 54

[106] Part II, Chapter 10, p. 227: https://youtu.be/z6kgvhG3AkI

[107] Part II, Chapter 11, p. 232: *God, Chance, and Necessity*, Keith Ward. Oneworld Publications, 1996. p. 11

[108] Part II, Chapter 11, p. 232: ibid. p. 11

[109] Part II, Chapter 11, p. 232: ibid. p. 12

[110] Part II, Chapter 11, p. 232: ibid. p. 12

[111] Part II, Chapter 11, p. 233: ibid. p. 11

[112] Part II, Chapter 11, p. 234: *Law and Order: Special Victims Unit (S.V.U.)*, "Fashionable Crimes," Season 17, Episode 20. 5/4/16

[113] Part II, Chapter 11, p. 235: *God, Chance, and Necessity*, Keith Ward. Oneworld Publications, 1996. p. 101

[114] Part II, Chapter 11, p. 235: ibid. p. 101

[115] Part II, Chapter 11, p. 235: ibid. p. 198

[116] Part II, Chapter 11, p. 235: ibid. p. 198

[117] Part II, Chapter 11, p. 235-236: ibid. p. 198

[118] Part II, Chapter 11, p. 236: ibid. pp. 198-199

[119] Part II, Chapter 11, p. 236: ibid. p. 199

[120] Part II, Chapter 11, p. 236: ibid. p. 204

[121] Part II, Chapter 11, p. 236-237: ibid. p. 204

[122] Part II, Chapter 11, p. 237: ibid. p. 204

[123] Part II, Chapter 11, p. 237: ibid. p. 204

[124] Part II, Chapter 11, p. 237: ibid. p. 204

[125] Part II, Chapter 12, p. 239: https://youtu.be/XjTZzP95ugo

[126] Part II, Chapter 12, p. 240: Session 2, November 5, 2006, https://youtu.be/bcTbGsUWzuw?list=PLCE8BF6B97FDDA910

[127] Part II, Chapter 12, p. 243: Session 2, November 7, 2006, https://youtu.be/6RjW5-4IiSc

[128] Part III, Chapter 1, p. 250: *Go Set a Watchman*, Harper Lee. HarperCollins Publishers, 2015. pp. 270-271

[129] Part III, Chapter 1, p. 254:
https://video.search.yahoo.com/yhs/search?fr=yhs-mozilla-102&hsimp=yhs-102&hspart=mozilla&p=kim+davis+september+23+2015+megyn+kelly#id=0&vid=46b4e3bf62fcf6784e9d0793c208d707&action=click

[130] Part III, Chapter 1, p. 255:
https://www.alternet.org/2012/05/joe_biden_endorses_same-sex_marriage/

[131] Part III, Chapter 1, p. 255:
https://www.youtube.com/watch?v=V_RkoMDv3fE&feature=youtu.be, and

https://video.search.yahoo.com/yhs/search?fr=yhs-mozilla-102&hsimp=yhs-102&hspart=mozilla&p=president+obama+endorses+gay+marriage#id=2&vid=e81a41fda8a2b3483db4d12900099fcd&action=click

[132] Part III, Chapter 1, p. 257: "We Are All Mutants," Gemma Tarlach interviewing Masatoshi Nei. *Discover*, March, 2014, p. 32

[133] Part III, Chapter 1, p. 261: Interview in *Playboy*, November 1999. https://www.celebatheists.com/wiki/Jesse_Ventura

[134] Part III, Chapter 1, p. 261: *I Ain't Got Time to Bleed*, Jesse Ventura. Random House, p. 290 https://www.ontheissues.org/Archive/Time_To_Bleed_Principles_+_Values.htm

[135] Part III, Chapter 1, pp. 267-268: *The Horse Whisperer*, Nicholas Evans. Delacorte Press, 1995. pp. 370-374

[136] Part III, Chapter 1, p. 268: *Pale Blue Dot*, Carl Sagan. Random House, November 8, 1994. https://www.goodreads.com/work/quotes/1816628-pale-blue-dot-a-vision-of-the-human-future-in-space (eighth quote on the page)

[137] Part III, Chapter 2, p. 274: *The Demon-Haunted World: Science as a Candle in the Dark*, Carl Sagan. Ballantine Books, N.Y. 1996. p. 429

[138] Part III, Chapter 2, p. 284: *Broca's Brain*, Carl Sagan. Ballantine Books, 1980 p. 330

[139] Part III, Chapter 3, p. 291: *Dying To Be Me: My Journey From Cancer, To Near Death, To True Healing*, by Anita Moorjani, Hay House, Inc. 2012 p. 6

[140] Part III, Chapter 3, p. 291: ibid. p. 68

[141] Part III, Chapter 3, p. 296: *The Universe In Your Hand: A Journey Through Space, Time, and Beyond*, Christophe Galfard. Flatiron Books, N.Y. 2015. p. 14

[142] Part III, Chapter 3, p. 296: *God: A Human History,* Reza Aslan. Random House 2017. p. 169

INDEX

A

Abel (Old Testament), 263–265
abortion
    Roe vs. Wade, 46–48
    suggested legislative compromise by Carl Sagan and Ann Druyan, 46–47
Abraham (Old Testament), 48, 135, 155
absolute, 42–46, 49–52, 55–57, 70, 73, 79, 83, 111, 141, 165, 177, 196, 233
accident
    accidental, 198, 204
ad infinitum, 95, 191
Adam (Old Testament), 10, 38, 79–80, 140, 154–155, 191, 196, 252, 263
Adams, John
    nothings, 191–192
        Mercutio, 191
        Romeo, 191
Afghanistan, 48
afterlife, 35, 202, 277
agnostic, 24, 134, 172, 174–175, 212, 260, 290, 292
Al-Anon
    God as we understood Him, 290
Alcoholics Anonymous
    AA, 13–14, 282
alien, 65–66, 114–115
Alliance of Baptists, 275
American Beauty, 68
Amish, 274

Anglican Communion, 170
antiquity, 141–142, 222
Arabians, 274
Asimov, Isaac
    15 billion years (previous age of the universe), 79–80, 195–196
    natural law, 81
Aslan, the Lion, 26
atheism, 56–57, 70, 95, 152, 202, 211–212, 275, 294
atheist, 24, 70, 75, 116, 134, 152, 196, 201, 219, 223, 225, 234, 290
atoms, 11, 113, 149, 162, 220
Audi Q5, 204–205
autistic, 298
automatic writing, 91, 153
autonomy
    autonomous(ly), 165, 168, 202–203, 220, 236, 289, 295
    Daniel Dennett, 236

B

Bacharach, Burt
    David, Hal, 294
    What the World Needs Now Is Love (song), 294
Begley, Sharon, 161
Behar, Joy, 147
belief
    believe, 15–17, 26, 30–35, 37, 66, 68–69, 84–85, 96–98, 100–101, 104–105,

INDEX

107, 115–116, 118, 120–121, 125, 130, 133, 135–138, 141, 143–144, 146, 150–153, 155, 162–163, 176–178, 200, 209, 212–213, 219–220, 222–223, 234, 241–242, 248, 257, 260–261, 263, 271–272, 276, 284, 289–290, 293
  believe, think, know (comparison), 30–35
believeth, 30
Bell, Rob
  Mars Hill Bible Church, 260
Ben-Hur, 127–128
Ben-Hur
  Messala, 127
  Quintus Arrius, 127
  Tirzah, 127
Bentall, Richard P., 161
Bi-Sexual, 250, 259
Bible
  biblical, 25–26, 55, 67, 107, 176, 194–196, 249, 256
  King James Bible, 263
Biden, Vice-President Joe, 255
Big Bang
  13.799 billion years (current age of the universe), 79, 195
biracial, 216
blasphemous, 9, 14, 134, 143, 151, 153
Blind Faith (rock group), 132
Blind following, 30, 132
Borden, Lizzie, 50
Borg, Marcus J., 27
Boston Tea Party
  Tea Party, 43–45, 256

brain
  Broca's Area, 161
  left-brain, 5, 15
  right-brain, 5, 15, 288
brain waves
  in utero, 47
breathing biology (personal), 12
British Parliament, 43
Broca's Brain, 26, 75, 89, 161
Brown, Dan
  The Da Vinci Code, 104, 177
Bryan, William Jennings, 219
Buddhism
  Buddha, 6, 185, 287, 291
  Buddhist, 12, 19, 134, 140, 168, 184–185
burden of proof, 135, 150–152
Bush, George W., 45

C

Cain, 263–265
Calvin, John
  Common Grace, 278, 280
  Reformed Church, 278
Canned Heat
  Let's Stick Together (song), 297
  Let's Work Together (song), 297
  Ricki and the Flash, 297
Carlin, George
  Humpty Dumpty, 192
  The Ten Commandments, 153
Carter, Brandon
  anthropic principle, 38, 112, 198–206, 209, 219, 259, 295
Catholicism
  Catholic, 7, 10, 18, 71, 74, 76, 111, 115, 134, 177, 183, 215, 248, 271, 273,

INDEX

288, 292
catholic, 7, 10, 18, 71, 74, 76, 111, 115, 134, 177, 183, 215, 248, 271, 273, 288, 292
Catholic Church, 115, 183, 248, 273
CBS This Morning
   The Waltons, 293
      Learned, Miss Michael (Walton, Olivia), 293
      Thomas, Richard (Walton, John Boy), 293
      Waite, Ralph (Walton, John), 293
Challenger Space Shuttle, 269
chaos
   blunder, 167
   chance, 118, 167, 194–195, 198, 200–201, 203, 205, 209, 232, 234, 282, 300, 303
   rolled the dice, 201
chaplain, 71, 76, 111
Christ, Jesus
   Divine Son of God, 176
   Son of God, 66, 139, 169, 174, 176
Christian Nation, 252, 272, 274
Christian Right, 49
Christianity
   Christian, 7–8, 18–19, 25, 27, 40, 46, 49, 55, 66, 73, 86, 116–117, 134, 147, 150, 159, 173–176, 194, 219, 222, 227, 248, 252–253, 271–272, 274, 289, 292
Christmas, 8, 224, 292, 295
Christmas, 8, 224, 292, 295
Church of England, 48, 170
Cinderella, 80, 196

Civil War, 48
Clarke, Arthur C., 80
CNN, 252
Cobb, John B., 150
coexistence
   coexist, 153, 156, 295
   coexisting, 101, 298
   cooperation, 118, 216–217, 272–273
Cold War
   Strategic Defense Initiative (SDI, "Star Wars"), 119
   Union of Soviet Socialist Republics, 119
Colonial States, 252
Comet
   Hale-Bopp, viii, x, 300
conductor
   authentic performance, 70
Constitution, 45, 51, 63–64, 251–252, 261, 272–273
Cooperative Baptist Fellowship, 275
Copernicus, Nicolaus
   heliocentric, 203, 215
cosmic speed limit
   light, 3, 6, 26, 31, 106, 148, 179, 185, 188, 190, 237, 244, 281, 303
cosmos, 8, 25, 28–29, 37–38, 65, 71, 76, 82, 91, 95–97, 100–102, 110–112, 137, 143, 149, 154, 156, 167–168, 183, 200, 203, 205, 207, 233, 237, 239, 243–244, 292
Cotton, John, 252
COVID-19, 156
Creative and critical thinking
   Four Fundamentals (personal), 58, 221
Creator, ix, 17, 20, 24–25,

INDEX

28–29, 38, 61, 65, 67, 70, 75, 79–80, 94–96, 99–100, 102, 106, 112, 142, 154–155, 166, 172, 189, 191, 195, 199, 201, 205–206, 210–212, 220, 222–223, 237, 241, 253, 265, 276, 284, 292, 298

D

dark energy, 239
dark matter, 148–149, 168, 239–240
Darrow, Clarence, 219
Darwin, Charles
    Origin of Species, 86
    Survival of the Fittest, 36, 140
Davidson
    Davidson College, 277, 280
Davis, Kenneth C., 82
Davis, Kim
    Kelly, Megyn, 254
Dawkins, Richard
    anthropic principle, 38, 112, 198–206, 209, 219, 259, 295
    Carter, Brandon, 199, 202, 206
    Glynn, Patrick, 112, 197, 199, 201–203, 205, 207, 209
    Hawking, Stephen, 35, 57, 149, 152, 186–187, 189, 191–192, 199, 211, 232, 284, 291, 299
    The God Delusion, 30, 83, 145, 199, 201
debate, 7, 46, 56–57, 69, 72, 82, 90, 102, 148, 215, 219, 227–228, 262, 272
Declaration of Independence, 48
Deism
    absentee Father, 8, 253

Deist, 253
Deity
    deities, 9–11, 16, 71, 99, 118, 120, 141, 163, 192, 219, 242, 295, 298
    deity, 7, 9, 11, 15–18, 20, 25–26, 28–29, 31, 36–37, 49, 60, 62–63, 70–71, 74–76, 79, 85, 92–93, 95, 99–102, 105–107, 110–113, 115, 128, 133–138, 140–147, 152–155, 162–163, 165, 167, 173, 182, 184, 189, 192, 199, 207, 221, 224–225, 239–240, 242, 262, 266, 289, 295, 298
denomination, 72, 86, 252, 275
Designer
    Devil, 160, 163, 244
    devil, 160, 163, 244
    devil's, 244
dimensions
    other dimensions, 113
dinosaur
    dinosaurs, 100, 194
Discover (magazine), 67, 84, 190, 257
Discovery, 5, 21, 24, 39, 71, 84, 86–87, 91–92, 96, 98–99, 142, 145, 149, 165, 188, 196, 203, 213, 232, 239, 241–245, 282, 290
discrimination, 253, 259, 274
divine
    divine gift, 220
    divinity, 6, 9–10, 35–36, 100, 119, 138–140, 147, 155, 175–176, 278
DNA, 11, 161, 219–220, 288

dogma
 private, 16, 64, 72, 99, 116, 184, 209, 251–252, 254, 258, 272–274, 284, 293
Doubting Thomas, 138, 145
Dr. Seuss
 The Sneetches, 39
Drake, Frank
 The Drake Equation, 97
Druyan, Ann, 3, 23, 34, 46, 59, 148, 183, 244

E

Earth, ix, 8, 10, 19–20, 34, 38–40, 57, 65, 84, 93–94, 97, 100, 114, 130, 140, 142, 148–149, 151, 168, 173, 175, 195, 198–200, 206, 223, 227, 231, 240–241, 244, 264, 295–296, 298, 301
Easter, 35, 55, 144, 271, 292
Easter Bunny, 35, 55, 144
eclipse
 eclipses, 300
 full corona, 300
 Solar Eclipse, 300–304
 totality, 28–29, 194, 292, 300–301, 303–304
ecstasy
 emotions, not drugs, 89–90, 96
Eden (Old Testament)
 Old Testament, 3, 155, 251
Einstein, Albert
 General Relativity, 188
 Special Relativity, 187–188, 196
 Theory of Relativity, 80, 94, 184, 187–188, 212, 228
elf, 144
emotional, 12, 14, 37, 55, 63–65, 71, 90, 102, 105, 108, 111, 128, 135, 149, 152, 166–167, 183–184, 210, 213, 231, 245, 265–266, 284, 288–289
emotions, 5, 15, 71, 75, 96, 111, 115, 148, 183, 231, 235, 266, 288
Enlightenment
 classical music, 253
 Classical period, 253
Entity
 entities, 9, 192, 222, 295
 entity, 8–9, 20, 24–25, 27–28, 37, 44, 67, 69, 74, 76, 81, 94, 101–102, 111–112, 136, 145, 154, 163, 167, 169–170, 173–174, 184, 189–190, 213, 222, 236, 265, 273, 284, 295–296, 298
Esther, 127–128
Euclidean Geometry, 61
evangelist, 38, 271
Evans, Nicholas
 The Horse Whisperer, 267–268
Eve (Old Testament)
 Genesis, 13, 24–26, 35–38, 79, 84, 86–87, 154–155, 195, 198–199, 227–228, 234, 237, 256, 263–264, 272
evolution
 fact, 6, 10, 13, 15, 23–24, 31–32, 38–39, 49, 51, 56–59, 65, 67, 71, 76, 80–87, 93–97, 100, 102, 106, 112–113, 124, 132, 139–140, 142, 148–150, 152, 156, 161–162, 164, 167, 177, 182–183, 185,

INDEX

188, 190, 195–196, 199–200, 202, 205, 211–212, 216, 220–221, 224, 228, 236, 240–242, 245, 248–249, 253, 255, 257–259, 264, 266, 278, 283, 289, 298, 301–302, 304
  theory, 20, 24, 49, 57, 70, 76, 79–86, 94, 113–114, 118, 160–161, 167, 184, 187–190, 196, 201, 211–212, 216, 228, 242–243, 257–258, 288
evolutionary picture-puzzle, 86
evolutionary puzzle, 85
extinction
  extinct, 84, 140–141
extraterrestrials, 97–98, 114, 143–144, 221

F

fact
  facts, 21, 58, 119, 132, 154, 164, 169, 185, 203, 215–216, 232–233
fairy, 35–36, 96, 144
Falwell, Reverend Jerry, 54
Federal Government
  Big Government, 48–49
  states' rights, 48
fellowship
  Fellowship, 19, 275, 296
Ferguson, Niall, 4
Ferris, Timothy, 183
First Amendment, 63–64, 216, 252–254, 261, 272, 274
Fitzroy, Vice-Admiral Robert, 86
fluke, 166–167
fossil, 82, 84, 87, 228
fossils, 194, 228

Fourteenth Dalai Lama
  The Universe in a Single Atom: A Convergence of Science and Spirituality, 182
Framers
  Constitution, 45, 51, 63–64, 251–252, 261, 272–273
  Founding Fathers, 252, 261
Free Agency, 136
Free Will, 17, 97–98, 129–130, 133, 135–139, 141–143, 145, 147, 149, 151, 153, 155–156, 159, 165, 192
free-thinker, 69, 292
fundamental
  Four Fundamentals (personal), 58, 221
    Creative and Critical Thinking, 58–59
    umbrella, 58–59, 63, 275
Fundamentalism
  Fundamentalist, 46, 55–57, 59–60, 64–72, 79, 84, 151, 227–228, 260–261, 273, 275, 290
  fundamentalist, 46, 55–57, 59–60, 64–72, 79, 84, 151, 227–228, 260–261, 273, 275, 290

G

Galfard, Christophe
  The Universe in Your Hand: A Journey Through Space, Time, and Beyond, 296
Galilei, Galileo, 215, 274
Gamow, George, 81
Gandalf
  (asterisk), 26

INDEX

Gay
  child-rearing, 255
    by gay couples, 255
  Gay marriage, 49, 249, 253, 255–257
  Supreme Court legalized gay marriage nationally, 249, 255–256
gheu, 29
Glynn, Patrick
  anthropic principle, 38, 112, 198–206, 209, 219, 259, 295
  anthropocentric, 198, 203
  God: The Evidence: The Reconciliation of Faith and Reason in a Postsecular World, 112, 202
  Hawking, Stephen, 35, 57, 149, 152, 186–187, 189, 191–192, 199, 211, 232, 284, 291, 299
    strong, 10–11, 20, 32–33, 37, 46, 57, 70–74, 97, 107, 111, 115, 133, 137, 148, 151, 179, 199–200, 202, 204, 213, 221, 289, 291
    weak, 16, 46, 113, 135, 175, 199–200, 202, 261–262
God
  Adonai, 262
  Allah, 9, 26, 135, 225, 262
  Elohim, 262
  existence of God, 7, 16, 24, 30, 34, 36, 55–56, 60–61, 70, 75–76, 85, 96–97, 113, 135, 137, 143, 148, 150, 152–153, 159, 163, 169, 173, 187, 199, 213, 219, 225, 264, 292, 294
  God Lives in Glass, 297
    Landy, Dr. Robert, 297
    Thompson, Keith, 297
  God of the Gaps, 239
    Tyson, Neil deGrasse, 183, 188, 238–239, 241, 243, 245, 295, 300
  God-fearing, 109
  Jehovah, 134, 262
  Krishna, 262, 291
  meaning of God, 13, 27, 68, 153, 161, 184, 295
  Para Brahman, 262
  ShangDi, 262
  Yahweh, 26
Gore, Al, 45
Graham, Billy, 38
gravity, 6, 10, 57, 79, 91, 94, 139, 149, 160, 188–190, 211, 228, 241–243
Great Britain, 273
Great Flood, 20, 173, 256, 265
Greeks, 141–142, 222
Gregory, David
  Biden, Vice-President Joe, 255
  Meet The Press, 254
Groundhog Day, 35
Gulf War, 48
Gushee, David, 73

H

Hall, Francis J.
  Dogmatic Theology, 29
Ham, Ken
  Is Creation A Viable Model of Origins? (debate), 227
  debate, 7, 46, 56–57, 69, 72, 82, 90, 102, 148, 215, 219, 227–228,

INDEX

262, 272
Hansberry, Lorraine
   A Raisin in the Sun, 125
Hanukkah
   (asterisk), 292
Harpur, Tom, 169
Hawking, Stephen
   A Brief History of Time, 187, 199
   anthropic principle, 38, 112, 198–206, 209, 219, 259, 295
      Carter, Brandon, 199, 202, 206
      Dawkins, Richard, 30, 82–83, 98, 104, 145, 199, 232
      Glynn, Patrick, 202–207
      strong, 10–11, 20, 32–33, 37, 46, 57, 70–74, 97, 107, 111, 115, 133, 137, 148, 151, 179, 199–200, 202, 204, 213, 221, 289, 291
      weak, 16, 46, 113, 135, 175, 199–200, 202, 261–262
   Big Bang to Black Holes, 187
   Curiosity, 19, 37, 64, 102, 107–108, 133–134, 190, 266
   Did God Create the Universe (PBS progarm), 190
   The Grand Design, 190
Heaven, 35, 37, 56, 65, 107, 178, 216, 223, 277
Heaven's Gate
   Applewhite, Marshall Herff ("Do"), 65
   Nettles, Bonnie Lou ("Ti"), 65
Heinlein, Robert, 80

heterosexual
   heterosexuality, 250, 259
Higher Power
   higher power, 13–15
Hindu, 134
Hiroshima, 72
Hitchens, Christopher, 16, 248
Holocaust, 72
Holy Ghost, 9
Holy Spirit, 9, 25
Homo Sapiens, 83, 114, 203
homosexual
   homosexuality, 250, 255–256, 259
How the Grinch Stole Christmas, 295
Hubble Space Telescope, 19
human sexual reproduction, 201
Hume, David, 211
Huxley, Aldous, 233
hypothesis
   hypotheses, 21, 58, 75, 136, 152

I

Idle, Eric
   Monty Python, 260
If...then... statements
   If...then... statement, 153, 284
immaculate (cleanliness), 10
Immaculate Conception, 10, 35
immigration, 33
immortal, 9–10, 29
incorporeal, 95, 142, 149, 162, 212, 222, 285
infinite
   infinite regression, 95
infinite dimensions, 113
inner voice
   imagination, 6, 26, 32–33, 35, 99, 119, 142, 145–148,

INDEX

151, 153, 161, 191, 219, 222, 295
interpretation, 10, 13, 56, 70, 74, 119, 146–147, 161, 199, 202, 205–206, 252, 256, 260, 263, 288, 296
Inquisition
  Inquisitions, 57, 72, 269
Instigator, 93–95, 205, 211
intellect
  intellectual, 5, 12, 14–15, 63, 71, 76, 90, 102, 107–108, 110–111, 142, 150, 188, 202, 213, 231, 233, 236, 239, 243, 245, 266, 285, 288
Intelligent Design, 159, 198–199, 204, 240–241, 243
Intelligent Design
  iron, 244, 300
    15-ton meteorite, 244
    in human blood, 244
    in the core of a star, 244
  philosophy of ignorance, 243
International Astronomical Union, 202
invention
  inventions, 58, 156, 295
Irving, John, 86
Is Creation A Viable Model of Origins? (debate)
  Answers in Genesis, 227
  Ark Encounter: A Life-Size Noah's Ark Experience, 227
  Creation Museum, 227
  debate, 7, 46, 56–57, 69, 72, 82, 90, 102, 148, 215, 219, 227–228, 262, 272
  Ham, Ken, 226–229
  Nye, Bill, 226–229
  Young Earth Creationist Ministry, 227
  6,000 years old, 228
Islam
  Islamic, 19, 72, 116–117
Izzard, Eddie, 26

J

Jackson 5
  ABC (song), 297
Jacobs, Harold
  B.C. (cartoon), 131
  Escher, M.C., 131
  Peanuts (cartoon), 131
  Volkswagen Station Wagon, 204
  Wilde, Oscar, 205
Jehovah's Witness, 134
Jennings, Gary
  Aztec, 109, 206
  Raptor, 87, 248, 271
  Sun Stone, 109
Jonah
  Old Testament, 3, 155, 251
Judaism
  Jewish, 116–117, 119, 127, 282–283
  Jews, 19, 127, 271, 274
Jupiter, 300

K

Kant, Immanuel
  Categorical Imperative, 159
  Good Will, 159
Keillor, Garrison
  A Praire Home Companion, 6
Kelly, Megyn
  Davis, Kim, 253
Kema, Ayya, 12, 295
Kerry, John, 49

INDEX

knowledge
  know, viii, 4, 6–7, 26, 28, 31, 33–37, 49–50, 65, 68, 70, 72, 75–76, 81–82, 86, 91, 93–96, 99–100, 102, 108, 110, 113, 116–118, 125–126, 136–138, 140, 145–150, 152, 156, 159–161, 164–169, 173, 176, 178, 182, 201, 203–204, 206, 219–221, 234, 243–245, 248–250, 255–256, 258, 260–262, 264, 268, 277, 280–283, 287–288, 291–293, 301, 303
  leche, 8
  ledge, 7
  rebinding, 7–8
  relinking, 7–8
  retying, 7–8
Krakauer, Jon, 56, 107
Kucinich, Dennis
  (asterisk), 9

L

Land, Judy, 131
Laplace, Pierre-Simon de
  Bonaparte, Napoléon, 192
Law and Order: Special Victims Unit (S.V.U.)
  Belzer, Richard (Munch, John), 233
  Hargitay, Mariska (Benson, Olivia), 233
  Ice T (Tutuola, Odafin "Fin"), 32
  William, Delaney (Buchanan, John), 32
Lee, Harper
  Go Set a Watchman, 250
  To Kill a Mockingbird, 50, 250
Lemaître, Georges, 81
Lesbian, 250, 255, 259
Levitical Law, 119, 253
Lewis, C.S.
  Chronicles of Narnia, 159, 169
  Law of Human Nature, 159–160, 164, 168–169
  Laws of Nature, 10, 39, 81, 159–160, 168–169, 189, 194, 204, 210–211, 219, 234, 236
  Life Force, 162, 289
  Mere Christianity, 159
  Mind, 162, 166
life force
  (asterisk), 289
light
  cosmic speed limit, 188, 237
Limbaugh, Rush, 45
Lincoln, Abraham
  Emancipation Proclamation, 251, 254, 256
logic, 17, 61–63, 65, 76, 99, 151–152, 190, 196, 201, 204, 206, 228, 237, 242
love, 4, 6–9, 12, 17, 20, 33, 36–40, 51, 58–59, 68–69, 73–74, 101–102, 106, 111, 114, 119, 121, 128, 142, 148, 154–155, 172–175, 178–179, 182–183, 185, 199, 211, 223, 234, 237, 249–251, 253–255, 258–260, 268–269, 275, 279–280, 282, 284–285, 288–289, 291, 293–299

INDEX

M

macroscopic, 11, 150, 187–188
Maker
  maker, 95, 223
Mandela, Nelson
  Apartheid, 251, 274
marijuana, 51
Mars, 19, 38, 149, 151, 260
materialism
  materialist, 11, 166–167, 231–232
Matthew 7:3-5, 249
McGovern, George, 49
McKelway, Adelaide ("Babs"), 277
McKelway, Alexander Jeffrey ("Sandy"), 277
meditation, 12, 17–19, 148, 161–162, 278
Mennonites, 274
Merali, Zeeya
  The Truman Show, 67
Messiah, 10, 141, 174
microscopic, 11, 91, 150, 188
Middle East
  comparison of the three regional monotheistic faiths, 116–119
Milky Way Galaxy, ix, 97
Milne, A.A.
  Binker, 145–146
  Christopher Robin, 145–146
  Now We Are Six, 145–146
  When We Were Very Young, 146
mind, 11, 17, 36, 49, 64, 69, 75–76, 78, 84, 102, 104, 106–107, 110, 115, 119, 121, 151, 159–160, 162, 166, 174, 184–185, 192, 210, 212, 219, 221, 223, 234–237, 241, 243–244, 261, 266, 287, 289–290
miracle
  111 (or 1:11 on a digital device), 126, 277, 297–298
  1111 (or 11:11 on a digital device), 126
  miraculum, 124
Mitchell, Joni (asterisk)
  Woodstock (song), 244
monotheism
  monotheistic, 9, 25–26, 29, 54, 62, 96, 116, 119, 141–142, 154, 163, 166, 222, 225
Montana, Cate, 11
Moon
  moon, 8–9, 19, 94, 156, 198, 240–241, 296, 300, 303
  moons, 38, 57, 300
Moonstruck
  Aiello, Danny (Cammareri, Johnny), 140
  Dukakis, Olympia (Castorini, Rose), 140
  Gardenia, Vincent (Castorini, Cosmo), 140
Mooreland, James Porter (J.P.)
  Davies, Paul, 219, 221
  epistemic rights, 219–220
Moorjani, Anita
  Dying To Be Me, 291
  near-death experience (NDE), 291
Moral Majority
  (epigraph), 54
morality, 45–47, 49, 52, 136–138, 159, 165, 169, 210–211, 216, 219–220, 222, 250, 262, 272–274

INDEX

Mormon Church
  ex-communication (shunning), 259
  Missionaries, 281
  Reed, Edith Carlquist, 281
  Reed, John Grant, 281
  Seven Lessons, 281
  Testimony, 116, 133, 147, 177, 227, 236
  The Church of Jesus Christ of Latter-Day Saints (LDS), 116
Mormons, 116, 274, 281–282
Moses
  Parting the Red Sea, 35, 55
Moyers, Bill
  Tyson, Neil deGrasse, 183, 188, 238–239, 241, 243, 245, 295, 300
Muhammad, 6, 135
multiverse, 24, 112, 156
murder
  absolutely wrong, 50–51
Mutation-Driven Evolution, 84, 257
myth
  Egyptian, 104, 169
  Greek, 12, 28, 30, 94, 96, 142, 198, 222
    Zeus, 222, 240
  mythology, 11, 36, 79, 94, 96, 141–142, 163, 169, 213, 222, 266

N

Nagasaki, 72
NASA
  Opportunity, 39, 72, 140, 149, 249, 255, 304
  Spirit, 9, 11–12, 14, 25, 27, 48, 75–76, 149, 265, 289
  water, 6, 9, 35, 38, 48, 127–128, 149, 155, 179, 294
  Mars, 19, 38, 149, 151, 260
natural law, 5, 20, 37, 81, 92, 100–101, 167, 189, 194, 199–200, 206, 234, 298
natural law, 5, 20, 37, 81, 92, 100–101, 167, 189, 194, 199–200, 206, 234, 298
Nei, Masatoshi
  Tarlach, Gemma, 257
  Tarlach, Gemma, 257
Nei, Masatoshi, 84, 257
New Horizons, 19
New Testament, 155
Nielsen, Kai
  incoherent, 222
  poy, 223, 225
  sui generis, 223, 225
Noah (Old Testament)
  Ark Encounter: A Life-Size Noah's Ark Experience, 227
  Noah's Ark, 20, 227
  The Great Flood, 20, 173, 256, 265
non-religious
  nones, 294
noun
  common noun, 29–30
  pronoun, 9, 17, 25, 105, 134, 283, 289
    pronoun projection, 9, 17, 25, 105, 134, 283, 289
  proper noun, 7, 14–15, 24, 28–30, 156, 224, 292
    confusion in clarity
      misusing common and proper nouns, 14–15, 24

INDEX

O

O'Donohue, John, 179
Obama, President Barack, 255
objective
    public, 44, 46, 48–49, 55–57, 64, 73, 86, 107, 109, 116, 120, 184, 216, 239, 241, 243–245, 251, 254–255, 261, 274, 292
observed physical universe, 154
Ockham's Razor, 84, 154
Oh God!
    film, 50, 68, 97, 102, 127–128, 134–135, 140, 187, 297
Old Testament
    Burning Bush, 35
omnipotent, 9–10, 63, 134, 142, 189
omnipresent, 212
omniscient, 156, 212
Order of Operations
    Comparison to scientific method/evolution, 6–62, 141
organized religion
    religion, 5, 7–11, 13–20, 25–27, 29–34, 37, 45, 54, 57, 59–65, 69–74, 76, 79–80, 82, 94, 96–100, 104–108, 111, 113, 115, 119–120, 133–134, 136, 139–144, 150, 152–154, 156, 159, 161–163, 165–166, 169, 172, 176, 182–185, 187, 189, 202, 209, 211, 215–217, 219, 221–222, 225, 227–228, 231–233, 235, 237, 239–240, 248, 251–253, 255, 257–258, 260–262, 265, 268–269, 272–274, 276–278, 281, 283–285, 288–290, 292–295
Origin of Species
    Darwin, Charles, 36, 78, 84
Originator, 199
orthodox, 151
Orwell, George
    1984, 172–173, 273
    Big Brother, 9, 164, 173, 175
    Orwellian, 164, 175

P

Palestinians, 274
pantheism, 27, 194
Parini, Jay, 252
Paris, 72–74, 300
partial theories, 187–188
particle
    behavior, 59, 91, 115, 150, 159–160, 165, 169, 188–189, 250, 253, 258–260, 265–266, 275, 285, 301
    intelligence, 20, 40, 43, 45–46, 52, 67, 75–76, 89, 102, 137, 149–150, 164–165, 183, 185, 194, 203, 206, 209, 212, 220–221, 242, 256, 297–299
Pascal, Blaise
    Pascal's Wager, 178
PBS, 190, 227, 239
Pence, Vice-President Mike, 147
perfect
    imperfection, 155–156
    perfect fifth, 156
    perfect fourth, 156
    perfection, 10–11, 155, 265

INDEX

persecution, 252, 274
personal, 3, 7–8, 10–11, 13, 15, 18–19, 23, 25, 30, 36–37, 55–56, 58, 64, 66, 69, 73, 94, 99, 116, 132–134, 145–146, 151, 153, 156, 179, 184, 209, 220, 224, 235–236, 241–242, 246, 251, 259, 272, 277, 282–284, 293–294, 300–301
perspicacious
    perspicacity, 6
philosophy
    philosophical, 68, 74, 169, 180, 210, 243, 294, 298
Phoenix Bird, 66
Pioneers 10 and 11, 19
Placher, William C., 150
Polkinghorne, John
    Artist, 212, 219, 266, 278
    Belief in God in an Age of Science, 210, 213
    Ex nihilo nihil fit, 211
    Family Values, 209
    So Finely Tuned a Universe, 211
    valuable, 39, 52, 58, 95, 203, 209
    value, 210
polytheism
    polytheistic, 142, 163
Pooka
    Harvey (the rabbit), 35
Pope John Paul II
    Encyclical, 115, 215
    Fides et Ratio, 115
        Faith and Reason, 115, 202
prayer
    pray, 18, 147, 173
prejudice, 92, 216, 232, 249–251, 253, 256, 259, 261, 273–274, 279, 282–283

Preston, Richard, 78
prior cause, 95
Priory, 177
privacy
    dogma, 21, 98, 107, 151, 177, 182–183, 185, 188, 191, 249, 251, 257–258, 275–276, 278
    faith, 7, 9, 17–19, 25, 27, 31–32, 60–64, 67–68, 71–73, 76, 86–87, 92, 103–111, 113–121, 130–135, 138, 140, 142–144, 147, 151–153, 155–156, 162, 176–177, 182–185, 202, 209, 223, 229, 232, 234, 237, 242, 248, 250, 252, 267, 272, 275–279, 281, 283–285, 288–290, 292–293
Pronoun projection
    Big Brother, 9, 164, 173, 175
        Orwell, George, 173, 273
    Brother Sun, Sister Moon, 8
        Zeffirelli, Franco, 8
    Father Christmas, 8
    Father Time, 8
    Founding Fathers, 252, 261
    Mother Earth, 8
    Mother Lode, 8
    Mother Nature, 8
    Mother Ship, 8
    Motherboard (computer), 9
        computer, 9, 35, 67, 164, 245
    Old Man River, 8
    Old Man Winter, 8
    Seven Sisters, 9
        Pleiades ("Seven Sisters"), 9
    The Man in the Moon, 9

INDEX

proof, 11–12, 27, 56, 59, 65–66, 98, 113, 121, 129–145, 147, 149–156, 163, 166–167, 185, 190, 199, 222, 225, 239, 244, 252–253, 284, 291, 294, 300, 302
proofs
  axioms, 61
  deductive reasoning, 61, 132
  Jacobs, Harold, 131, 204
  postulates, 61, 131
  theorems, 61, 131
  University of North Carolina School of the Arts, 131, 306
Protestant, 134, 274
Ptolemy, Claudius
  geocentric, 38, 198, 240
public
  citizens, 43–45, 48, 251, 254
  civil law, 251, 273
  community, 55, 64, 68, 73, 81, 83, 85, 91–92, 96, 107, 118, 132, 137, 143–144, 168, 187, 239, 251, 255, 258–259, 261, 294, 298
  secular, 8, 13, 25, 63, 76, 101, 105, 118, 156, 202, 234, 251, 260, 293
pulsar, 143–144
purpose
Pyle, Howard
  (epigraph), 287

Q
Quakers, 274
Quantum physics, 24, 39, 94, 150, 212
quantum physics
  quantum mechanics, 91, 187–188
  subatomic, 76, 91, 113, 149, 188
Quantum Theory of Gravity, 188–189
Queer, 250
queer, 250
Qur'an
  (Koran), 107

R
radio waves, 148
Ramachandran, Vilayanur, 161
random, 20, 25, 60, 86, 91, 100, 150, 167, 200–203, 205, 209, 234, 264, 301
reality, 27, 29, 37, 67, 92, 95, 109, 113, 119, 128, 148, 164, 167–169, 173, 184–185, 196, 202, 210–211, 223, 235, 245, 261, 292, 295
reason-for-being, 168
Redmayne, Eddie, 187
Reeve, Christopher
  Still Me, 100
Reflexive Property of Equality, 84, 97
Relativity, 42, 79–80, 82, 94, 184, 187–188, 196, 212, 228
religion
  organized, 18, 72, 80, 96, 131, 152, 209, 216, 252, 258, 261–262, 274, 277, 284–285
religious
  religiosity, 243, 279, 283
Resurrection
  resurrection, 35, 66–68, 138, 155
Richey, David Frank, iii, 125, 305
Richey, Elaine Lee, iii, 90, 305
Right to Choose, 46
Right to Life, 40, 46

INDEX

Robinson, Bishop V. Gene
  U.S. Episcopal Church, 259
Roe vs. Wade, 46–48
Ruiz, Don Miguel
  Four Agreements, 58, 221
  Second Agreement, 117
  Third Agreement, 221, 225, 298
Rushdie, Salmon
  Khomeini, Ayatollah, 274
Russell, Bertrand
  Russell's Teapot, 151

S

sacred
  faith, 7, 9, 17–19, 25, 27, 31–32, 60–64, 67–68, 71–73, 76, 86–87, 92, 103–111, 113–121, 130–135, 138, 140, 142–144, 147, 151–153, 155–156, 162, 176–177, 182–185, 202, 209, 223, 229, 232, 234, 237, 242, 248, 250, 252, 267, 272, 275–279, 281, 283–285, 288–290, 292–293
  private, 16, 64, 72, 99, 116, 184, 209, 251–252, 254, 258, 272–274, 284, 293
Sagan, Carl
  apocrypha, 112
  Billions and Billions, 40, 46, 112
    (apocryphal), 112
  Contact, 38, 94, 98, 100, 134–135, 220, 295
  Demon-Haunted World, The, 67
  prime numbers, 221
Sandman, 35
Santa Claus, 35, 55, 144, 224
Satan, 136
Saturn
  Enceladus, 38
    (water discovery on), 38
  Titan, 38
    (water discovery on), 38
Schaef, Ann Wilson, 115
Schroeder, Gerald L.
  Genesis and the Big Bang, 79, 195
  stretching time, 196
    6,000 years of human history, 195
science
  scientia, 7
  scientific, ix, 3, 17–21, 23, 30, 34, 59–63, 65–66, 69, 81, 84–85, 88, 90–102, 111, 118–119, 121, 131–132, 137–142, 144–145, 148, 152–154, 162, 166–168, 177, 180, 182–183, 185, 187–188, 194–196, 198–199, 209, 211–213, 215, 219, 222, 228, 231–233, 235, 239–240, 242–245, 257–258, 269, 272, 274, 283, 288, 290, 292–294, 298, 301
  scientific method, 17–19, 59–63, 65, 69, 84, 90–92, 94, 96, 98–100, 111, 119, 131–132, 137, 144–145, 152–154, 222, 231, 235, 272, 290
Scopes Monkey Trial, 219
secular
  civil law, 251, 273
  public, 44, 46, 48–49, 55–57,

INDEX

64, 73, 86, 107, 109, 116, 120, 184, 216, 239, 241, 243–245, 251, 254–255, 261, 274, 292
Secularists, 253
self-centered
right to be themselves, 117, 156
self-preservation
right to be themselves, 117, 156
selfish, 8, 117, 154, 259
Serenity Prayer, 304
Serenity Prayer
Niebuhr, Reinhold, 304
SETI (Search for Extraterrestrial Intelligence), 220–221
Shuck, John
Shuck and Jive, 276
sin
my personal meaning of, 117, 156
right to be themselves, 117, 156
sinful, 154–155
Snowbird Summer Arts Institute
Little Cottonwood Canyon, 281
Solar Eclipse
eclipse, 300–304
Solar System, viii, 19, 34, 38, 65, 80, 94, 142, 156, 192, 198, 200, 215, 240–243
Solomon, R. J.
Life Coach, 282–283, 285
soul, 11–12, 75, 101, 191, 202, 215
Southern Baptist Alliance
Alliance of Baptists, 275
Southern Baptist Convention, 275

Spellman, W. M., 81
Spinoza, Baruch, 26
spiritual
spirit, 9, 11–12, 14, 25, 27, 48, 75–76, 149, 265, 289
Spiritual, But Not Religious, 11
spirituality, 8–9, 11–13, 18, 182, 184–185, 235, 244, 294–295
stardust, 244, 300
starstuff, ix, 244
Steinbeck, John, 18
Stephen Jay Gould
Humani Generis, 215
NOMA, 215–216, 272
Pope Pius XII, 215
Rocks of Ages, 215
Stevens, Cat
The Boy with a Moon And Star on His Head, 296
Stevenson, Robert Lewis
Kidnapped, 179
subatomic
quantum mechanics, 91, 187–188
quantum physics, 24, 39, 94, 150, 212
subjective
private, 16, 64, 72, 99, 116, 184, 209, 251–252, 254, 258, 272–274, 284, 293
Sumerians, 4
Summit of Spirituality (personal), 12
Sun, 6, 8, 33, 65–66, 109, 125, 151, 156, 241, 243, 300, 303
supernatural
supernatural phenomena, 153
supernatural theism, 27
superstition, 222

INDEX

Supreme Being, 28, 35, 92, 106, 174, 213, 235, 265, 299
Supreme Court, 45–46, 48, 249, 255–256
Sykes, Margaret, 47

T

Taylor, Barbara Brown
    red "X", 101
technology, 4, 19, 91, 108, 120–121, 135, 154
Tegmark, Max, 190
teleology, 194–195, 209
terminology
    terms, 17, 27–28, 36–38, 42, 96, 111, 115, 140, 156, 160, 169, 198, 224, 232, 260, 290, 292, 298
terrestrial, 97, 115, 142, 206, 221
Terrorism
    Al Qaida, 72
    claimed responsibility (news phrase), 73
    ISIL, 72
    ISIS, 72
    Paris, 72–74, 300
    World Trade Center, 72, 119
texting, 4
The Golden Rule, 117, 165, 261
The Grapes of Wrath, 18
The Simpsons
    (asterices), 178, 216
The Theory of Everything, 187
The Ultimate 747 Gambit
    The Tornado in the Junkyard, 201
Theism
    theology, 23, 29, 79, 150, 169, 191, 210–211, 233, 277, 290
theocracy, 252

theory
    theories, 21, 58, 81, 136, 187–189
Thinking
    Creative and Critical Thinking, 58–59
Three Dog Night
    Celebrate, 266, 298
Tillich, Paul, 23–24, 27, 42, 97, 145, 154, 291, 299
Tooth Fairy, 35, 144
totality of the observable universe
trance channelers, 153
transcendent, 27, 220, 223, 236–237
Transgender, 249–250
Transitive Property of Equality, 30, 162, 284
Tree of the Knowledge of Good and Evil, 55
Trinity
    personal trinity, 8, 58, 69, 156
    three-in-one, 9
    trinity-in-unity, 9
    Triune, 9
Trump, President Donald J.
    (asterisk), 174
Twelve-Step meetings, 13–14, 283
Twentieth (20th) Century, 49, 55, 120
tyrannies, 253
Tyson, Neil deGrasse
    American Museum of Natural History, 239
    Beyond Belief: Science, Religion, Reason, and Survival, 240
    Cosmos: A Spacetime Odyssey, 239

God of the Gaps, 239
Hayden Planetarium, 239
Moyers, Bill, 239
National Academy of Sciences, 241
Newton, Isaac, 187, 240–241
PBS, 190, 227, 239
Philosopiae Naturalis
   Principal Mathematica (Mathematical Principles of Natural Philosophy), 240
Ptolemy, Claudius, 38, 198, 240
   Almagest (The Greatest), 240
   (The Greatest), 240
Rose Center for Earth and Space, 244
science, ix, 5, 7–8, 15, 18–20, 24, 27, 33, 35, 39, 45, 49, 57, 59, 61–65, 67, 70–71, 75–76, 79–80, 82, 84–85, 87, 89, 91–94, 97–99, 104, 106, 111, 113, 118, 128, 136, 141–142, 150, 152–153, 156, 166–168, 182–185, 187, 189–190, 194–195, 202–203, 209–213, 215–217, 219, 221, 225, 227–228, 231–237, 239–243, 245, 257–258, 260, 268, 272–273, 283, 290, 292, 294–295, 301
   philosophy of discovery, 243
theory of the large, 188
theory of the small, 188

U

ultimate answer, 70
unified theory, 57, 187–189, 211–212, 228
Unitarian Church
   Unitarian Universalist Church, 12, 296
United States, 7, 33, 43–45, 51, 119, 251–252, 255–256, 261, 272–273, 275, 300–301
United States Constitution, 51, 251
universe
   13.799 billion years old (current age of the universe), 79, 195

V

value, 68–69, 85, 118, 163, 165, 203, 209–211, 216, 219–221, 232–234, 236–237, 242, 259, 290
various values of currency and coins, 85
Vaunauken, Sheldon
   A Severe Mercy, 172–173, 175–176
   If This Be All, 175
   Shining Barrier, 172, 175–176
   The Last Long Dive, 175
Ventura, Jesse
   I Ain't Got Time to Bleed, 261
   Jefferson, Thomas, 191
   Playboy, 261
   Queen Mab, 191
   via negativa, 191
Vietnam, 48
Virgin Mary, 8, 10
visceral, 5–6, 12, 15, 111, 245, 290

Voyager 1, 19
Voyager 2, 19
Voyager Interstellar Record, 148, 244

W

Walsch, Neale Donald, 146
Ward, Keith
    God, Chance, and Necessity, 232
    Materialism, 231–235
    Materialistic, 231, 290
Watts, Alan W., 106, 194
We Are the World (song), 295
Welsh, Constance Debear ("Connie"), 159
Whigs, 48
Whos, 295
Wildernesse (Secondary) School, 280
William Shakespeare (Isaac Azimov's Guide to), 80
William, Bramley
    Custodians, 114
Williams, Robin, 164
Williams, Roger
    Colony of Rhode Island and Providence Plantations, 252
    Garden of the Church, 252
    Wilderness of the World, 252
Wizard of Oz
    Dorothy, 102, 123, 275, 295
    Glenda, The Good Witch of the North, 102, 123
    Scarecrow, 102
    Tin Man, 102
Wolff, Baron Christian Von, 194
Word of God, 153
Word was God, 25

Y

Young, William P.
    The Shack, 172
Youngs, Pastor Sharon
    First Presbyterian Church (Oak Ridge, TN), 276

Z

Zeffirelli, Franco, 8

CPSIA information can be obtained
at www.ICGtesting.com
Printed in the USA
LVHW081036190520
656043LV00019B/1322